Defamation and the Right to Freedom of Speech

In an effort to balance the protection of reputation and the right to free speech, the UK Parliament attempted to fundamentally transform English libel law through the Defamation Act 2013. This book evaluates the success of this attempt by means of a comparative analysis of relevant law in the United States of America (US), Germany, and the European Court of Human Rights. It examines the reasons that it was deemed necessary to reform the common law of defamation in England and Wales, the changes wrought by the act, and the case law it has engendered. As defamation often occurs internationally, the book also takes a broad comparative look at the way in which other relevant jurisdictions attempt to balance reputational protection and free speech. The natural starting point is the US where freedom of expression is strongly protected by the US Constitution. From there the focus shifts to Germany where both competing legal interests are likewise given constitutional protection. The European Court of Human Rights' jurisprudence is also examined because of its highly developed balancing approach and its general reflection of European legal thinking. Recent high-profile defamation cases such as those concerning the actors Johnny Depp and Amber Heard, decided in the UK as well as the US, form interesting and informative case studies. The final section of the work rates the libel reform attempted in the UK against its own benchmarks, provides suggestions about the way in which it is developing, and concludes that valuable lessons can still be learnt from the comparator jurisdictions. The book will be essential reading for those working in the areas of human rights law and media law.

Mariette Jones is Senior Lecturer in Law at Middlesex University, UK.

Routledge Research in Human Rights Law

The Rohingya Crisis
Humanitarian and Legal Approaches
Edited by Manzoor Hasan, Syed Mansoob Murshed and Priya Pillai

Sports Investigations Law and the ECHR
Collection, Use and Exchange of Intelligence
Björn Hessert

The Right of the Child to Play
From Conception to Implementation
Naomi Lott

Social Media, Fundamental Rights and Courts
A European Perspective
Edited by Federica Casarosa and Evangelia Psychogiopoulou

Housing, Land and Property Rights
Residential Justice, Conflict Zones and Climate Change
Scott Leckie

The European Convention on Human Rights and the COVID-19 Pandemic
Ronagh J.A. McQuigg

International Human Rights and Local Courts
Human Rights Interpretation in Indonesia
Edited by Aksel Tømte and Eko Riyadi

Defamation and the Right to Freedom of Speech
The UK in Comparative Perspective
Mariette Jones

For more information about this series, please visit: www.routledge.com/Routledge-Research-in-Human-Rights-Law/book-series/HUMRIGHTSLAW

Defamation and the Right to Freedom of Speech

The UK in Comparative Perspective

Mariette Jones

Routledge
Taylor & Francis Group
LONDON AND NEW YORK

First published 2024

by Routledge
4 Park Square, Milton Park, Abingdon, Oxon OX14 4RN

and by Routledge
605 Third Avenue, New York, NY 10158

Routledge is an imprint of the Taylor & Francis Group, an informa business

British Library Cataloguing-in-Publication Data
A catalogue record for this book is available from the British Library

Library of Congress Cataloging-in-Publication Data
Names: Jones, Mariëtte, author.
Title: Defamation and the right to freedom of speech : the UK in comparative perspective / Mariette Jones.
Description: Abingdon, Oxon [UK] ; New York, NY : Routledge, 2024. | Series: Routledge research in human rights law | Includes bibliographical references and index.
Identifiers: LCCN 2024001179 | ISBN 9781032520025 (hardback) | ISBN 9781032542638 (paperback) | ISBN 9781003416005 (ebook)
Subjects: LCSH: Libel and slander—England. | Libel and slander—Wales. | Great Britain. Defamation Act 2013 | Libel and slander—Germany. | Libel and slander—United States. | Freedom of speech.
Classification: LCC KD1960 .J66 2024 | DDC 346.4203/4—dc23/eng/20240129
LC record available at https://lccn.loc.gov/2024001179

ISBN: 978-1-032-52002-5 (hbk)
ISBN: 978-1-032-54263-8 (pbk)
ISBN: 978-1-003-41600-5 (ebk)

DOI: 10.4324/9781003416005

Typeset in Galliard
by Apex CoVantage, LLC

Contents

Introduction

Freedom of speech is one of the almost universally accepted cornerstones of liberal democracy. However, its status as a cornerstone never quite seems assured, for it so often clashes with a variety of other rights and interests. These range from the ancient, such as the right not to have your reputation unlawfully besmirched, to the more recent, such as the right to privacy and personal data protection. The English common law protecting reputation metastasised into such a restraining influence on freedom of speech that around ten years ago, the UK legislator found it necessary to attempt comprehensive reform by enacting the Defamation Act 2013.

Free speech advocates had long argued that the UK's common law on defamation was too claimant friendly and, as such, either potentially or actually chilled free speech. The phenomenon of libel tourism to the UK, illustrated by several high-profile cases and arguably the result of the claimant friendly tilt of the law, served to prompt various actors including the United States federal government, the European Parliament, and the UK government itself, to call for reform. This culminated in Parliament's ambitious attempt to fundamentally transform libel law in the UK: The Defamation Act, 2013 ('the Act'). A decade hence and significant case law on the Act mean that it is now possible to analyse the success of this attempt. Specifically, the question may be asked whether the Act succeeds in redressing the balance between the protection of reputation and freedom of speech,[1] one of the stated aims of the legislative reform.

To answer this question, an examination of the Defamation Act 2013 itself and the case law it has engendered is the obvious starting point. In addition, a comparative analysis of other jurisdictions is not only useful in this analysis but arguably imperative: Transnational pressures played a significant role in prompting the local calls for reform that culminated in the Act. Furthermore, in an increasingly globalised and interconnected world, reputation rights and freedom of speech are both issues that transcend borders. National

1 Throughout the book, the terms 'freedom of expression,' free speech,' and 'freedom of speech' are used synonymously.

DOI: 10.4324/9781003416005-1

and international courts continue to grapple with how, and how far, to protect personality rights, such as privacy, dignity and reputation, and freedom of speech and how to balance them when they so often conflict with each other. Many lessons can therefore be learned from key jurisdictions.

Much has been written about the disparate topics covered in this research, i.e. defamation and freedom of speech, broadly speaking. This book offers a comparative analysis of select jurisdictions, chosen for their differing stances, which assist in shedding light on the way in which the Defamation Act 2013 has so far been and may be developed and interpreted in order to truly redress the balance in favour of freedom of expression in England and Wales.[2]

General background

A wealth of information exists about both the right to freedom of speech and defamation,[3] and much has also been said about the cross-boundary implications of differential national treatment of (especially) libel and freedom of speech.[4] However, it had been argued for some time that the English common law was inordinately biased in favour of defamation claimants – England was routinely referred to as the world's defamation capital,[5] and the European Parliament, for example, in May 2012 termed England and Wales 'the most claimant-friendly in the world.'[6] These factors combined to have a chilling effect on freedom of expression, in that the mere threat of a libel action could serve as a deterrent to fearless expression.[7] Since such a chilling effect is in reality a form of self-censorship, it is particularly difficult to gauge. Nevertheless, as will become clear from the discussion in chapters 1 and 2, there was compelling evidence of this chilling effect – enough concern was raised both internationally and locally to more or less lead to the very enactment of the Defamation Act 2013.

This has also led to concerns about 'libel tourism' – the practice of forum-shopping for a jurisdiction favourable to libel claimants. This term referred specifically to England and Wales for its relatively generous, jury-driven libel

2 References to English law throughout this book should be read as the law applicable to England and Wales. Note that Northern Ireland declined to adopt the Defamation Act 2013.

3 Barendt, E *Freedom of Speech* (2nd edn, OUP, Oxford, 2005), chapter 19 'Libel and Invasion of Privacy,' 198–230.

4 Jones, M 'EU Law Relating to Online Infringement of Personality Rights – is EU Law Effective in Preventing Forum Shopping for the Pursuit of Actions Arising from Online Infringement of Personality Rights?' in Weaver, RL, Gilles, W *et al.* (eds), *Privacy in a Digital Age: Perspectives from Two Continents* (Carolina Academic Press, Durham, North Carolina, 2017), 47–72.

5 Kenyon, Andrew T *Defamation: Comparative Law and Practice* (UCL Press (now Routledge), London, 2006), 6.

6 European Parliament Resolution of 10 May 2012 (2013/C 261 E/03), paras C–E.

7 The chilling effect in the UK has been proven empirically for as long as 20 years: Barendt, E, Lustgarten, L, Norrie, K and Stephenson, H *Libel Law and the Media: The Chilling Effect* (Clarendon Press, Oxford, 1997), 191.

awards. In a way, libel tourism itself could be viewed as merely a symptom of the bigger problem – namely, the chilling effect English common law of defamation had on the right to freedom of speech. One could also approach this problem from the other direction by examining the extent to which the right to freedom of expression itself figures in defamation law. The notion of freedom of expression as a defence is not foreign to UK jurisprudence: Barendt points out that prior to its recognition as a fundamental right in the Human Rights Act 1998 (HRA), freedom of expression had 'mostly been treated as a *defence* or as an *exception* or *qualification* to other well-established legal rights, such as the right to reputation.'[8] The question is whether the legislative reform in the Defamation Act 2013 sufficiently addresses the inhibitory effect of the common law of defamation on free speech – and to what extent freedom of expression as such play a role in the application of the reformed law.

The central aim of this book is to evaluate whether the Defamation Act 2013 adequately addresses these free speech concerns, thereby providing a mechanism for balancing reputational rights and the right to free speech in England and Wales. Given the existence (and problem) of libel tourism, and the fact that the chilling effect is a concern shared by many jurisdictions, the book compares the way in which these are addressed in a choice of key jurisdictions – the United States of America (US), Germany, and the European Court of Human Rights (ECtHR). Globalisation of necessity entails that the UK at least notes and perhaps learns from the way in which common issues of concern are addressed in key jurisdictions.

Since the coming into effect of the Defamation Act 2013 several important cases have been decided which signal the direction in which the Act's impact is heading. But further developments and interpretations may yet signal a change of course. In a newly reformed and developing area of law, it is useful to compare developments in other key jurisdictions. A good place to start is by examining practice and regulation in a jurisdiction where freedom of expression is strongly protected, such as the United States of America.[9] In addition, given the European Union's concerns about libel tourism in England and Wales, it is useful to examine also a continental jurisdiction – such as Germany, being a leading EU state. Germany also makes a natural choice as it is a jurisdiction in which freedom of speech and the right to a reputation are constitutionally balanced[10] and therefore German law seems to occupy the middle ground between the perceived primacy of freedom of speech in the USA versus the perceived primacy of defamation in England and Wales (at least, prior to the reforms in 2013). Relevant jurisprudence from the European Court of

8 Barendt, note 3, 41.

9 For example, the First Amendment accords protection against pre-publication censorship or 'prior restraint' – see the landmark cases of *Near v Minnesota*, 283 US 697 (1931) and *New York Times Co. v US*, 403 US 713 (1971).

10 German Constitution, article 5.

Human Rights (ECtHR) also deserve scrutiny due to its continuing gravitas in the development of UK law in general and personality rights in particular.

This book proceeds from the fact that the UK recognised that freedom of speech was being limited in England and Wales through its defamation laws, and acted on that recognition by promulgating the Defamation Act 2013. The question is whether this goes far enough to adequately redress the balance with freedom of expression. Put another way, the question is whether the enactment of the 2013 Act rings the death knell for defamation's chilling effect on free speech in England and Wales. If the number of suits pursued is any indication, the answer may be positive. There has been a pronounced drop in the number of libel suits pursued,[11] to such an extent that England and Wales can no longer be termed the 'libel capital of the world.'[12] But does that necessarily translate to a positive effect on free speech in England and Wales?

Enough time has now lapsed since its enactment for an in-depth and systematic look at the courts' interpretation of the Defamation Act 2013 in this regard. This, in turn, would benefit from an examination of the jurisdictions chosen for the focus of this study. There are several excellent comparative analyses of defamation in a number of jurisdictions, but most of these predate the 2013 legislative reform. An up-to-date comparative analysis of key jurisdictions is necessary to gauge the direction that UK defamation law is taking *vis-à-vis* the promotion of free speech in England and Wales.

Chapter summaries

The book comprises seven chapters: The first chapter provides a brief synopsis of the central theme and the balance between speech rights and reputation rights, and sets the scene for the more detailed discussions in the chapters to follow.

Chapter 2 explains why the UK Parliament deemed a wholesale reform of English defamation law necessary. In the main, there were a few key failings in the pre-reform common law of defamation which, it was argued, skewed the law in favour of defamation claimants at the expense of free speech. As such,

11 For example, in 2016 there were only 37 decisions in defamation proceedings, down from 56 in 2015, and only eight of these cases went to trial; see the Inforrm blog of 5 September 2017 at <https://inforrm.org/2017/09/05/using-data-protection-law-to-defend-your-reputation-what-about-the-new-data-protection-bill-michael-patrick-and-alicia-mendonca/> accessed 22 November 2017. There were 49 reported defamation cases in the UK over the year to the end of June 2017 that made it to a court hearing, down from 86 three years ago, according to research by Thomson Reuters; see Mayhew, F 'Higher Threshold of Harm Has Seen Number of UK Defamation Cases Drop as Celebs Look to Privacy Actions to Fight Libel' *Press Gazette* (London, 23 April 2018), <www.pressgazette.co.uk/higher-defamation-threshold-has-seen-number-of-uk-cases-drop-as-celebs-look-to-privacy-actions-to-fight-libel/> accessed 25 February 2020.

12 This prompted Barendt to remark that this dubious distinction 'probably now belongs to Sydney' in his review of Rolph, D's *Defamation Law* (Thomson Reuters, Sydney, 2016): Barendt, E 'Defamation Law' (2017) 9(2) *Journal of Media Law* 291–295.

it fuelled the forum-shopping phenomenon that came to be known as 'libel tourism' to England, which in turn became known as the 'libel capital of the world.' This chapter also revisits the reasons for the protection of freedom of expression and of reputation.

Chapter 3 examines the reforms in the Defamation Act 2013, its interpretation in significant cases, and its impact on the way libel actions specifically are pursued in England and Wales. It evaluates the efficacy of its reforms against its stated aims, focusing on whether the overarching goals of addressing the problems of libel tourism and the chilling of free speech have been achieved.

Throughout chapters 2 and 3, the focus remains on the role of freedom of speech in English libel actions past, present and future. The interaction of the right to protect one's reputation with the right to freedom of speech in England and Wales is examined, followed by an attempt to answer the question whether these rights are now equally balanced. The tentative answer, given parallel developments in privacy and data protection laws in the UK, is that the reforms do not go far enough in redressing the balance in favour of free speech. This in turn will set the scene for the next chapter's discussion of the jurisdiction where the opposite seems to hold.

Chapter 4 thus turns the attention to the United States and the way in which defamation actions are conducted according to US Federal Supreme Court guidelines in order to give effect to the constitutional entrenchment of the First Amendment right to free speech. Having examined the English law in the preceding two chapters, comparative analysis is now possible between these two seemingly disparate jurisdictional positions.

From there the focus shifts to Germany in chapter 5: Given its constitutional balancing of freedom of speech and 'personal honour,' it seems to occupy the middle ground between the perceived extremes exemplified in the USA on the one hand and the common law of defamation prior to its reform in England and Wales on the other.

Chapter 6 analyses relevant decisions handed down by the European Court of Human Rights. The European Court of Human Rights' jurisprudence is very valuable for its highly developed balancing approach and its general reflection of European legal thinking.

Chapter 7 summarises key conclusions from the preceding chapters and offer some ideas about the likely and/or desirable directions further interpretation of the Defamation Act 2013 may take. Best practices identified in the comparator jurisdictions are revisited, as well as pitfalls to avoid. The chapter also briefly examines other, newer legal threats to the exercise of free speech, such as the rapidly developing law of privacy, data protection, and cybersecurity.

The final chapter ends with conclusions about where the law is, where it is headed and whether it has properly dealt with the problems identified with the English common law of defamation. The chapter includes best practices and lessons from the comparator jurisdictions. A few conclusions are proffered regarding the extent to which the Act achieved significant gains in redressing the balance in favour of free speech in the UK.

1 Defamation and freedom of speech

Before embarking on detailed discussion of the defamation law in the UK and its reform, and then comparing it to defamation regimes in the comparator jurisdictions, the underlying principles at issue deserve some unpacking. Defamation is the part of the law that protects an individual's reputation. In England and Wales, vindicating one's reputation is an ancient right. More recently, other personality rights have become more significant, such as the right to privacy. In Germany, constitutional protection is given to 'the personality right' which in turn is an umbrella term encompassing, inter alia, reputation, dignity, and privacy. These rights in their observance or enjoyment often conflict with another important legal right, the right to freedom of speech. Concerns about its chill on free speech, in their turn, were the main drivers for the legislative reform of defamation law in England and Wales. This introductory chapter explores these core concepts by re-examining the reasons that they are deemed worthy of legal protection. No discussion of free speech and the challenges it faces nowadays in any of the jurisdictions covered in this book would be complete without at least some attention to the 'new kids on the block,' such as the expanded personality rights. But the discussion there must be brief, to not stray too far from the main focus namely the reform of English defamation law mandated by free speech concerns.

Freedom of speech

Western philosophy recognised freedom of speech[1] and its importance long before its inclusion in the 1948 Human Rights Declaration: John Stuart Mill's classic essay 'Of the Liberty of Thought and Discussion,' dating back to 1859, has proven to be an enduring starting point on the topic.[2] Today freedom of speech is one of the most highly valued human rights, with almost universal acceptance as a *sine qua non* for democratic societies. It is included in

1 Throughout this work, the terms 'free speech,' 'freedom of speech,' and 'freedom of expression' are used interchangeably.

2 Mill, JS *On Liberty* (Longman, Roberts & Green, London, 1869, originally published 1859).

DOI: 10.4324/9781003416005-2

international conventions such as the Universal Declaration of Human Rights (article 19), the European Convention of Human Rights (article 10) and the Charter of Fundamental Rights of the European Union (article 11), to name but a few. Free speech is protected in some form in every modern liberal democracy. It could even be argued that a state does not merit being called either liberal or a democracy, if it does not protect freedom of speech. Indeed, so well entrenched is this right that nowadays debate is usually constrained to its limitation rather than its substantive nature. Because of its wide acceptance, Barendt remarks that free speech is prized by liberals for reasons that they may not understand.[3] But in deciding how to weigh up competing interests, the normative value of the interests should determine their relative weight, which in turn should dictate where the balance should lie should these interests in fact come into conflict. It therefore makes sense to first pause and revisit the reasons that free speech and reputation are deemed worthy of protection before examining the balancing act attempted by the Defamation Act 2013.[4]

It is submitted that both freedom of speech and defamation could fruitfully be viewed by focusing on societal interests. Several of the most important theoretical bases underlying the value of free speech allocate the benefit of free speech in this manner.[5] A good place to start is John Stuart Mill's classic essay mentioned earlier.[6] Mill's stated goal in *On Liberty* is to identify the nature and limits of the power which can be legitimately exercised by society over the individual. His famous argument from truth emphasises the interests of society in discovering the truth. For this, he argues, society should not merely tolerate but embrace speech that is considered objectionable. The reasons for this are fourfold: Nobody is infallible, and therefore, we must be open to the possibility that an opinion that deviates from the mainstream might be true. Next, even where an argument is substantially wrong, it may still contain a portion of truth that is missing from the accepted opinion. If the prevailing opinion is completely true, it still needs to be open to challenge for it is only through frequent challenge and vigorous defence that those who hold the opinion can fully understand the rational grounds for the opinion. Finally, related to the last point and of particular importance to our current analysis, Mill argues that in the absence of vigorous debate, the meaning of the doctrine itself will be in danger of being lost, or enfeebled, and deprived of its vital effect on character and conduct.[7] In short, an argument may persuade the audience members to change their minds, or it may cause them to defend their stance on the matter.[8] Either way, the focus is on the

3 Barendt, E *Freedom of Speech* (2nd edn, OUP, Oxford, 2005), 1.
4 For an explanation of these theories, see Barendt, note 3, chapter 1 ('Why Protect Free Speech?').
5 Ibid.
6 Mill, note 2.
7 Ibid.
8 For a critical view of the relevance of Mill's argument from truth to modern jurisprudence, see Wragg, P 'Mill's Dead Dogma: The Value of Truth to Free Speech Jurisprudence' (2013) *Public Law* 363–385.

argument, the message, the speech, rather than the speaker. The speaker has the right to free speech only as a function of delivering the message.

This is also the case in the next theory, the argument from citizen participation in a democracy. Meiklejohn, a leading exponent of political speech, emphasised the importance of the electorate being able to access a variety of opinions on political and social matters. This at the least equals, and probably outweighs, the individual speaker's interest in participating in the discourse.[9] A further theory, best framed by Scanlon, explores free speech as an aspect of individual self-fulfilment or autonomy and holds that the justification for freedom of speech proceeds from the right of an individual to consider all the arguments and views that may determine their course of action.[10] Of course the liberal notion of individual autonomy also includes the speaker's right to determine the content of their speech.[11] But given the fact that the arguments from truth, citizen participation in democracy and from autonomy have been influential in shaping the development of constitutional free speech rights, it is fair to say that recipients, rather than speakers, are the primary object of free speech interests.[12] The categorisation of the right as being a societal good is clear.

However, freedom of speech is not an absolute right, and it often conflicts with other important rights, such as the right to privacy and the right to preserve a good reputation. It is now recognised that article 8 of the European Convention on Human Rights (ECHR),[13] which protects the right to privacy, also includes the 'right to reputation.'[14] Reputational rights are accorded protection to varying degrees. For example, in international law the Universal Declaration of Human Rights (article 12) and the International Covenant on Civil and Political Rights (article 17) recognise the right to legal protection from attacks on individual honour and reputation. On the national level many jurisdictions protect individual reputation through defamation laws specifically. In Germany, both rights are included in the Constitution: The German Constitution in article 5(1) guarantees the right to freedom of expression but in article 5(2) states that the right is subject to limitations, including the right to personal honour. In the United Kingdom, reputation has long been vindicated in the courts, with the common law action in defamation stretching back to the 1600s.[15]

9 Meiklejohn, A *Political Freedom* (Harper Collins, New York, 1960), 64.
10 Scanlon, T 'A Theory of Freedom of Expression' (1972) 1 *Philosophy and Public Affairs* 204.
11 Dworkin, R *Philosophy of Law* (OUP, Oxford, 1977), introduction.
12 Barendt, E *Anonymous Speech: Literature, Law and Politics* (Hart Publishing, Oxford, 2016), 62.
13 Convention for the Protection of Human Rights and Fundamental Freedoms (adopted 4 November 1950) 213 UNTS 221.
14 Mullis, A and Scott, A 'The Swing of the Pendulum: Reputation, Expression and the Recentering of the English Libel Law' (2012) 63 *Northern Ireland Legal Quarterly* 27–58.
15 See McNamara, L *Reputation and Defamation* (OUP, Oxford, 2007), chapter 3 'Reputation and the History of Defamation.' Post, RC 'The Social Foundations of Defamation Law:

Freedom of expression includes the right to impart statements, regardless of the subject matter and via any medium, such as online, in print, in speech or otherwise. This includes expression of a wide range of artistic, scientific, political, religious, cultural, and other perspectives, including deeply offensive or controversial statements, although harmful speech may be restricted under strict conditions. International law recognises that the right to freedom of expression imposes both positive and negative obligations on states: On the one hand, there is the negative obligation on states to refrain from interfering with the exercise of the right. On the other, they are also at times under a positive obligation to take steps to ensure the full realisation of freedom of expression. In the UK the state felt obliged to take positive steps to redress the defamation law in favour of free speech. But first, let us examine the *raison d'être* for defamation law, i.e. the reputational interest.

Reputation

It is useful at this point to take a step back and examine reputation as the *raison d'être* of defamation. It is trite that the tort protects an individual's reputation. But what makes reputation a right worthy of protection in the first place? Post argues that the protection of reputation is informed by the core values of property, honour, and dignity.[16] In other words, reputation could be regarded as personal property, or as part of a person's honour, or as a function of the inherent dignity of all human beings, and thus worthy of protection for one or all or a combination of these reasons. An analysis of all three of these values indicates that protecting reputation serves an overarching societal interest. As such, it accords with the classic view of Mills' espousal of free speech as inherently being a societal rather than just an individual good. That there is also a clear societal interest underlying these values if often overlooked.

The image of the market society underlies and informs the view of reputation as property.[17] This view resonates strongly with the pervasive neoliberal worldview and also explains why non-human entities such as companies are able to sue in defamation. Honour and dignity are after all not aspects that can be ascribed to the corporate form. Lord Hoffman pointed out that a commercial company has no soul and therefore its reputation is more correctly seen as a valuable commercial asset, something attached to its trading name which brings in customers.[18] In short, this view of reputation sees it as a form of intangible property that may be damaged and, as such, result in monetary loss which can be compensated. However, the 'property' argument alone

Reputation and the Constitution' (1986) 74 *California Law Review* 691 provides a good discussion of the foundations of defamation law in both England and the United States.

16 Post, note 15.

17 Milo, D *Defamation and Freedom of Speech* (OUP, Oxford, 2008).

18 *Jameel v Wall Street Journal Europe SPRL (No. 3)* [2006] UKHL 44 at 91.

cannot explain why reputation is deemed worthy of protection, as it cannot, for example, explain fundamental aspects of defamation law such as the rule that an action for defamation dies with the claimant, or the legal presumption of damage.[19]

When looking at the next view of reputation, that of 'honour,' it is interesting to remember that the civil law of defamation in England in large part developed because the Star Chamber outlawed duelling, the traditional means of restoring honour.[20] The modern conception of 'honour' arguably relates more to the inherent dignity of man and may be reflected in the grand and ongoing project of the current and previous century – namely, the idea and practice of human rights. However, all the elements of a cause of action in defamation confirm that what is protected is an *external* conception of image rather than an internal conception of self. Everything that the claimant needs to prove focus on the attitudes of the community – that the statement identified the claimant directly or indirectly, that it was defamatory, and that it was made public through publication to a third party. As such, it is the projection of the self to society that the law protects.[21] Reputation, like beauty, is in the eyes of the beholder.

The common denominator in reputation as property and as honour is the involvement of society, of other people. The value of the company's reputation is determined by society's view, as is the *de facto* reputation of the individual. This chimes with the definition of reputation as 'the respect or esteem which a person enjoys in society.'[22] This clearly differentiates reputation from self-esteem, which is the esteem a person has for themselves. It is therefore submitted that reputation as the focus of defamation law is a societal construct that seeks to mediate the relationship between individuals and the society in which they exist. Lord Nicholls in *Reynolds v Times Newspapers Ltd* [1999] explained how reputation is important both to the individual concerned and to society more generally:

> Reputation is an integral and important part of the dignity of the individual. It also forms the basis of many important decisions in a democratic society which are fundamental to its well-being: whom to employ or work for, whom to promote, whom to do business with or vote for. Once besmirched by an unfounded allegation in a national newspaper, a reputation can be damaged forever, especially if there is no opportunity to vindicate one's reputation. When this happens, society as well as the individual is the loser. For it should not be supposed that protection of

19 Milo, note 17, 30.

20 Holdsworth, WS *A History of English Law* (Methuen, London, 1948), vol VIII, 336.

21 Milo, note 17, 30. See also Brown, RE *The Law of Defamation in Canada* (Carswell, Toronto, 1994), vol 1, 17.

22 Weir, T *An Introduction to Tort Law* (2nd edn, Clarendon Press, Oxford, 2006), 175.

> reputation is a matter of importance only to the affected individual and his family. Protection of reputation is conducive to the public good. It is in the public interest that the reputation of public figures should not be debased falsely. In the political field, in order to make an informed choice, the electorate needs to be able to identify the good as well as the bad.[23]

To this must be added that allowing someone to safeguard a false or misleading reputation surely damages the public good severely. Jimmy Savile is a case in point.

Societal interests in free speech and reputation can therefore be brought squarely into Mill's argument from truth, and this is also the basic perspective from which this book evaluates the Defamation Act 2013.

Other threats to free speech

For free speech advocates, current trends in liberal democracies must be worrying. In fact, legal measures restricting speech have reached such saturation point that instead of thinking of speech as 'free,' one could be forgiven to observe that the adjectives that more accurately describe the situation in the UK nowadays is 'restricted,' 'permitted,' 'proscribed,' or even 'censored.' What you can say now very much depends on who you are, what you are saying, and where you are saying it. For example, draconian provisions and amendments in the areas of new anti-terror legislation,[24] rapidly expanding privacy and data protection,[25] and the ever-expanding regulation of 'hate speech'[26] all have a direct impact on the ability to speak freely and to communicate ideas.

The UK is not alone in this arena, of course. Legal regulation of online content, under the guise of protecting citizens against 'fake news' and a plethora of other perceived online threats, is being increasingly and fervently pursued across many if not most liberal jurisdictions.[27] These include recently enacted

23 *Reynolds v Times Newspapers Ltd* [1999] 3 WLR 1010, para 201D with Lord Cooke of Thorndon and Lord Hobhouse of Woodborough concurring.

24 For an in-depth discussion of the far-reaching free speech implications of the UK's Counter-Terrorism and Border Security Act 2019 and its amendment of the Terrorism Act 200, *see* Bechtold, E and Phillipson, G 'Glorifying Censorship? Anti-Terror Law, Speech and Online Regulation,' in Stone, A and Schauer, F (eds), *The Oxford Handbook of Freedom of Speech* (Oxford University Press, Oxford, 2021), chapter 28.

25 On the proliferation of privacy and data protection suits, *see* Goutzamanis, Y 'Closing the Floodgates on Privacy Class Actions: *Lloyd v Google LLC*' (2023) 86(1) *Modern Law Review* 249–262.

26 Law Commission, 'Hate Crime Laws' *Law Com No. 402*, 2021, paras 1.35–1.37, 1.49, 4.220. *See* also Law Commission, 'Modernising Communications Offences' *Law Com No. 399*, 2021.

27 Haciyakupoglu, G, Yang Hui, J, Suguna, VS, Leong, D and Rahman, MFBA 'Front Matter', in *Countering Fake News: A Survey of Recent Global Initiatives* (S. Rajaratnam School of International Studies, 2018), 22–26.

laws that amount to compulsory state-directed content moderation, such as Germany's NetzDG,[28] the EU's 2021 Regulation on online terrorism content and its Strengthened Code of Practice on Disinformation 2022, and Australia's Online Safety Act 2021, as well as proposed laws such as the European Media Freedom Act which was proposed in September 2022. Australia seems to want to moderate content further than the provisions of that act allows, as a bill focusing on misinformation specifically is currently being considered.[29] All of these focus on external regulation, i.e. states relying on privately owned social media companies to control expression through the imposition of liability and a duty to actively monitor, control, and remove content.[30]

Perhaps in order to catch up with its European and other Western liberal democratic neighbours, the UK legislator set its sights on the online environment, specifically social media platforms. The UK's Online Safety Act 2023 goes much further than the notice-and-take down regime that has made its insidious way into so much of European online content regulation by placing a positive duty of care on social media platforms.[31] Instead of the usual notice and takedown regime, corporations are now legally required to proactively seek out and limit online content.[32] The Online Safety Act's core operational feature entails the state compelling private companies to actively monitor, evaluate, and remove content created by third parties. The act aims to establish a new regulatory regime to address illegal and 'harmful' content online, by means of imposing legal requirements about this kind of content on providers of internet user-to-user services and internet search engines. In order to enforce the newly created duties, the act confers extensive new powers on the Office of Communications (OFCOM) enabling them to act as the online safety regulator.[33] This role will include overseeing and enforcing the new regulatory regime. The duty of care imposed by the act is analogous to the duty of care in tort or health and safety laws, but with the key difference that the duty would be based on a *precautionary principle*, i.e. by prior constraint.[34]

28 Netzwerkdurchsetzungsgesetz 2019. See Mchangama, J and Fiss, J 'The Digital Berlin Wall: How Germany (Accidentally) Created a Prototype for Global Online Censorship' (2020) *Justitia* 1.

29 Michelle Rowland, MP The Albanese Government will legislate to provide the Australian Communications and Media Authority (ACMA) with new powers to hold digital platforms to account and improve efforts to combat harmful misinformation and disinformation in Australia. (Media Release, 20 January 2023), https://minister.infrastructure.gov.au/rowland/media-release/new-acma-powers-combat-harmful-online-misinformation-and-disinformation.

30 David Kaye, Report of the special rapporteur on the promotion and protection of the right to freedom of opinion and expression (June 6–23, 2017, A/HRC/35/22, Agenda Item 3), para 1.

31 Online Safety Act (2013), chapter 50, section 1(2).

32 See Jones, M 'Regulation of Online Speech in the UK' (2024) 55(2) *University of the Pacific Law Review* 261–275 for a discussion of the Online Safety Act 2023.

33 Section 1(2)(b).

34 Coe, P 'The Draft Online Safety Bill and the Regulation of Hate Speech: Have We Opened Pandora's Box?' (2022) 14(1) JML 50.

Put another way, whereas in tort a wrongdoer is punished for breaking the law, here the balance is shifted to state-sanctioned private censorship of content, without any *judicial* consideration of whether or not the content was in fact illegal. Index on Censorship rightly points out that this shift would mark 'the most significant change in the role of the state over free speech in the UK since 1695.'[35]

There is also the concern that defamation claims may be replaced by misuse of private information (MOPI) claims as the weapon of choice by rich and powerful claimants to try and silence critics – a trend that started to be noticeable soon after the Defamation Act 2013 came into operation.[36]

The current legal landscape can therefore accurately be termed challenging to freedom of speech, and what further complicates matters is the fact that many interests overlap, lines are blurred. In the chapters discussing the German law and jurisprudence from the European Court of Human Rights, for instance, it is shown how fundamentally different legal concepts such as privacy and reputation are conflated into one personality right. The effects of developing and evolving privacy law, data protection, cybersurveillance, etc. on freedom of speech all deserve and give rise to detailed discussion outside the confines of this book. What needs to be borne in mind throughout is that the current legal landscape includes a variety of threats to freedom of speech, of which a claimant-friendly defamation regime forms but one part.

The balancing exercise

Before describing in broad terms what the chosen jurisdictions do about defamation and freedom of speech, it is necessary to first explain a juridical concept that will form the basis of much of the discussion in this book – namely, the balancing exercise. Most jurisdictions subject to a constitution containing a bill of rights have a balancing mechanism to assist the judiciary in instances where rights conflict with each other. For example, the Canadian constitution states in section 1:

> The Canadian Charter of Rights and Freedoms guarantees the rights and freedoms set out in it subject only to such reasonable limits prescribed by law as can be demonstrably justified in a free and democratic society.[37]

35 Index on Censorship, *Online Safety Bill will 'Significantly Curtail Freedom of Expression'* (4 May 2022), <www.indexoncensorship.org/2022/05/online-safety-bill-will-significantly-curtail-freedom-of-expression/>.

36 Greenslade, R 'Privacy Claims Reach Record Level as Defamation Cases Fall Away' *The Guardian* (13 June 2016), <www.theguardian.com/media/greenslade/2016/jun/13/privacy-claims-reach-record-level-as-defamation-cases-fall-away> accessed 31 October 2023.

37 Canada Act 1982 c. 11.

How the decision is reached as to what exactly is justified in a free and democratic society is left up to the courts. In a more recent constitution, the drafters attempted to assist the courts in this function: Section 36 of the Constitution of the Republic of South Africa[38] entrenches a balancing mechanism with more explicit instructions as to what should be considered in a free and democratic society. Section 36(1) states the following:

> The rights in the Bill of Rights may be limited only in terms of law of general application to the extent that the limitation is reasonable and justifiable in an open and democratic society based on human dignity, equality and freedom, taking into account all relevant factors, including –
>
> (a) the nature of the right;
> (b) the importance of the purpose of the limitation;
> (c) the nature and extent of the limitation;
> (d) the relation between the limitation and its purpose; and
> (e) less restrictive means to achieve the purpose.

The European Convention on Human Rights also relies on the idea of balancing rights with each other, and several of the articles specifically spell out what they need to be balanced against. The right to freedom of expression is a good example. Article 10 of the ECHR[39] reads as follows:

> (1) Everyone has the right to freedom of expression. This right shall include freedom to hold opinions and to receive and impart information and ideas without interference by public authority and regardless of frontiers. This article shall not prevent States from requiring the licensing of broadcasting, television or cinema enterprises.

This freedom is not absolute and should be balanced against competing rights in the relevant context. Article 10 also contains its own constraints in paragraph 2 including a specific mention of the protection of reputation (which is not otherwise specifically mentioned in the Convention):

> (2) The exercise of these freedoms, since it carries with it duties and responsibilities, may be subject to such formalities, conditions, restrictions or penalties as are prescribed by law and are necessary in a democratic society, in the interests of national security, territorial integrity or public safety, for the prevention of disorder or crime, for the protection of health or morals, *for the protection of the reputation or rights of others*, for preventing the disclosure of information received

38 Act 108 of 1996.
39 This article is now incorporated into English law through the Human Rights Act 1998, S 12.

in confidence, or for maintaining the authority and impartiality of the judiciary. [my emphasis]

In the other three national jurisdictions under discussion, the balancing exercise is neither prescribed nor described in such detail.[40] Nonetheless, a balancing exercise still happens in each. As will be seen in the following brief introductory discussions, exactly *what* gets to be 'put on the scales of the balance,' as it were, *how* these factors are weighted and to which extent the courts have freedom to decide for themselves on this, and to which extent they have to follow prescribed methodolcgies will form much of the comparative element of this study.

England and Wales

It is necessary to examine defamation law and its recent changes in England and Wales in a bit more detail at this stage (than defamation laws in the US and Germany), as an analysis of the English and Welsh reforms is the focus of this book. First, however, it needs to be stated that whereas the balancing exercise mentioned earlier is no stranger to English jurisprudence, it would be over-simplifying it tremendously to state that where the right to reputation clashes with the right to freedom of expression, a straight-forward balancing mechanism exists in English law: It does not. For this reason, we need to keep in mind the common law 'wrongs-based' approach to the tort of defamation and the fact that this does not always comfortably fit in with the rights-based approach developing since the incorporation of ECHR rights in the HRA.[41] Still, examples of the courts balancing competing rights are not difficult to find. The right to freedom of expression incorporated in section 12 of the HRA is a good starting point.[42] For present purposes, section 12(4) is the most relevant:

(4) The court must have particular regard to the importance of the Convention right to freedom of expression and, where the proceedings relate to material which the respondent claims, or which appears to the court, to be journalistic, literary or artistic material (or to conduct connected with such material), to –

40 Although para 5(2) of the German Constitution lists possible limits.

41 The 'culture clash' between these two approaches are explored in detail by Gilliker, P *The Europeanisation of English Tort Law* (Hart Publishing, Oxford and Portland, Oregon, 2014).

42 Section 12(1) incorporates article 10 of the ECHR in the following manner: '(1) This section applies if a court is considering whether to grant any relief which, if granted, might affect the exercise of the Convention right to freedom of expression.' Section 12(3) contains a prohibition of prior constraint: '(3) No such relief is to be granted so as to restrain publication before trial unless the court is satisfied that the applicant is likely to establish that publication should not be allowed.'

(a) the extent to which –
 (i) the material has, or is about to, become available to the public; or
 (ii) it is, or would be, in the public interest for the material to be published;

(b) any relevant privacy code.

Section 12 was designed to allay fears by the press about privacy rights trumping freedom of expression, and at first glance it appears to prioritise freedom of expression over competing rights such as the right to privacy. However, the courts soon stated that the correct interpretation is that freedom of expression must be balanced against competing Convention rights and interests: Sedley LJ in *Douglas v Hello!* [2001][43] interpreted the right as including the restrictions that form part of article 10 of the ECHR, i.e. with regard to, for example, the right to reputation. This view was confirmed by the House of Lords in *Campbell v MGN* [2004].[44] Logically, it follows that this balancing exercise would apply to all the Convention rights in the HRA.

Having said that, there was, and remains, a perception that the right to reputational protection was unfairly prioritised through the way in which UK defamation laws operated. This merits an in-depth discussion of English defamation law, its reform in the 2013 Act, and the impact of such reform, the topics explored in chapters 2 and 3. For now, a brief introduction to the problem suffices.

Based on Lord Atkin's test for the word 'defamatory' in *Sim v Stretch* [1936],[45] defamation can be defined as 'the publication of a statement which reflects on a person's reputation and tends to lower him in the estimation of right-thinking members of society generally or tends to make them shun or avoid him.'[46] The tort aims to protect a person's reputation, which is still seen as distinct from privacy protection in English law: The latter is protected to a large extent by the rapidly developing tort of misuse of private information.[47] Given the recognised importance placed on the right to privacy, which includes the right to one's reputation, it is necessary to explore the reasons for the reform of England and Wales's common law of defamation. These, the reasons for the legislative reform culminating in the Defamation Act 2013, are explored in detail in chapter 2. As already mentioned, one of, if not the main,

43 *Douglas v Hello!* [2001] QB 967, paras 133–135.
44 *Campbell v MGN* [2004] 2 AC 457, paras 55 (Hoffmann), 111 (Hope) and 138–141 (Hale).
45 *Sim v Stretch* [1936] 2 All ER 1237.
46 Rogers, WVH *Winfield and Jolowicz on Tort* (18th edn, Sweet & Maxwell, London, 2010), para 12.3.
47 This tort developed from the tort of breach of confidence, and protects against the disclosure of confidential information (and is therefore largely equivalent to privacy protection). A few examples of successful use of this tort includes Catherine Zeta Jones's suit (note 43) and Naomi Campbell's (note 44).

reason for enacting the Defamation Act 2013 was the concern that the English common law of defamation was chilling free speech, which in turn was driven by inequality under the common law between defamation claimants and defendants. The structure of defamation law and litigation itself handed an advantage to the claimant for which, it is argued, there exists no justification.

Several characteristics of the common law combined to give an unfair advantage to libel claimants. The costs associated with bringing or defending a defamation claim were prohibitive. In the absence of a tribunal or other alternative dispute resolution forum for defamation, the court remained the only option for such disputes, with the result that it seemed that only the rich and powerful had unfettered access to legal protection of their reputations. Impecunious defendants, faced with potentially being bankrupted by defending their words in a libel claim, could be bullied into silence by the mere threat of being sued.[48] So while in theory the courts were open to all to vindicate either their reputation or their right to free speech, the costs associated with this meant in reality this was akin to stating that the Ritz-Carlton hotel is open to everyone. The matter ended up as an access to justice issue that went to the European Court of Human Rights via the famous McLibel litigation.[49]

Furthermore, three principles peculiar to the common law fundamentally favoured defamation claimants: A legal presumption that the allegedly defamatory statement was false combined with an irrebuttable presumption of damages, and finally the strict liability nature of libel and some slander claims. Milo referred to these as the 'potent trilogy of defamation law,'[50] which combined to place a *de facto* reverse burden of proof on the defamation defendant.

If one accepts that there is no inherent reason to accord such advantage to the defamation claimant, and that such advantage unfairly tilts the balance in favour of reputation and away from speech, the logical conclusion is that in order to address free speech concerns the advantage given to defamation claimants need to be removed. A level playing field needs to be ensured in the defamation trial. This is a useful benchmark against which the Defamation Act 2013 is scrutinised in chapter 3 before the focus shifts in chapter 4 to the jurisdiction in which freedom of speech is protected more than anywhere else.

The United States of America

The Constitution of the United States of America guarantees and protects freedom of speech. This could be explained as a result of American history,

48 See Singh, H 'The Libel Survivor' (2011) 13(32) *Legal Week* 20–21.

49 *McDonald's Corp. v Steel* [1995] 3 All ER 615; *Steel and Morris v UK* [2005] 18 BHRC 545. The latter case led to the legal aid regime to be reformed so that defendants sued by large multinational corporations are now entitled to legal aid. However, for all other parties to defamation claims, legal aid remains unavailable.

50 Milo, note 17, 11.

a detailed analysis of which goes beyond the scope of this book. Suffice it to say that Thomas Jefferson's sentiment that freedom of expression 'cannot be limited without being lost'[51] found expression in the First Amendment to the Constitution, which states that (*inter alia*) 'Congress shall make no law . . . abridging the freedom of speech, or of the press.' At this stage it is important to note that the First Amendment and the free speech protection it offers are binding only on the *state:* In its literal sense it only refers to laws of Congress, but the due process clause of the Fourteenth Amendment makes clear that it also applies to the individual states.[52] Freedom of speech, then, is protected from infringement by government at federal and state level.

A prohibition on any laws prohibiting freedom of speech seems absolute, but this does not mean that the right to freedom of expression trumps all other fundamental rights in the US. From a practical point of view alone, this absolutist position is impossible to sustain, and an examination of case law shows that the US courts, including the federal Supreme Court, do indeed depart from a literal or absolute interpretation of the First Amendment. Many cases can be quoted as examples where free speech was restricted,[53] but perhaps Holmes J put it best when he stated with true common law common sense, in the landmark decision on the First Amendment in *Schenk v US* (1919),[54] that the 'most stringent protection of free speech would not protect a man falsely shouting fire in a theatre and causing a panic.' To start with, freedom of speech sometimes needs to be restricted in order to enable others to exercise their own right to freedom of speech.

Barendt points out that in the US, freedom of speech is not regarded as an undifferentiated monolith; as such, various forms of speech are given differing levels of protection with particularly strong protection being accorded to political speech as opposed to, for example, commercial speech or advertising.[55] Whilst the courts perform a balancing exercise when free speech conflicts with other rights, as courts do in other jurisdictions, in the US there is a strong presumption in favour of free speech. The US Supreme Court has specifically formulated principles intended to guard against the danger of according the First Amendment right to freedom of speech less protection than it should enjoy, i.e. to guard against it being ranked as just another factor to consider in combination with other factors in a constitutional democracy.

Examining these guiding principles, it is clear that the threshold to infringe free speech is set very high. Foremost there is the 'clear and present danger'

51 Letter to James Currie, 28 January 1786, Library of Congress.

52 As was clear since the decision in *Gitlow v New York*, 268 US 652 (1925).

53 A select sample would include the 'prior restraint' cases, of which the prime example is the famous *Pentagon Papers* case: *New York Times v US*, 403 US 713 (1971).

54 *Schenk v US*, 249 US 47, 52 (1919).

55 Barendt, note 3, 48.

test: Free speech is allowed unless it can be shown that allowing it presents a clear and present danger intended to, and likely to, produce imminent lawless behaviour.[56] Indeed, if one compares the use of this test to the practice in other common law jurisdictions, including England and Wales, insulting and inflammatory speech that would almost certainly fall foul of contempt of court proceedings in these jurisdictions would be protected under the First Amendment in the US.[57] The same is true *mutatis mutandis* for defamation proceedings.

Further, US courts recognise the strong prohibition against prior constraint: Following the famous *Pentagon Papers* case (1971),[58] courts can only grant a prior restraint if the state concerned showed that it would otherwise suffer direct, immediate, and irreparable damage. The utility of recognising this will be important in the discussion of the chilling effect evidenced by UK defamation law. Finally, and most importantly, a state cannot restrict freedom of speech (based on the content of the offending speech) unless it can prove a compelling reason to do so. If there is any other less draconian way of protecting the interest concerned, that state will not be able to do so by restricting freedom of speech.[59]

Turning to defamation specifically, the almost visceral distrust of governmental restriction of free speech is particularly evident here, to such an extent that the Supreme Court has formulated guiding principles and rules for lower courts when faced with libel actions. Principled guidelines are given here for the balancing exercise (as opposed to leaving it up to the courts to decide on an ad hoc basis which factors to consider when balancing competing interests in this regard).[60] Where the claimants are public officials, a libel claim cannot succeed unless the claimant can prove clearly that the aggrieving statement was not only false but that the author demonstrably knew that the statement was false. The rule was stated in *New York Times v Sullivan* (1964)[61] by Brennan J and imposed as a constitutional safeguard against the possible chilling effect of libel law, as follows:

> [A] federal rule that prohibits a public official from recovering damages for a defamatory falsehood relating to his official conduct, unless he proves that the statement was made with 'actual malice' – that is, with knowledge that it was false or with reckless disregard of whether it was false or not.[62]

56 *Brandenburg v Ohio*, 395 US 444 (1969).

57 Barendt, note 3, 50.

58 *New York Times v US*, 403 US 713 (1971).

59 Barendt, note 3, 51.

60 For a discussion of this approach, see Schauer, F 'Categories and the First Amendment: A Play in Three Acts' (1981) 34 *Vanderbilt Law Review* 265, 296–307.

61 *New York Times v Sullivan*, 376 US 254 (1964).

62 At 279–280.

The discussion of *New York Times v Sullivan* in chapter 4 examines the importance of setting this threshold so high in more detail. The short summary in this introductory chapter suggests that the First Amendment to the US Constitution accords, on the face of it, absolute protection to freedom of speech: Nevertheless, the courts do recognise that in certain cases this right needs to be restricted. However, the right to freedom of expression is regarded as superior to other rights, and this is evidenced in setting the threshold for its legitimate infringement very high indeed, especially in defamation suits.

Germany

Paradoxically, it can be said that freedom of expression in Germany is accorded both more and at the same time less protection than in the US: Regarding the former, in Germany the state is under a positive duty to promote freedom of expression in ways which the US judiciary, with its constitutionally imposed distrust of government would find almost unimaginable. Regarding the latter, in Germany the right to freedom of expression is not constitutionally ranked as superior to other rights – that distinction belongs to the right contained in article 1 of the GG which guarantees the inviolable right to dignity of man (*Ehre*) and which cannot be amended.

Article 5 of the German Constitution deals with freedom of expression and is noticeably more detailed than the First Amendment. In the same manner as article 10 of the ECHR (and section 12 of the HRA) do, it includes recognition of the idea that freedom of expression relates to both the freedom to express an opinion and the right to receive information. The relevant part reads as follows:

> (1) Everyone shall have the right freely to express and disseminate his opinion by speech, writing and pictures and freely to inform himself from generally accessible sources. Freedom of the press and freedom of reporting by means of broadcasts and films are guaranteed. There shall be no censorship.
>
> (2) These rights are limited by the provisions of the general laws, the provisions of law for the protection of youth, and by the right to inviolability of personal honour.[63]

Given the not-too-distant history of Germany, it is unsurprising that a strong commitment to human dignity pervades its Constitution and is accorded supreme protection in article 1. All other rights are to be interpreted in a manner consistent with paragraph 1. Barendt points out that this partly explains

63 Markesinis, B, Bell, J and Janssen, A *Markesinis's German Law of Torts: A Comparative Treatise* (5th edn, Hart Publishing, Chicago, 2019), 218. Unless otherwise stated, all translations of German statutes and case law are from this source.

why the German Constitutional Court had upheld statutory provisions proscribing Holocaust denial (a clear restriction of freedom of speech);[64] it also explains in part the decision reached in *Mephisto* (1971).[65] This case concerned a novel satirising the claimant's father courting Nazi leadership – when the court had to balance the publisher's right to freedom of expression enshrined in article 5 with the claimant's right to human dignity in article 1, the latter triumphed. Although the case was not couched in defamation terms, it is interesting to note that had it been, and had it been pursued in England and Wales, there would have been no prospects of success as only living persons are accorded the protection of defamation laws in English law. By contrast in Germany, deceased persons' reputations are potentially protected. This is an indication of how seriously 'personal honour' or the inviolable dignity of man is taken in that jurisdiction.

Returning to the 'balancing exercise' – in the seminal case of *Lüth* (1958)[66] (another case dealing with allegations of Nazi links, which is discussed in detail in chapter 5) – the German Constitutional Court established a balancing formula stating that the right to freedom of expression as enshrined in paragraph 5(2) is limited not only by paragraph 1 but also by provisions in general laws, including provisions concerning defamation both in the criminal law and in tort.[67]

On the face of it then, it seems as if the net of reputation protection is cast wider in Germany, but that presumption is wrong, at least as far as political and other public discourse is concerned. In this case there is a presumption in favour of freedom of expression.[68] In the same way opinion is accorded more protection than statements of fact. From a reading of relevant case law, it is clear that the balancing exercise is more nuanced and competing rights may be treated differently in differing cases, depending on the circumstances surrounding the facts. In this way, German jurisprudence in this area of law proceeds in a more ad hoc manner than in the US, where there are strict guidelines from the US Supreme Court on to the way in which rights should be balanced. It must be noted that there are indeed guidelines from the German Constitutional Court,[69] particularly emphasising that due weight should be given to the character of the statement, but that these guidelines are not as rigid as those in the USA and allow for far more contextual flexibility in the lower courts.

64 Barendt, note 3, 61, commenting on the '*Auschwitz Lies*' case, 90 BverfGE 241 (1994).

65 *Mephisto*, 30 BVerfGE 173 (1971).

66 *Lüth*, BVerfGE 198 (1958).

67 The German Criminal Code, paragraphs 185–94 and the German Civil Code paras 823 and 826. Nolte, G *Beleidigungsschutz in der freiheitlichen Demokratie* (Springer, Heidelberg, 1992) provides a thorough exposition of defamation law in Germany (as well as under the ECHR and in the USA).

68 For a comparative analysis, see Nieuwenhuis, A 'Freedom of Speech: USA vs. Germany and Europe' (2000) 18 *Netherlands Quarterly of Human Rights* 195.

69 See the '*Soldiers are murderers*' case, 93 BVerfGE 266 (1995) discussed in chapter 5.

The European Court of Human Rights

The penultimate chapter of this book examines the way in which the European Court of Human Rights (ECtHR) seeks to balance the rights to free speech and reputation. The first and key observation that must be made here is the ECtHR's conflation of reputational rights with the right to privacy. Much of the jurisprudence therefore proceeds from the balancing of the rights in article 10 and article 8 of the ECHR. For now it should be noted that the ECtHR had long recognised that chilling free speech could also be seen as self-censorship,[70] and that free speech may be chilled in various ways and for a variety of reasons. For example, people may self-censor due to fear of disproportionate sanctions.[71]

Another example relates to the nature of possible consequences of speaking up: The possibility of incurring criminal sanctions for defamation may inevitably have, by their very nature, an inhibiting effect on free speech. In *Altuğ Taner Akçam v Turkey* (2011), the ECtHR held:

> Furthermore, it is also open to a person to contend that a law violates his rights, in the absence of an individual measure of implementation, if he is required either to modify his conduct because of it or risk being prosecuted or if he is a member of a class of people who risk being directly affected by the legislation. The Court further notes the chilling effect that the fear of sanction has on the exercise of freedom of expression, even in the event of an eventual acquittal, considering the likelihood of such fear discouraging one from making similar statements in the future.[72]

Unpredictably large damages are also capable of chilling free speech. In *Independent News and Media v Ireland* (2006) the issue of large damages was addressed:[73]

> [I]t is not necessary to rule on whether the present damages award had, as a matter of fact, a chilling effect on the press: as matter of principle, unpredictably large damages' awards in libel cases are considered capable of having such an effect and therefore require the most careful scrutiny. Accordingly, and even if, as the Government argued, the assessment of damages in libel cases is inherently complex and uncertain, any such uncertainty must to be kept to a minimum.

70 *Vajnai v Hungary*, No. 33629/06, ECHR 2008, para 54.

71 *Cumpănă and Mazăre v Romania*, [GC] No. 33348/96, ECHR 2004-XI, para 114.

72 *Altuğ Taner Akçam v Turkey*, No. 27520/07, 25 October 2011, (2016) 62 EHRR 12, para 68.

73 *Independent News and Media and Independent News Ireland Limited v Ireland*, No. 55120/00, ECHR 2005-V, (2006) 42 EHRR 46, para 114.

Finally, the ECtHR recognises that chilling free speech is detrimental to the whole of society.[74] In *Bladet Tromsø and Stensaas v Norway* it reiterated that, when measures taken or sanctions imposed by the national authority are capable of discouraging the participation of the press in debates over matters of legitimate public concern, it is the duty of the court to accord the issue the most careful scrutiny.[75]

Over the past decade or so, two major channels of development in the field of defamation and freedom of expression are of interest. On the one hand, there has been a move in England and Wales to right the balance between a tilt in favour of defamation claimants at the expense of the principle of freedom of expression in general. Almost during the same time frame, it can be safely said that European Court of Human Rights jurisprudence has been moving away from the notion of giving precedence to freedom of expression (when competing with reputation rights) to regarding these as two equal rights to be balanced in the context of their own specific circumstances. These decisions followed from and built upon the recognition given by the ECtHR of reputation forming part of the article 8 of the ECHR right to respect for private life.

To fully understand the jurisprudence from the ECtHR on defamation, one therefore needs to also examine the relevant development in its treatment of the right to privacy, and this is explored in chapter 6. Given the continued importance of Strasbourg jurisprudence in this area of law, this chapter's comparative analysis could arguably provide a barometer of shifting perspectives on the continent.

Conclusion

From a preliminary analysis of the positions in England and Wales, compared to the other three jurisdictions examined in this book, the following tentative statements can be made: Of the three national jurisdictions, freedom of speech is protected most vigorously in the US, with a concomitant lower likelihood of defamation actions being pursued successfully in cases where freedom of speech may arise as a defence, or as a balancing factor.

In Germany (as in the other jurisdictions) freedom of speech is differentiated according to the kind of speech concerned: Political speech and opinion, for example, are accorded higher protection than other forms of speech. But all of them are subject to a balancing exercise with relevant competing constitutional rights where these come in conflict. Therefore, a defamation suit may well be trumped by judicial consideration of the right to freedom of speech.

74 *Cumpănă*, note 71, para 114.

75 *Bladet Tromsø and Stensaas v Norway*, No. 21980/93 ECHR 20 May 1999, (2000) 29 EHRR 125, para 64. See also *Jersild v Denmark*, No 15890/89 (A/298), (1995) 19 EHRR 1, paras 31 and 35.

The relative weights given to competing rights depend on the context of each case, and therefore, the balancing exercise tends to be rather ad hoc. One also needs to keep in mind that under the right circumstances, the personality right protected by a defamation claim in Germany may overlap with the paragraph 1 GG right to human dignity which is sacrosanct in German constitutional law: In such a case, this will then trump the freedom of speech consideration.

In England and Wales, it was recognised that defamation law operated in such a manner that there were legitimate concerns that it was stifling freedom of expression. To that end, a major legislative reform process culminated in the Defamation Act 2013. This act attempts to redress the balance by, *inter alia*, addressing concerns that defamation laws were particularly claimant friendly, setting the threshold for instituting claims higher, discouraging libel tourism and abolishing the right to trial by jury for defamation claims. The extent to which these concerns are addressed and the way in which they are handled in case law can be fruitfully analysed from a free speech perspective.

Against the broad brush-strokes of this initial introduction, the next chapters will focus in more detail on each of the selected jurisdictions, starting with the English common law of defamation in chapter 2.

2 Common law of defamation in England and Wales prior to the Defamation Act 2013

Introduction

Chapter 1 explored the two fundamental legal interests examined in this book – reputation and freedom of expression. Both trace their roots far back in the common law, and cogent and enduring arguments remain valid for their raisons d'être and continued legal protection alike. This chapter describes how the conflict between these two legal interests intensified to the extent that, by the start of the second decade of this century, calls for reform were insistent and loud enough to trigger extensive legislative reform of the defamation law of England and Wales.[1] The core reason that Parliament enacted the Defamation Act 2013 is because certain characteristics of the common law of defamation rendered it problematic – in particular, those that Milo characterised as the 'potent trilogy of fundamental principles' of the common law of defamation – the presumption of falsity, the nature of defamation as a no-fault/strict liability tort, and the presumption of damages.[2] The tort was actionable *per se*, which means that the claimant need not prove that they suffered any damages. The defamation claimant was further assisted in this regard by the irrebuttable presumption of harm which was triggered upon proof of a defamatory statement identifying the claimant. The result was a series of high-profile incidents of 'libel tourism' where claimants domiciled abroad chose to sue in England.[3] This forum shopping led to the abuse of process doctrine being applied vigorously in defamation cases in order to discourage the pursuit of a number of frivolous cases. A threshold of seriousness was set, but the legal presumptions of harm and of falsity were firmly retained, as well as the nature of the tort as being actionable *per se*.

1 For a more extensive discussion of the common law of defamation see Milmo, P and Rogers, WVH (eds), *Gatley on Libel and Slander* (10th edn, Sweet & Maxwell, London, 2004) and Collins, M *Collins on Defamation* (OUP, Oxford, 2014).

2 Milo, D *Defamation and Freedom of Speech* (OUP, Oxford, 2008), 11.

3 As stated in chapter 1, reference to England includes Wales, and 'English law' means English and Welsh law.

DOI: 10.4324/9781003416005-3

Under the common law, defamation was also the only civil action in England and Wales that was routinely tried by jury. A pattern developed where disproportionately large awards were given by juries, which then later had to be reduced on appeal. This both led to the ECtHR signalling its disapproval,[4] as well as legislative reform which effectively placed a cap on the awards that could be given with libel damages now subject to a notional ceiling which rises with inflation.[5] The legal costs associated with pursuing or defending a defamation trial was also very high, and no state legal aid was available to either party to a defamation suit. These considerations meant that many people or institutions, including academics and consumer groups could be silenced with the mere threat of a libel suit. This of course was inhibiting, or 'chilling,' free speech and the main reason for the eventual reforms that passed in 2013. Before examining these issues in more detail, it is useful to briefly summarise the main elements of the common law tort of defamation.

The common law tort of defamation

Based on Lord Atkin's test for the word 'defamatory' in *Sim v Stretch* [1936],[6] defamation can be defined as 'the publication of a statement which reflects on a person's reputation, and tends to lower him in the estimation of right-thinking members of society generally or tends to make them shun or avoid him.'[7] In order to succeed with a common law claim in defamation, the claimant had to prove the publication of a defamatory statement referring to them. Under the common law harm to reputation is presumed upon proof of the defamatory meaning of the statement. In addition, the common law then presumes that the statement is false, placing the burden to prove otherwise on the defendant. This presumption, one of Milo's 'potent trilogy' mentioned earlier, indicates the gravity with which the law regarded reputation.[8]

Defamatory statement

To succeed in a common law defamation suit in England and Wales, the claimant had to prove the publication of a defamatory statement identifying the claimant. There was no need to prove damages to the claimant or fault on the part of the defendant. Once these elements were proven, the burden

4 *Tolstoy Miloslavsky v United Kingdom* [1996] EMLR 152.

5 A significant change in the civil costs-regime was initiated by Sir Rupert Jackson's reforms (*Final Report on Civil Litigation Costs* (December 2009)) and enacted by the legislature in Legal Aid, Sentencing and Punishment of Offenders Act 2012 (LASPO).

6 *Sim v Stretch* [1936] 2 All ER 1237.

7 Rogers, WVH *Winfield and Jolowicz on Tort* (18th edn, Sweet & Maxwell, London, 2010), para 12.3.

8 See the following discussion of this and the other two issues in the 'potent trilogy.'

then shifted to the defendant who had a plethora of disparate defences at their disposal.

Since the clear formulation in *Webb v Bloch* (1928),[9] it is generally accepted that publication occurs when a person intentionally or negligently communicates, or takes part in communicating, material. To establish publication for defamation, a third party needs to have heard or seen the statement – a statement made solely to the claimant, without anybody else hearing it, can therefore not be defamatory, regardless of how insulting it is.[10] The reason once again is that defamation is concerned with protecting an individual's reputation, and a reputation, whilst belonging to an individual, depends for its existence on others' opinions.

It is worth noting that at common law, not only those who composed the statement could be held responsible for publication. Such responsibility was extended to those who participated in the preparation of the statement, in its communication, including, for example, typists, editors, media proprietors, online content moderators, and television affiliates, reflecting the principle dating back to *R v Paine* (1696):

> [I]f one dictate, and another write, both are guilty of making it . . . If one repeat and another write a libel, and a third approve what is wrote, they are all makers of it; for all persons who concur, and shew their assent or approbation to do an unlawful act, are guilty: so that murdering a man's reputation by a scandalous libel may be compared to murdering his person; for if several are assisting and encouraging a man in the act, though the stroke was given by one, yet all are guilty of homicide.[11]

What is more, at common law even secondary distributors of defamatory statements were treated as publishers. These included, for example, libraries,[12] retailers, and wholesalers.[13]

Claimants in defamation actions must prove that the publication conveyed a defamatory meaning. How difficult a task they face depends on the statement itself. The law recognises several levels of defamatory meaning. In *Chase v News Group Newspapers Ltd* [2002][14] the Court of Appeal held that a defamatory

9 *Webb v Bloch* [1928] 41 CLR 331 (HCA), 363–366.

10 *Pullman v Walter Hill & Co Ltd* [1891] 1 QB 524 (CA), 527, 529, 530; *Powell v Gelston* [1916] 2 KB 615, 619. See however, instances where publication only to the defamed person may be sufficient, such as where further communication should have been anticipated, *Theaker v Richardson* [1962] 1 WLR 151 (CA); or, for example, where the recipient is a trade union official under an obligation to further disseminate to union members the material defaming himself, see Collins, note 1, 70.

11 *R v Paine* [1696] 5 Mod 163 (KB), 167; ER 584, 586–7.

12 Martin v Trustees of the British Museum (1894) 10 TLR 338 (QB).

13 *Emmens v Pottle* [1885] 16 QBD 354.

14 *Chase v News Group Newspapers Ltd* [2002] EWCA Civ 1772.

statement may involve three levels: Level 1 comprises a clear imputation of guilt on the part of the claimant, level 2 entails that there are reasonable grounds to suspect that the claimant is involved, and finally, level 3 comprises grounds to investigate what the claimant has done. When exactly a statement is defamatory is by its nature a vexing question. Lord Justice Neill famously said in *Berkoff v Burchill* [1996][15] that he was not aware of any entirely satisfactory definition of the word 'defamatory.' However, it seems to be broadly agreed that a statement is defamatory if it has some (negative) bearing on the reputation of the claimant, and again Neil LJ in *Berkoff* gave what may be the most important modern consideration of the relationship between defamatory meaning and reputation, with reputation 'to be interpreted in a broad sense as comprehending all aspects of a person's standing in the community.'[16] McNamara points out that to understand what is defamatory, one needs therefore to understand properly what is meant by 'reputation,' and that it is here that the law is lacking.[17] It is worth pausing to consider whether this question has been (or indeed can ever be) satisfactorily answered. It certainly forms the basis of an enquiry of its own,[18] but for present purposes the discussion of reputation in chapter 1 and the ways in which the courts and other legal thinkers have attempted to define 'defamatory meaning' must suffice, with the caveat to the reader that a final answer has not been formulated yet, and perhaps never could be.

In general, Parke B's statement in 1840 in *Parmiter v Coupland* (1840) is seen as the starting point: A statement that 'is calculated to injure the reputation of another by exposing him to hatred, contempt or ridicule' is defamatory.[19] Since then the law changed significantly, and McNamara describes three tests for defamatory meaning that can be identified as having crystallised over the last seven decades.[20] The principal test is the 'lowering the estimation' test quoted earlier from *Sim v Stretch*.[21] In this case the *Parmiter v Coupland* position was watered down – instead of having to prove that the statement inspired feelings as strong as hatred, ridicule, or contempt, Lord Atkin held that it was enough that the plaintiff was lowered 'in the estimation of right-thinking members of society generally.'[22] A more recent iteration of this test

15 *Berkoff v Burchill* [1996] 4 All ER 1008, 1011, CA.

16 Ibid, 151.

17 This question informs the entirely of the work in McNamara, L *Reputation and Defamation* (OUP, Oxford, 2007).

18 See on the relationship between defamation and reputation also: Post, RC 'The Social Foundations of Defamation Law: Reputation and the Constitution' (1986) 74 *California Law Review* 691; and Rolph, D *Reputation, Celebrity and Defamation Law* (Routledge, Abingdon, 2008).

19 *Parmiter v Coupland* [1840] 6 M&W 105, 108, Exch.

20 McNamara, note 17, 2–3.

21 *Sim v Stretch*, note 6.

22 Ibid, 1240. It is interesting to note that a diverse society brings its own problems in this regard. Suffice it to note here that the orthodox view as expressed by Warby J in *Monroe v*

is found in the Faulks Committee on Defamation's 1975 formulation of a statement as defamatory if it would be likely to affect a person adversely in the estimation of reasonable people generally.[23]

Two other tests are also generally recognised. The first is as follows: Even if there is no 'moral discredit,' a statement is defamatory if it will lead to the claimant being 'shunned and avoided.'[24] The final test is whether or not the statement subjects or exposes a person to ridicule.[25] McNamara points out that the second test is almost never applied by the courts but is nevertheless regularly cited as part of the law, and that the third test appears in case reports more often but is still only applied occasionally.[26] Although the first test remains primary, and the others tend to be used only when the first test cannot yield an answer, the three together can be regarded as a synopsis of the law.

'Single meaning' rule

Statements that are ambiguous or that could be interpreted differently by different persons are problematic and become more so because English defamation law allows for only one interpretation. The common law 'single meaning' rule states that, as in the construction of contracts or statutes, a given set of words is to be treated as having only one meaning.[27] This means that, when faced with the question of whether the defendant has committed the tort of defamation, the courts dismiss the possibility that a statement may be genuinely ambiguous and must instead adhere to 'the fiction that there is a single reasonable reader, so that the words, duly taken in context, have only one meaning.'[28] In practice, the judge would determine which meanings the allegedly defamatory words were capable of bearing and exclude those which they were considered not capable of bearing. The judge would then put to the jury the various possible meanings and, with appropriate directions, invite the jury to decide which of those adumbrated meanings was the one to be attributed

---

Hopkins [2017] EMLR 16, paras 50–51 states: 'The demands of pluralism in a democratic society make it important to allow room for differing views to be expressed, without fear of paying damages for defamation. Hence, a statement is not defamatory if it would only tend to have an adverse effect on the attitudes to the claimant of a certain section of society.' Some argue for a sectional test (i.e. whether a specific section of the population would find the statement defamatory). Cf. Speker, A *Paradise and Prostitutes: Time for a Sectional Standards Test?* <https://inforrm.org/2017/11/16/paradise-and-prostitutes-time-for-a-sectional-standards-test-adam-speker/#more-38727> accessed 19 November 2017.

23 Report of the Committee on Defamation CMND 5909, 1975, para 65.

24 *Youssoupoff v Metro-Goldwyn Mayer* [1934] 50 TLR 581, CA.

25 *Berkoff v Burchill*, note 15.

26 McNamara, note 17, 3.

27 *Charleston v News Group Newspapers Ltd* [1995] 2 AC 65, 71–72.

28 *Ajinomoto Sweeteners Europe SAS v Asda Stores Ltd* [2010] EWCA Civ 609, [2010] 4 All ER 1029, 3 per Sedley LJ.

to the words said to be defamatory. Sir Anthony Clarke MR in *Jeynes v News Magazines Ltd* [2008] summarised the legal principles by which such single meaning was to be identified:

> (1) The governing principle is reasonableness. (2) The hypothetical reasonable reader is not naïve but he is not unduly suspicious. He can read between the lines. He can read an implication more readily than a lawyer and may indulge in a certain amount of loose thinking but he must be treated as being a man who is not avid for scandal and someone who does not, and should not, select one bad meaning where other non-defamatory meanings are available. (3) Over elaborate analysis is best avoided. (4) The intention of the publisher is irrelevant. (5) The article must be read as a whole, and any 'bane and antidote' taken together. (6) The hypothetical reader is taken to be representative of those who would read the publication in question. (7) In delimiting the range of permissible defamatory meanings, the court should rule out any meaning which, 'can only emerge as the product of some strained, or forced or utterly unreasonable interpretation . . .' (8) It follows that 'it is not enough to say that by some person or another the words might be understood in a defamatory sense.'[29]

The 'single meaning' rule was, and remains, subject to criticism. It might even be seen as contradictory that a single statement can qualify as defamatory in order to found a claim on the basis of one set of criteria when it does not make the grade based on another, without any clear reason why this should be so. The exercise of choosing a single immutable meaning from a series of words which are capable of bearing more than one has therefore rightfully been described as artificial.[30] Defenders of the rule usually point out that the identification of a single meaning to be accorded a statement arose in many areas of law, most notably in the interpretation of statutes, contracts, and notices.[31] However, as a sceptic, Lord Reed pointed out recently: 'Whether the analogy between a single defamatory meaning and a sole meaning to be given to a contractual term, statutory provision or notice is apt (which I take leave to doubt), it is clear that the single meaning approach is well entrenched in the law of defamation.'[32] At least the rule provides a practical, workable solution in cases where a statement has more than one plausible meaning. The question of whether defamation has occurred can only then be answered by deciding that one particular meaning should be ascribed to the statement.

29 *Jeynes v News Magazines Ltd* [2008] EWCA Civ 130, para 14.

30 *Slim v Daily Telegraph Ltd* [1968] 2 QB 157, 172 per Diplock LJ.

31 *Oriental Daily Publisher Ltd v Ming Pao Holdings Ltd* [2013] EMLR 7, 138 per Lord Neuberger of Abbotsbury.

32 *Stocker v Stocker* [2019] UKSC 17, 34.

Of course, the fact remains that until 2013 it was for the jury to decide whether the aggrieved statement was defamatory. Despite the directions given to the jury on how to make their decision, the decision itself was not reasoned. In the end it largely came down to something best defined as 'we know it when we see it.'

Finally, it bears repetition that reputation is very much dependent on the opinions or judgements of the beholder and is not solely a function of personality such as informs the basis for privacy rights. The complications of conflating these concepts are explored in subsequent chapters and in more detail in the discussion of the jurisprudence of the European Court of Human Rights. If the claimant cannot be identified from the statement, there is no defamation. This does not mean that the claimant has to be specifically named: They may be identified by implication. The test is whether the hypothetical reasonable reader/viewer, with knowledge of any special circumstances would believe that the claimant is being referred to. The requirement that the claimant has to be identified/identifiable reinforces the principle that defamation is concerned with reputation as a construct that exists primarily in the opinion of members of a community.

Peculiar characteristics of the tort of defamation which may have led to the imbalance *vis-à-vis* free speech

In England and Wales, the common law tort of defamation differed substantially from other torts in several significant ways. It was the only tort of strict liability that was also actionable *per se*. By putting the defendant to the proof as to the truth of the allegedly defamatory statement (which in itself was subject to an irrebuttable presumption of harm), the burden of proof shifted to the defendant in a way that clearly departs from the rule of civil procedure that 'he who avers has to prove.' It is therefore useful to examine more closely this 'potent trilogy of fundamental principles' of the common law of defamation – namely, the presumption of falsity, strict liability, and the presumption of damages.[33]

Strict liability

Initially defamation was a tort based on fault in the form of malice, but it underwent a metamorphosis – in a transition that was 'neither smooth nor unanimous'[34] to a tort of strict liability.[35] The general position therefore was that under the common law, the defamation claimant did not need to prove

33 Milo, note 2.

34 Mitchell, P *The Making of the Modern Law of Defamation* (Hart Publishing, Oxford, 2005), 101–113, 112–113.

35 *Jones v E Hulton & Co* [1910] AC 20 HL.

fault on the part of the defendant, be it malice, intention, or negligence, and neither could the absence of fault be raised as a defence.[36] Innocent defamation therefore means that a defendant could be held liable for the purely unintended consequences of a statement.[37] One of the classic formulations of the rule concerns a case where the author of a statement believed it to be fictitious, whereas the 'fictitious' name used turned out to belong to a real person, who successfully vindicated it in a libel action: In the House of Lords' decision in *E Hulton & Co v Jones* [1910], the applicable principle was stated as follows:

> Libel is a tortious act. What does the tort consist in? It consists in using language which others knowing the circumstances would reasonably think to be defamatory of the person complaining of and injured by it. A person charged with libel cannot defend himself by shewing that he intended in his own breast not to defame, or that he intended not to defame the plaintiff, if in fact he did both.[38]

The principle of strict liability was held in *O'Shea v MGN Ltd* [2001][39] to be in violation of the right to freedom of expression guaranteed in article 10 of the ECHR. However, this did not put paid to the principle of strict liability for libel in English common law. Subsequent cases held otherwise, clarifying that the decision in *O'Shea v MGN Ltd* merely meant an extension of the common law Reynolds defence, which protected *prima facie* defamatory statements published on matters of public interest.[40] In *Baturina v Times Newspapers Ltd* [2011],[41] for instance, Lord Neuberger MR stated that article 10 of the ECHR did not require any modification of the strict liability principle for instances of 'reference innuendos'[42] as the Reynolds defence would usually apply.

This means that strict liability is indeed capable of being successfully challenged as being incompatible with article 10 of the ECHR, but it seems that it is possible only on an *ad hoc* basis, depending on each case's facts, rather than on a systemic and principled basis. In *O'Shea*, for instance, the court held that the particular facts of the case placed an impossible burden on the defendant and served no pressing social need: Clearly here a factual weighing up/

36 Milo, note 2, 185, 186.

37 As will be seen in chapter 3, this characteristic of the common law survived the 2013 reforms.

38 *E Hulton & Co v Jones* [1910] AC 20 (HL).

39 *O'Shea v MGN Ltd* [2001] EMLR 40 (QB).

40 This defence was formulated in the case of *Reynolds v Times Newspapers Ltd* [1999] 4 All ER 609, and was the closest the UK common law came to a 'responsible journalism' defence. For a discussion of the Reynolds defence, see Barendt, E 'Reynolds Revived and Replaced' (2017) 9(1) *Journal of Media Law* 1–13.

41 *Baturina v Times Newspapers Ltd* [2011] EWCA Civ 308, [2011] 1 WLR 1526, para 27.

42 These are statements that are prima facie defamatory but where external knowledge is then further necessary to link the statement to a specific person.

balancing exercise was undertaken by the court. In this case, a pornographic website used in its advertisement a photograph of a woman bearing a striking resemblance to the claimant, who alleged that she was identified by the photograph. In the judgment of the court, article 10 of the ECHR in this instance outweighed the claimant's dependence on the strict liability characteristic of English libel law.

Presumption of harm: actionable per se

In the English common law libel (and some instances of slander[43]) were actionable *per se*, meaning the claimant did not have to prove damages. For the majority of defamation claims, all the claimant had to prove therefore was that there was a defamatory statement which identified the claimant. Not only was there no need to prove damages, the claimant also did not need to prove that their reputation was in fact harmed. The presumption survived the introduction of the Human Rights Act 1998.

Nor was the presumption displaced by considerations relating to article 10 of the ECHR: In *Jameel v Dow Jones* [2005] it was held that the presumption of damage that forms part of the English law of libel is not incompatible with article 10 of the Convention.[44] The claimant, a Saudi national, issued defamation proceedings in England against the publisher of the *Wall Street Journal* based on an article it posted on its website in the US, which was available to subscribers in England. The claimant alleged that the article and its hyperlinks identified him as a donor to Al-Qaeda. The defendant pointed out to the court that very few (as few as five) people in England had accessed the article and that the claimant had therefore in fact suffered no or minimal damage to his reputation. This brought them to the issue of presumption of harm. The defendant argued that this presumption was in conflict with the right to freedom of speech. The Court of Appeal held that the presumption of harm in the tort of defamation was irrebuttable. However, the court then held that in cases where actual damage to the claimant's reputation was minimal, the claim could be struck out as an abuse of process. In what subsequently came to be known as the 'Jameel exception,' the courts, although stopping short of removing the presumption of harm, thereafter required as a minimum

43 In cases of slander the claimant had to prove special damages: cf. *Chamberlain v Boyd* [1883] 11 QBD 407 (CA). There were four exceptions where slander too was actionable *per se* – namely, if the aggrieved statement alleged that the claimant was an unchaste woman, suffered from a communicable disease, had committed a serious crime, or that the claimant was incompetent, unfit or dishonest in her business, profession or trade: cf. Slander of Women Act 1891, s 1; *Taylor v Perkins* [1606] CroJac 144 (KB), 79 ER 126; *Webb v Beavan* [1883] 11 QBD 609; *Jones v Jones* [1916] 2 AC 481 (HL).

44 *Jameel (Yousef) v Dow Jones & Co Inc* [2005] QB 946, para 41. See also *Jameel (Mohammed) v Wall Street Journal Europe Sprl* [2007] 1 AC 359.

threshold for defamation actions that the claimant must have, in fact, suffered harm to their reputation.

The next significant development in this area of the law occurred in the first instance decision of Tugendhat J in *Thornton v Telegraph Media Group Ltd* [2011].[45] It is clear that Tugendhat J was concerned, particularly in the context of article 10 of the ECHR and proportionality considerations, about the need to exclude trivial claims. He concluded that there was a requirement for a 'threshold of seriousness'[46] and that the correct formulation was 'the publication of which he complains may be defamatory of him because it *substantially* affects in an adverse manner the attitude of other people towards him, or *has a tendency so to do*' (emphasis in original).[47]

A threshold of seriousness, phrased in terms of substantiality, was thereby introduced. In fact, Tugendhat J reasoned that such a threshold is the logical *sine qua non* for the very existence of the presumption when he explained his understanding of the reason that the law presumes damage in libel as follows:

> If the likelihood of adverse consequences for a claimant is part of the definition of what is defamatory, then the presumption of damage is the logical corollary of what is already included in the definition. And conversely, the fact that in law damage is presumed is itself an argument why an imputation should not be held to be defamatory unless it has a tendency to have adverse effects upon the claimant. It is difficult to justify why there should be a presumption of damage if words can be defamatory while having no likely adverse consequence for the claimant.[48]

In developing the threshold of seriousness requirement, the courts mitigated the effects of defamation's strict liability nature. Nevertheless, the presumption of harm itself remained intact.

Presumption of falsity

At common law, upon proof by the claimant that a defamatory statement of fact[49] identifying the claimant had been published, a presumption arises that the statement is false. The legal burden of proof then shifts to the defendant to prove that the statement is substantially true, or failing that, is covered by one

45 *Thornton v Telegraph Media Group Ltd* [2011] 1 WLR 1985.

46 Ibid, paras 90 and 92.

47 Ibid, para 96.

48 Ibid, para 94.

49 As opposed to opinion, in which case the defendant could possibly rely on the defence of honest comment – but would still bear the burden of proving the veracity of the underlying facts upon which the opinion is based.

of a number of defamation-specific defences.[50] This reverse burden of proof has been criticised consistently over the years. Lord Lester, who long campaigned for libel reform, arguably voiced the frustration of many critics when he stated that '[v]illains can (and frequently do) recover substantial damages in libel without having to show that what has been published about them is false.'[51] Nevertheless, jurists have been remarkably resistant to the idea of abolishing this presumption, and it remains firmly entrenched. Both the Faulks Committee[52] and the Neil Committee[53] rejected changing it. The ECtHR has also stated that placing the burden to prove substantial truth on the defendant in the way that the common law does is not in principle incompatible with article 10.[54]

When given the opportunity to address the issue, albeit of necessity *obiter*, the Court of Appeal declined to consider the point in *Jameel (Mohammed) v Wall Street Journal Europe SPRL (No.3)* [2005].[55] It did, however, take the time to remark that suggesting a removal of this reverse burden of proof was going too far, and that it would require a major change in the law of defamation.[56] Arguments in favour of retaining the presumption can be summarised as comprising a reluctance to break with longstanding precedent,[57] the notion that reputation deserves to be protected robustly in this way by the courts, that the existence of defences such as honest opinion and justification mitigated the harshness of the presumption, and the argument that burdening the claimant with proving falsity requires of them the difficult, if not at times impossible, task of proving a negative.

50 Parkes, R *et al. Gatley on Libel and Slander* (12th edn, incorporating Second Supplement, Sweet & Maxwell, London, 2017), para 11.4.

51 *Hansard* HL Deb Col 240 (2 April 1996), where Lord Lester unsuccessfully moved an amendment to the Defamation Bill 1996 that would have placed the burden to prove falsity of the defamatory statement on the claimant.

52 Report of the Faulks Committee on Defamation (Cmnd 5909) (1975). The Committee on Defamation was appointed by the Lord Chancellor and the Lord Advocate in June 1971 under the chairmanship of The Honourable Mr. Justice Faulks, MBE, TD. Its terms of reference, which applied to Scotland as well as to England and Wales, were as follows: 'To consider whether, in the light of the working of the Defamation Act 1952, any changes are desirable in the law, practice and procedure relating to actions for defamation.' The Committee's report was published in 1975 (Cmnd. 5909).

53 UK Supreme Court Procedure Committee *Working Group on Practice and Procedure in Defamation* (1991). This committee, chaired by Sir Brian Neill reviewed some aspects of defamation law by the Faulks Committee and updated a previous statute dating from 1952. The findings were instrumental to the enactment of the Defamation Act 1996.

54 *EuropaPress Holding DOO v Croatia* [2011] 53 EHRR 27, para 63. See also *McVicar v UK* [2002] 35 EHRR 22; *Steel and Morris v UK* [2005] 41 EHRR 22, para 93.

55 *Jameel (Mohammed) v Wall Street Journal Europe SPRL (No. 3)* [2005] EWCA Civ 74, para 57. (For the appeal to the HL on other issues, see [2006] UKHL 44; [2007] 1 AC 359).

56 Ibid, para 55.

57 Ibid.

As to the contention that reputation needs to be favoured in this way, the reasons for this argument seem unclear, especially given that the English law of defamation remains committed to the proposition that a claimant is not entitled to recover damages for injury to a (good) reputation which he does not in fact have.[58] For this purpose the reputation a person possesses is determined as a matter of objective fact.[59] But there is still no logically valid reason that this evidentiary burden is placed on the defamation defendant, rather than on the defamation claimant, as is usual in other civil actions. After all, there are other related areas of law in which the claimant is required to prove falsity, such as malicious falsehood and negligent misrepresentation. What is more, this argument conflates evidentiary difficulty with evidentiary burden and therefore rests on a less than firm basis.[60] Finally, claimants remain in the best position to say precisely what is true and what is false about defamatory statements.[61]

One of the arguments for this reverse burden of proof is the notion that being required to think about whether one could prove the truth of what gets to be said or published, acts as a necessary restraint on publishers. In other words, the argument goes that, together with the defence of truth, this injects a much-needed element of caution into decisions about publication.[62] However, that does not consider the fact that proving truth is often very difficult, especially in the publication of more contentious issues – journalists may wish to protect their sources, and some sources may be anonymous or have died or moved abroad.[63] The argument that this presumption helps to ensure that only deserving statements are published can be countered by the argument that requiring the claimant to prove falsity will go some way towards ensuring that 'only claimants with deserved reputations succeed.'[64]

In the final analysis, it seems that with this presumption the common law places a premium on reputation, compared to other considerations such as free speech. Why this is so remains unclear and, '[a]t bedrock, the allocation of the burden of proof depends upon ***public policy***' (own emphasis).[65]

58 *McPherson v Daniels* [1829] 10 B & C 263 at 272. *Chase v News Group Newspapers Ltd* [2002] EWCA Civ 1772; [2003] EMLR 218, para 33.
59 Gatley, note 1, para 11.1.
60 Hagans, WG 'Who Does the First Amendment Protect? Why the Plaintiff should Bear the Burden of Proof in any Defamation Action' (2007) 26 *Review of Litigation* 613, 635–636.
61 Butterworth, S 'Lord Lester's Defamation Bill should be more Radical' *The Guardian* (London, 23 June 2010).
62 Mullis, A and Scott, A 'Lord Lester's Defamation Bill 2010: A Distorted View of Public Interest?' (2011) 16(1) *Communications Law* 6–18.
63 Butterworth, note 61.
64 Milo, note 2, 163.
65 Ibid, 182.

Free speech rationale for defamation reform

In the preface to his book on defamation law, Milo recognised that it is trite that the law of defamation contemplates the clash of two fundamental rights, the right to freedom of expression and the right to reputation.[66] Indeed the fact that the right to reputation may be and often is in conflict with the right to freedom of expression continues to exercise the courts: In *Re S*, the House of Lords held that balancing these rights would have to consist of a two-way exercise involving an intense scrutiny of all the circumstances of the case.[67] It should therefore come as no surprise that rebalancing the law in favour of promoting free expression was one of the stated aims of the reforms that culminated in the Defamation Act 2013. In fact, this was identified in the report of the Joint Committee on the draft Defamation Bill[68] as one of four key areas of concern.[69]

Based on what evidence, however, was it alleged that the common law on defamation tilted in favour of reputation, at the cost of free speech? In addition to the 'triumvirate of presumptions' in favour of defamation claimants discussed earlier, the following issues were paramount – the chilling effect of the threat of defamation suits, the perceived phenomenon of libel tourism to England, and characteristics of the common law that fuelled these phenomena, such as the inequality of arms inherent in equating corporate claimants with natural persons, the 'multiple publication' rule, and the growth of the internet outpacing the common law rules on publication.

The chilling effect

The 'chilling effect' refers to the kind of self-censorship induced by the fear, real or perceived, of being sued. Threats of defamation suits especially tended to silence would-be speakers subject to the (very wide) jurisdiction of the English common law of defamation. The reality of this chilling effect was proven empirically more than twenty years ago through research conducted by Prof. Eric Barendt[70] and has been confirmed in related research at multiple points since then by equally distinguished scholars, based on both content analysis as well as wide-ranging interviews.[71]

In this way English libel laws favoured the rich and powerful who could, with the mere threat of a defamation claim, silence an impecunious critic.

66 Ibid, ix.

67 *Re S (A Child) (Identification: Restrictions on Publication)* [2004] UKHL 47, para 17.

68 Joint Committee on the Draft Defamation Bill, *Draft Defamation Bill* (2011).

69 Milo, note 2, 3.

70 Barendt, E, Lustgarten, L, Norrie, K and Stephenson, H *Libel Law and the Media: The Chilling Effect* (Clarendon Press, Oxford, 1997), 191.

71 See for instance Dent, C and Kenyon, AT 'Defamation Law's Chilling Effect: A Comparative Content Analysis of Australian and US Newspapers' (2004) 9 *Media & Arts Law Review* 89.

Moreover, this was a one-way street as impecunious victims of libel or slander found their access to justice barred by the costs of litigation. A further reason for the chilling effect of the common law of defamation therefore relates to costs – of the suit itself, as well as potential damage awards that were inflated by defamation juries. These two drivers of the chilling effect bear closer scrutiny.

Costs

It is highly likely that the costs involved in defending a defamation claim had at least the potential to chill free speech. Such restraint on the free and frank exchange or expression of views in turn has dire consequences for scientific or academic discourse, consumer awareness, legitimate criticism, political discourse, and the practical exercise of democratic functions, to name but a few. Vindicating one's reputation was (and remains) an expensive affair in the UK. In the absence of a tribunal or other alternative dispute resolution forum for defamation, the court remains the only option for such disputes. Conditional fee arrangements, which are discussed in detail in chapter 3, only addressed this partially. The result was that it seemed that although any individual referred to in a defamatory statement could sue, and despite robust free speech precedent, only the rich and powerful had unfettered access to legal protection of their reputations. In that sense, stating that the courts were open to anybody to enforce their reputation rights was similar to saying that the Ritz-Carlton hotel is open to everybody: In theory, yes, they are; in practice, they are not. Since either pursuing or defending a defamation claim required deep pockets this meant that the playing field was not level – the impecunious, or those simply without the time and resources to devote to defending a costly defamation suit, definitely needed to think twice about what they said publicly about the rich and powerful. This is aggravated by the fact that not only natural persons but also legal persons, such as corporations, have legal standing to sue. In a globalised world with multinational corporations wielding enormous power, this is highly significant to free speech advocates – the so-called 'McLibel case'[72] discussed immediately below being the prime example of how this can all go wrong.[73]

Also, to make matters worse for litigants, under the common law there was no legal aid for defamation. Although legal aid in general is being cut and this has an impact on society, campaigners have pointed out that the fact that there was no legal aid for defamation actions impacted disproportionately on ordinary or impecunious parties. The lengthy and expensive court battle waged by McDonald's is a prime example – a multinational corporation with teams of lawyers against two indigent individuals dependent on the good will

72 *McDonald's Corp. v Steel* [1995] 3 All ER 615; *Steel and Morris v UK* [2005] 18 BHRC 545.

73 See the discussion of reputation as property in chapter 1: The idea of a corporate reputation is based on the marketplace ideology informing one of several understandings of reputation.

of pro bono lawyers in what came to be known as the McLibel case.[74] McDonald's successfully sued two environmental campaigners for allegedly defamatory statements about the company. The case is famous for being the longest civil action in English history and for the large amount of damages (£60,000) awarded to McDonald's, which paled in significance compared to the costs of pursuing the claim: It was rumoured that McDonald's legal costs ran into millions of pounds.

The defendants in the McLibel case took the matter to the ECtHR, where it was held that the fact that they had not been given legal aid when they were defending themselves in the UK courts was an infringement of the right to a fair trial.[75] As a consequence of this decision by the Strasbourg court, legal aid is now available to the defendant in a libel action, but only if they are sued by a multinational corporation.

Defamation claims constitute the only civil actions in English law that can potentially be heard by a jury. As stated earlier, it fell to the jury to decide whether or not the statement complained of in a defamation trial carried a defamatory meaning. This finding on the facts, being made by a jury, was not accompanied by reasons and arguably this meant that a full theory of what comprises defamatory meaning was lacking. There was also a tendency for juries to award disproportionately high damages awards, which often required the Appeal Court to later on reduce the amount. For example, in *John v Mirror Group Newspapers* [1996][76] the jury awarded Elton John a total of £350,000 in defamation damages. The Court of Appeal later reduced this to £75,000 and directed that in future judges should give clear guidance to juries on damages.[77] It could be argued that these high awards, coupled with the extra layer of complexity added by jury trials, further tended to have a chilling effect on free speech. The ECtHR seemed to agree: In *Tolstoy Miloslavsky v United Kingdom* [1996][78] it held that an award of £1.5 million made by a jury against the defendant was an infringement of article 10 of the ECHR.

Libel tourism

A further driver for defamation's chilling effect on speech could be found in the phenomenon which came to be known as 'libel tourism,' a term first coined by a *Guardian* journalist in 2008 and which entails the practice of forum-shopping for a jurisdiction favourable to libel claimants.[79] This was widely

74 *McDonald's v Steel*, note 72.
75 *Steel and Morris v UK*, note 72.
76 *John v Mirror Group Newspapers* [1996] 2 All ER 35.
77 *John v Mirror Group Newspapers* [1997] QB 586.
78 *Tolstoy Miloslavsky v United Kingdom* [1996] EMLR 152.
79 Wheatcroft, G 'The Worst Case Scenario' *The Guardian* (London, 28 February 2008).

recognised as a concern for UK defamation law, with England and Wales being seen as a prime destination for libel claimants.[80] For instance, libel tourism to England and Wales was identified and acknowledged as a problem by stakeholders as diverse as the US federal government,[81] the European Parliament,[82] and the UK government itself[83] – the Government Explanatory Notes to the Defamation Act accepted that concern about libel tourism was valid.[84] The phenomenon meant that cases with only a tenuous link to England and Wales were instituted there because the jurisdiction was seen as very favourable to defamation claimants. The fact that libel claims were actionable *per se* made this jurisdiction particularly attractive. Two well-known examples will suffice to illustrate the point. In *Bin Mahfouz v Ehrenfeld* [2005][85] a wealthy Arab businessman sued an American academic, Dr Rachel Ehrenfeld, in London for defamatory statements about him in her book entitled *Funding Evil.* Only 23 copies of her book had been sold in the UK, and it was pointed out that the claimant chose England rather than the US to sue, as the latter's constitutional protection of freedom of expression[86] effectively cancelled his suit's prospect of success. When he won his case in England, the US reacted by passing the Securing the Protection of our Enduring and Established Constitutional Heritage (SPEECH) Act 2010 (which followed the enactment in New York of 'Rachel's Law,' the Libel Terrorism Protection Act 2008).[87] This act made foreign libel judgments unenforceable in US courts, unless those judgments are compliant with the US constitutional protection of freedom of speech.

80 For a discussion of the problem of libel tourism as it manifests across jurisdictions, see Garnett, R and Richardson, M 'Libel Tourism or Just Redress? Reconciling the (English) Right to Free Speech in Cross-border Libel Cases' (2009) 5(3) *Journal of Private International Law* 471; Hartley, TC 'Libel Tourism and Conflict of Laws' (2010) 59(1) *International & Comparative Law Quarterly* 25 and Stavely-O'Carroll, S 'Libel Tourism Laws: Spoiling the Holiday and Saving the First Amendment?' (2009) *New York University Journal of Law & Liberty* 252.

81 In order to protect its citizens' constitutional freedom of speech, the US enacted the Securing the Protection of our Enduring and Established Constitutional Heritage (SPEECH) Act in 2010.

82 The European Parliament in its Resolution of 10 May 2012 (2013/C 261 E/03) made recommendations to the Commission of the European Union on the amendment of Regulation (EC) No. 864/2007 on the law applicable to non-contractual obligations (Rome II), in order to attempt to prevent libel tourism to the UK – despite noting the potentially positive effect of the then proposed Defamation Act 2013.

83 Paragraph 65 of the Explanatory Notes to the Defamation Act 2013 acknowledges the existence of libel tourism to England and Wales, and explains how the 2013 Act seeks to address this issue.

84 Para 65 of the Explanatory Notes to the Defamation Act 2013.

85 *Bin Mahfouz v Ehrenfeld* [2005] EWHC 1156.

86 The US constitutional protection of free speech and its effect on US defamation law are discussed in detail in chapter 4.

87 For a discussion of this Act see Feldman, M 'Putting the Brakes on Libel Tourism: Examining the Effects Test as a Basis for Personal Jurisdiction under New York's Libel Terrorism Protection Act' (2010) 31 *Cardozo Law Review* 2457, 2461.

The fact that a traditional ally such as the US deemed it necessary to protect its citizens' right to freedom of speech against English laws by enacting legislation to that effect was seen as hugely embarrassing: The House of Commons Culture Select Committee Report on Press Standards, Privacy & Libel 2010 termed it a 'national humiliation.'

Similar factors also made suing (or silencing critics by threatening to sue) in London attractive to multinational corporations with only the most tenuous links to the UK. Without doubt, the fact that defamation actions could be pursued without having to prove damages made this jurisdiction inviting to multinational corporate litigants. This was illustrated in *Jameel v Wall Street Journal Europe SPRL (No. 3)*[88] where the House of Lords held that a company which had a trading reputation in England and Wales was entitled to pursue a remedy in a defamation action without being required to allege or prove that the publication complained of had caused it actual damage on the basis that companies as legal persons were being treated in the same way as human beings (natural persons).

The common law also worked in such a way that the net for possible defendants could be cast to such a wide extent that it had the potential to silence entire sections of society. There may be several possible defendants and several possible actions. The originator of the statement would be held liable for their own *prima facie* defamatory publication. Under the common law, every repeat publication of a defamatory statement constituted a cause of action *de novo*, with a new prescription period running from the date of the repeat publication. In this way, defamation actions could be pursued many years after the original publication would have prescribed.

The common law position that each publication of the same defamatory statement gave rise to a separate cause of action is known as the 'multiple publication' rule. At common law, a statement is published at the time when and the place where it is received, i.e. read, heard, or seen.[89] Each repetition is therefore seen as a fresh defamation and actionable in its own right.[90] This meant the original publisher could potentially be held liable at common law for the additional damage caused by all further publications of the statement. The reason for this was because the limitation period was calculated from various times including when the original and the repetitions occurred.

88 Note 55.

89 For written material, see *Pullman v Walter Hill & Co Ltd* [1891] 1 QB 524 (CA); *Hebditch v MacIlwaine* [1894] 2 QB 54 (CA); *Shevill v Presse Alliance SA* [1995] 2 AC 18 (ECJ), para 41; and *Shevill v Presse Alliance SA* [1996] AC 959 (HL) 983.

90 *Pullman v Walter Hill & Co Ltd*, note 89, 527; *Berezovsky v Michaels* [2000] UKHL 25; *Godfrey v Demon Internet Ltd* [2001] QB 201, 208–209; *Loutchansky v Times Newspapers Ltd (nos. 2–5)* [2001] EWCA Civ 1805, [2002] QB 783, para 57. In *Times Newspapers Ltd (Nos. 1 and 2) v United Kingdom No. 3002/03 (ECHR, 10 March 2009)* [2009] EMLR 14, the ECtHR held that the common law 'multiple publication' rule did not violate the ECHR article 10 right to free expression.

Therefore, given various repetitions, an originally prescribed defamation action may revive as a new prescription period started afresh after each repetition. There were common law defences to this, but they were not satisfactory. For instance, the original publisher could argue that they should not be liable for the consequences of a republication because these were too remote, or that the republication was a *novus actus interveniens* that broke the chain of causation between the original publication and the damage suffered by reason of the republication.[91]

The rule also had the effect that publications of the same statement could occur (and give rise to separate actions) in multiple jurisdictions. The classic case illustrating the problem with this rule is *Duke of Brunswick v Harmer* (1849).[92] In 1830, the duke was defamed by a newspaper article. Eighteen years later, the duke sent his agent to find a copy of the newspaper, upon which procurement it was held that such acquisition sufficed to found a cause of action in defamation against the proprietor of the newspaper. Although the court in *Jameel* remarked that this would probably now be struck out as an abuse of process, the consequences of the 'multiple publication' rule for, for instance, internet publications, remained very grave.[93]

Conclusion

This chapter explored the relevant characteristics of the common law of defamation which led to calls for reform in the law of England and Wales. After briefly examining the structure and purpose of the common law of defamation, certain peculiarities of the law were highlighted. These include the fact that defamation was by and large a tort of strict liability, meaning that the claimant did not need to prove any fault on the part of the defendant, be that intention or negligence. A person could therefore be held liable for completely unintentional or innocent defamation. There are of course other torts where the liability imposed by law is strict. For instance, the modern statutory tort of product liability imposes strict liability on the manufacturers of products that cause damages to consumers.

91 In *McManus v Beckham* [2002] EWCA Civ 939, [2002] 1 WLR 2982, para 43, Laws LJ held that the test is one of foreseeability: the defendant would be held liable for the consequences of further publication if they foresaw, or reasonably ought to have foreseen, that the further publication would take place. See also *Shendish Manor Ltd v Coleman* [2001] EWCA Civ 913, paras 47–50 and *Campbell v News Group Newspapers Ltd* [2002] EWCA Civ 1143, [2002] EMLR 43, 977.

92 *Duke of Brunswick v Harmer* [1849] 14 QB 185, 199–209.

93 *Jameel*, note 44, discussed earlier. See also *Godfrey v Demon Internet*, note 90, 208–209 re bulletin board postings; *Loutchansky v Times Newspapers Ltd*, note 90 re online archives; *Harrods Ltd v Dow Jones & Co Inc* [2003] EWHC 1162 (QB), para 36 re web pages; *King v Lewis* [2004] EWCA Civ 1329, [2005] EMLR 4, para 2 re postings being published when downloaded.

There are also torts in the law of England and Wales where a defendant could be held liable without having to prove damages. These torts are termed actionable *per se* and include trespass to land, assault, battery, and false imprisonment. However, defamation remained the rare exceptional tort that was both one of strict liability as well as actionable *per se*. Not only did the burden of proof placed on the defamation claimant not require of them to prove fault on the part of the defendant, but they also did not need to prove that they suffered any damages. This is unusual in itself. But the defamation claimant was further aided by two legal presumptions: Upon production of a statement which had a defamatory meaning identifying the claimant, the court had to infer that the claimant's reputation was harmed and, further, that the statement itself was false. These powerful presumptions meant that the evidentiary burden on the claimant was very light and that the burden of proof in fact shifted for the bulk of the suit to the defendant. The Court of Appeal in *Jameel* held that the presumption of damage in UK defamation is not incompatible with article 10 of the ECHR and therefore stopped short of removing the presumption. However, in what subsequently became known as the 'Jameel exception,' the courts thereafter required as a minimum threshold for defamation actions that the claimant must have, in fact, suffered harm to their reputation. If they did not, their claim would be struck out as an abuse of process.[94]

The Jameel exception was further strengthened when Tugendhat J in *Thornton v Telegraph Media Group Ltd* [2011][95] signalled that in order to exclude trivial claims, and particularly in the context of article 10 of the ECHR and proportionality considerations, a 'threshold of seriousness' must be applied in defamation claims. These cases could be interpreted as a move in the right direction, i.e. to rebalance free speech and defamation law. However, they could also be interpreted as the need for reform being acknowledged at the highest level: But the courts could not, nor did they, change the law in substance. For that to happen, the legislator needed to act. What the courts did was using existing law, such as the 'abuse of process' norm, to interpret the defamation law more strictly. The law itself and its presumptions remained firmly in place.

The costs of defending a defamation trial remained an issue. Coupled with unpredictable and often excessive jury-driven awards, financial concerns meant that often the mere threat of a claim could silence critics. The claimant-friendly nature of the English common law of defamation acted as a driver for libel tourism. It was therefore clear that the law was ripe for reform by 2013.

94 *Jameel*, note 44.
95 *Thornton*, note 45.

To conclude this chapter, the words of Lord Lester, introducing his Defamation Bill, are perhaps the most apt:

> Our law suffers from the twin vices of uncertainty and overbreadth. The litigation that it engenders is costly and often protracted. It has a severe chilling effect on the freedom of expression not only of powerful newspapers and broadcasters, but also of regional newspapers, NGOs and citizen critics, as well as of scientific discourse. That chilling effect leads to self censorship. It impairs the communication of public information about matters of legitimate public interest and concern.[96]

The next chapter examines the reforms of the common law by the Defamation Act 2013, together with subsequent case law by examining them against the problems identified in this chapter. More specifically, a stab is made at determining whether or not the balance between free speech and the protection of reputation is restored in England and Wales.

96 Lord Lester of Herne Hill 'These Disgraceful Libel Laws Must be Torn Up' *The Times* (London, 15 March 2011).

3 Defamation law in England and Wales after the 2013 reforms

Introduction

The preceding chapters examined some of the most prominent concerns about the common law of defamation which led to the reforms in the Defamation Act 2013 ('the Act').[1] These included inequality of arms between the defamation claimant and defendant, due mostly to what Milo dubbed the 'potent trilogy' of common law defamation characteristics namely the presumption of harm, the presumption of falsity and the strict liability nature of the common law of defamation.[2] Furthermore, costs associated with bringing or defending a claim and the scope of potential liability were perceived to be so severe as to constitute an access to justice concern. It was believed that these, added to the de facto reversal of the burden of proof plus the cost and complexity of defamation actions, acted as a driver of forum shopping/libel tourism. The most troubling issue, however, was the concern that free speech was being chilled.

It now falls to try and determine whether and to what extent the Defamation Act 2013 succeeds in addressing these issues, the main being whether the reform has levelled the playing field for the defamation claimant and defendant.[3] Weir called the common law of defamation a 'blot on the lawscape'[4] because it accorded protection to reputation similar in strength to protection of liberty, which must surely outrank reputation as the more important right. Would he still be able to say this after the 2013 reforms? This chapter answers 'No': Broadly speaking, the 2013 Act succeeds in addressing the concerns

1 As stated already, reference to the England and English law in this book includes Wales and Welsh law.

2 See Milo, D *Defamation and Freedom of Speech* (OUP, Oxford, 2008), chapters V and VI and the discussion in chapter 2.

3 Few authors have examined the Defamation Act 2013 in general, with most seeming to focus on particular or discrete aspects of the Act. For more general critique see Rolph, D 'A Critique of the Defamation Act 2013: Lessons for and from Australian Defamation Law reform. (United Kingdom)' (2016) 21 *Communications Law* 116 and Johnson, H 'The Defamation Act 2013 – Reform or Tinkering? (Editorial)' (2014) 19 *Communications Law* 1.

4 Weir, T *An Introduction to the Law of Tort* (2nd edn OUP, Oxford, 2006), 190.

DOI: 10.4324/9781003416005-4

raised in the previous chapter. However, it could and arguably should have gone much further. This chapter explores these two aspects of the Act.

Before starting thematic analysis as set out earlier, a brief contextual overview of the Defamation Act 2013:[5] The Act is relatively short, consisting of only 17 sections that in turn codify, revise, or in some instances, change the common law. At first glance it becomes obvious that the Act does not fundamentally alter the overarching structure of defamation law in England and Wales, as the main focus remains on defences rather than on a reconceptualisation of the tort as such. A substantial part of the Act deals with defences: Sections 2 to 7 mostly abolish but also replace the common law defences, in the main with similar or at least analogous defences. Nevertheless, if one stands back and takes a broad view, the Act in short makes it more difficult to prove the tort, complemented by simultaneously making it easier to prove a defence. The question is whether this redresses the balance to a degree that levels the playing field in defamation claims.

For the defamation claimant, the Act's most far-reaching changes are twofold: Firstly, section 1 introduces a 'serious harm' threshold for a defamation claim, in effect abolishing the common law presumption of harm and adding a substantial hurdle for the claimant to clear. Secondly, for all intents and purposes section 11 abolishes the use of juries in defamation trials. This means that defamatory meaning is now determined by the judge alone, on an objective basis. Juries were also seen as notoriously claimant-friendly – an issue which is explored further here by contrasting the outcomes in the Johnny Depp defamation trials in England and Virginia respectively.

For the defendant, the following sections are significant in that they simplify, extend, or otherwise alter the common law in various ways that assist in countering a defamation claim. Section 3 makes it much easier to defend an opinion (as opposed to a statement of fact), and section 4, publication on a matter of public interest ('the public interest defence'), significantly widens the law's understanding of responsible journalism and also widens the defence's protection to defendants other than journalists. Other sections also work towards rebalancing the playing field in favour of the defamation defendant. Section 8 replaces the 'multiple publication' rule with a 'single publication' rule (but *only* for defence purposes), while section 9 attempts to address libel tourism by putting in place jurisdictional constraints on the adjudication of defamation suits pursued by non-domiciled claimants in England and Wales. Section 10 attempts to further restrict access to the libel court by limiting possible defendants to authors, editors, or publishers of defamatory statements – so limiting actions against, for example, internet service providers, search engines or other non-editorial 'secondary publishers.' Section 11 in effect abolishes jury trials in defamation actions, a significant change with

5 For a brief snapshot of the Act, see Farrer & Co 'A Quick Guide to the Defamation Act 2013 (United Kingdom)' (2014) 25 *Entertainment Law Review* 55.

far-reaching consequences. Sections 12 and 13, dealing with remedies, are also important as the expanded basket of remedies available to courts have the potential to limit costs. The remaining general provisions deal with administrative issues[6] and a confirmation that the common law meaning of 'publish' and 'statement' remain unaltered.[7] Against this broad outline, the Act can now be more closely examined.

The Defamation Act 2013: the claimant

It is trite that the key aim of statutory interpretation is to consider the mischief which the Act in question is intended to remedy, first by reading the Act and, if necessary, looking 'at the facts presumed to be known to Parliament when the Bill which became the Act in question was before it.'[8] Should the legislation itself prove ambiguous, it has been permitted since the decision in *Pepper v Hart* [1993][9] that the court may have regard to any report which informed the framing of the statute, provided that the report clearly discloses the mischief aimed at, or the legislative intention underlying the obscure or ambiguous words of the statute. Rarely, and as a last resort,[10] it is also permissible to have regard to statements made in the course of parliamentary debates by the promoters of the Bill. In this respect there are three key reports: The Ministry of Justice's consultation paper on the draft Defamation Bill,[11] the report of the Joint Committee on the draft Defamation Bill,[12] and the government's response to the Joint Committee's report.[13] The Joint Committee's report identified four main areas of concern:[14] balancing freedom of expression with the protection of reputation; reducing costs, as it is recognised that the reduction in the extremely high costs of defamation proceedings is essential in order to limit the chilling effect and making access to legal redress a possibility for the ordinary citizen;[15] accessibility in the sense of demystifying defamation law for the ordinary citizen; and cultural change in order to reflect the realities of

6 Section 16 concerns consequential amendments and savings, etc., and section 17 provides the short title and extent and commencement of the Act.

7 Section 15.

8 *Black-Clawson International Ltd v Papierwerke Waldhof-Aschaffenburg AG* [1975] AC 591 (HL), 614.

9 *Pepper v Hart* [1993] AC 593, 634 (Lord Browne-Wilkinson).

10 *Campbell v MGN Ltd* [2002] EWCA Civ 1373, [2003] QB 633, para 126.

11 Ministry of Justice, *Draft Defamation Bill: Consultation* (2011).

12 Joint Committee on the Draft Defamation Bill, *Draft Defamation Bill* (2011).

13 Ministry of Justice, *The Government's Response to the Report of the Joint Committee on the Draft Defamation Bill* (2012).

14 Joint Committee Report, note 12, 3.

15 Ibid. The Joint Committee further noted in this respect that 'early resolution of disputes is not only key to achieving this, but is desirable in its own right – in ensuring that unlawful injury to reputation is remedied as soon as possible and that claims do not succeed or fail merely on account of the prohibitive cost of legal action. Courts should be the last rather than the first resort.'

modern life, in particular modern communication culture. The government's response strongly stressed redressing concerns about free speech:

> [W]e are firmly committed to reform of the law on defamation and the protection of free speech. The right to speak freely and debate issues without fear of censure is a vital cornerstone of a democratic society. We believe that it is important that our defamation laws strike a fair balance so that people who have been defamed are able to take action to protect their reputation where appropriate, but so that free speech and freedom of expression are not unjustiably [*sic*] impeded by actual or threatened defamation proceedings.[16]

The government also explicitly stated as a goal improving accessibility and clarity of the law of defamation[17] and reducing costs.[18] The concerns highlighted in chapter 2 clearly mirror these stated aims.

From a free speech perspective, did the Act bring about significant changes to defamation law and how it operates in England and Wales? As defamatory meaning is the first element for the defamation claimant to prove, it makes for a good starting point.

Defamatory meaning

It used to fall to the jury to decide whether or not the statement complained of in a defamation trial carried a defamatory meaning. Section 11 now places this task in the hands of the trial judge, and the hope that this would engender more reasoned decisions by judges on why a statement is deemed defamatory seems justified. Indeed, the post-2014 case law mostly include very thoughtful and careful findings on meaning. It has now become standard practice in defamation claims to have a trial of preliminary issues at which the court (i.e. the judge) determines the natural and ordinary *single* meaning of the words complained of, to what extent the words were a statement of fact or an expression of opinion, and to what extent they were defamatory of the claimant. Nicklin J explained the 'single meaning' rule in *Koutsogiannis v The Random House Group Ltd* [2019] as follows:[19]

> The Court's task is to determine the single natural and ordinary meaning of the words complained of, which is the meaning that *the hypothetical*

16 Ministry of Justice Response, note 13, 4.

17 Ibid.

18 Ministry of Justice Response, note 13. The government specifically stated that costs should be reduced by reducing jury trials (17) and procedural changes to encourage early dispute resolution (18–20).

19 *Koutsogiannis v The Random House Group Ltd* [2019] EWHC 48 (QB), [2020] 4 WLR 25, paras 11–16.

> *reasonable reader* would understand the words bear. It is well recognised that there is an artificiality in this process because individual readers may understand words in different ways.[20] [Own emphasis]

He summarised from the common law the following key principles to aid the hypothetical reasonable reader's determination of the single and natural meaning of the words complained of:[21] The governing principle is reasonableness. The intention of the publisher is irrelevant. The hypothetical reasonable reader is not naïve but also not unduly suspicious, can read between the lines and may indulge in a certain amount of loose thinking but is not avid for scandal, and does not, and should not, select one bad meaning where other non-defamatory meanings are available.[22] Therefore, over-elaborate analysis must be avoided and the court should certainly not take a too literal approach to the task and should not fall into the trap of conducting too detailed an analysis. Any meaning that emerges as the produce of some strained, or forced, or utterly unreasonable interpretation should be rejected and furthermore, it is not enough that some person or another might understand the words as being defamatory. The publication must be read as a whole, and in context.

Nicklin J uses the example of the classic 'rogues' gallery' cases, where the context will tend to clothe the words in a more serious defamatory meaning, versus, on the other hand, the 'bane and antidote' cases, where the context will weaken or even extinguish altogether the defamatory meaning that the words would bear if they were read in isolation.[23] The mode of publication is also important in terms of context. The hypothetical reader is representative of those who would read the publication in question, but the court should beware of making a stereotypical assessment of the characteristics of a publication's readership.[24] In fact, the judges should include themselves and the impression the words make on them in the 'reasonable reader' hypothesising. Finally, the court is not bound by the meanings advanced by the parties – it is free to choose the correct meaning save that it cannot find a meaning that is more injurious than the claimant's pleaded meaning. The most important development arising out of the legislative reform in terms of this key element of a defamation claim, defamatory meaning, is the fact that it is clear that identifying the single natural and ordinary meaning of a statement is recognised and applied as an *objective* test. The intention of the publisher is irrelevant, and no evidence is admissible other than the publication complained of itself.[25]

20 Ibid, para 11.
21 Ibid, para 12 and the cases referenced there.
22 Ibid, para 12(iii).
23 Ibid, (iii).
24 Ibid, (xii).
25 *Riley v Murray* [2022] EWCA Civ 1146, para 12; *Koutsogiannis*, note 19, para 12(ii), (x).

A good example of the way meaning is now determined in defamation trials is the Supreme Court's judgment overruling both the first instance and appeal court findings in *Stocker v Stocker* [2019].[26] In this case, the respondent to the appeal, Ronald Stocker, was the former husband of the appellant, Nicola Stocker. After their marriage ended acrimoniously, Mrs Stocker said this to her ex-husband's new partner in a Facebook post: 'He tried to strangle me.' The issue before the court was purely that of meaning. The judges had to decide what those words would convey to the 'ordinary reasonable reader' of a Facebook post. At first instance and on appeal, the words were given their dictionary definitions, which accorded to the respondent's claim that it conveyed the meaning 'He tried to kill me.'[27] The Supreme Court held that by taking this as their starting point, the judges erred in law, and they also failed to consider the context of a Facebook post. The words had to be taken together so as to determine what the ordinary reasonable reader would understand them to mean.[28] Affirming the 'single meaning' rule, the court emphasised that the primary role here was to focus on how the ordinary reasonable reader would construe the words complained of, in the event of several possible meanings. To fulfil that obligation, the court should be particularly conscious of the context in which the statement was made.[29] The fact that the statement under scrutiny was made in a Facebook post was very pertinent: It was unwise to search a Facebook post for its theoretical or logically deducible meaning. It should be recognised that Facebook was a casual medium; it was in the nature of a conversation rather than carefully chosen expression. People scrolled through Facebook quickly and their reaction to posts was impressionistic and fleeting.[30] The court held that the ordinary reader of the Facebook post would unquestionably have interpreted the post as meaning that the respondent had grasped the appellant by the throat and applied force to her neck rather than trying deliberately to kill her. Because this was, in fact, what had happened, the court held that the appellant's defence of truth succeeded.[31]

The procedural stage at which the court examines meaning is also significant, but here the implications for the libel defendant were less clear. On the one hand, the procedure which is now accepted practice for the determination of meaning could entail significant costs savings, as meaning can be determined as a preliminary issue by the judge. A number of cases decided by Nicklin J indicate that in accordance with the overriding objective of the Civil Procedure Rules, a hearing to determine meaning should be held at an

26 *Stocker v Stocker* [2019] UKSC 17.
27 Ibid, para 16.
28 Ibid, paras 23–26.
29 Ibid, paras 34–38.
30 Ibid, paras 39–44.
31 Ibid, paras 61–62.

early stage and before service of the defence.[32] But this timing, on the other hand, initially made it unclear whether the procedure would also allow the defendant to dispute the issue of meaning. There was no clear obligation on a defendant to plead the meaning they said the words bore at such a preliminary hearing, and it was argued that there may even have been a rule preventing such a pleading.[33] Nicklin J, however, indicated that this is not the case anymore and that indeed it now falls to both parties to fully address meaning at an early stage. What is more, failure to do so could entail costs penalties: In *Poroshenko v BBC* [2019] the judge awarded costs against the claimant for unduly obstructing an early resolution of meaning.[34]

Serious harm to reputation

At common law a statement is defamatory if it conveys an imputation with an inherent tendency to cause substantial harm to a person's reputation. Once this was established, harm was *presumed* as a matter of law, and the publication of such a statement was actionable *per se*, i.e. without proof of actual damage. It has now been clearly established that this is no longer the case and that the Act burdens the claimant with a substantial additional element to prove – serious harm to reputation. It may well be argued that for the libel claimant, this additional evidential burden is the most far-reaching reform of the law of defamation. Section 1(1) of the Defamation Act 2013 states: 'A statement is not defamatory unless its publication has caused or is likely to cause serious harm to the reputation of the claimant.' Warby J said in *Doyle v Smith* [2018]:[35] 'This is a beguilingly simple sentence.' It proved to be a *misleadingly* simple sentence, as the debate as to its meaning and effect started before and continued long after the Act came into force on 1 January 2014. The question as to what constitutes serious harm proved at first to be difficult to resolve, and gave rise to debate about whether or not this section abolished the common law presumption of harm, meaning that libel would no longer be actionable *per se*, or whether it merely raised the threshold of harm, meaning that the presumption of harm would be retained and with it the nature of libel as being actionable *per se*. The Act itself is clear on this only in section 14(2), where it confirms the common law position that certain limited instances of slander are not actionable *per se*. Whether or not libel in general remained actionable *per se* fell to be determined by the courts.

The issue was addressed first in *Lachaux* [2015],[36] a case which concerned serious allegations made in British newspapers against the claimant by his

32 *Morgan v Associated Newspapers Ltd* [2018] EWHC 1850 (QB), *Bokova v Associated Newspapers Ltd* [2018] EWHC 2032 (QB).

33 *Bokova*, note 32, para 7.

34 *Poroshenko v BBC* [2019] EWHC 213 (QB), para 51.

35 *Doyle v Smith* [2018] EWHC 2935 (QB).

36 *Lachaux v Independent Print Ltd, Lachaux v Evening Standard Ltd, Lachaux v AOL (UK) Ltd* [2015] EWHC 2242 (QB), [2016] 2 WLR 437.

ex-wife. The defamatory meanings of the words complained of in various publications included serious allegations of, among others, domestic abuse and kidnapping of the couple's child.[37] The 'meaning hearing' was relatively straightforward, with the statements relied on by Mr Lachaux found to be defamatory. The next question was whether the common law inference of harm should follow, or whether the claimant now faced an additional evidential hurdle.

At first instance section 1(1) was interpreted as impliedly abolishing the presumption of harm. Warby J held that a proper construction of section 1(1) meant that 'libel is no longer actionable without proof of damage, and . . . the legal presumption of damage will cease to play any significant role.' He went so far as to say that '[t]hese . . . are necessary consequences of what I regard as the natural and ordinary, indeed the obvious meaning of section 1(1).'[38] However, the Court of Appeal reversed this decision, instead finding that the common law presumption of harm in fact survived the enactment of section 1(1).[39] The Court of Appeal agreed with the 2011, i.e. pre-reform reasoning of Tugendhat J in *Thornton v Telegraph Media Group Ltd*,[40] and declared that the existence of the presumption of damage is compatible with a raised threshold of harm. The court, therefore, found that section 1(1) had merely raised the threshold from one of 'substantiality' to one of 'seriousness,' with the latter conveying something 'rather more weighty' than the former.[41] Following this judgment, some disappointed commentators rightly observed: 'it seems fair to say that reports of the death of the libel writ have been greatly exaggerated.'[42]

But the Supreme Court disagreed with the Appeal Court's interpretation of section 1(1) of the Defamation Act 2013.[43] Lord Sumption gave a brief overview of the history preceding and culminating in the Defamation Act 2013 and set out the court's ruling on how section 1 should be interpreted and applied in defamation cases. The Supreme Court unanimously held if 'serious harm' within the meaning of section 1(1) can be demonstrated only by reference to the inherent tendency of the words themselves, then no change in the law would have been achieved – and the Defamation Act 2013 is clear that it intended in section 1 to make a significant amendment to the common law.[44]

37 Ibid, paras 5 to 21.

38 Ibid, para 60. On the facts, i.e. given the repute and scale of the publications, the judge held that serious harm was made out. He rejected the suggestion that an absence of tangible adverse reactions by publishees undermined his conclusions.

39 *Lachaux v Independent Print Ltd, Lachaux v AOL (UK) Ltd* [2017] EWCA Civ 1334, [2018] QB 594.

40 *Thornton v Telegraph Media Group Ltd* [2011] 1 WLR 1985, para 94.

41 *Lachaux*, Appeal note 39, para 44.

42 See Bennett, TDC 'Why so Serious? Lachaux and the Threshold of "Serious Harm" in Section 1 Defamation Act 2013' (2018) 10(1) *Journal of Media Law* 1.

43 *Lachaux v Independent Print Ltd and another* [2019] UKSC 27.

44 Ibid, para 13.

Section 1 raised the threshold of seriousness above the tendency of defamatory words to cause damage to reputation; the application of the test of serious harm must be determined by reference to actual facts about its impact and not just to the meaning of the words. This means that not only is the threshold of seriousness raised, but proof is also now required, on the facts, that the impact of the words was to harm the claimant's reputation.[45] Further proof of this is the fact that section 1(2) requires an actual impact assessment – and the two sections need to be read together.[46](Section 1(2) states: 'For the purposes of this section, harm to the reputation of a body that trades for profit is not "serious harm" unless it has caused or is likely to cause the body serious financial loss.')

The reference to 'has caused' in section 1(1) relates to the consequences of publication and thus points to harm which has actually occurred/'historic harm.' This is a matter of fact and evidence must be led as to the impact which the statement has actually had, which in turn depends on a combination of the inherent tendency of the words and their actual impact on the publishees. It does not merely refer to the publication itself. In short, the focus therefore is no longer only on the meaning of the words but on their actual or likely impact.[47] The term 'likely to cause' in turn points to possible future harm. The Supreme Court held that this too must be established as a fact.[48] Where the statement 'is likely to cause' serious harm, this is not synonymous with 'liable to cause' in the sense of the inherent tendency of defamatory words to cause damage to reputation. Instead, the factual conditions set under section 1 now necessarily call for an investigation of the actual impact of the statement because if serious harm could be demonstrated simply by the inherent tendency of statements to damage reputation, then the Act would have made very little substantive change.[49]

Lord Sumption in *Lachaux* clearly meant that the common law presumption of harm was dealt a fatal blow by section 1 of the Act when he stated the following:

> The main reason why harm which was less than 'serious' had given rise to liability before the Act was that damage to reputation was presumed from the words alone and might therefore be very different from any damage which could be established in fact. If . . . the presumption still works in that way, then this anomaly has been carried through into the Act. Suppose that the words amount to a grave allegation against the claimant, but they are published to a small number of people, or to

45 Ibid, para 12.
46 Ibid, para 15.
47 Ibid, para 14.
48 Ibid, para 14.
49 Ibid, paras 34(iii)–(iv).

> people none of whom believe it, or possibly to people among whom the claimant had no reputation to be harmed. The law's traditional answer is that these matters may mitigate damages but do not affect the defamatory character of the words. Yet it is plain that section 1 was intended to make them part of the test of the defamatory character of the statement.[50]

In short, the Supreme Court confirmed the demise of the common law presumption of harm. The logical next question is then how the libel claimant should go about proving not only harm but serious harm to their reputation.

Sobrinho v Impresa Publishing SA [2016] provides a useful summary of the evidentiary burden regarding serious harm.[51] The uncontroversial aspects of section 1 are set out as including the following: In order to prove 'serious harm to reputation' it is open to the claimant to call evidence in support of their case – and likewise it is open to the defendant to call evidence to demonstrate that no serious harm has occurred or is likely to occur. It would be up to the court to draw inferences based on the admitted evidence, on the understanding that mass media publications of very serious defamatory allegations are likely to render the need for evidence of serious harm unnecessary, whilst at the same time it should be stressed that the issue of serious harm is not a 'numbers game,' as it is acknowledged that very serious harm to a reputation can be caused by the publication of a defamatory statement to one person.[52] The court also pointed out that there are evidential difficulties in proving serious harm, such as an 'understandable desire not to spread the contents of the article complained of by asking persons if they have read it and what they think of the claimant, and because persons who think badly of the claimant are not likely to co-operate in providing evidence.'[53] The claimant may also find it difficult to get witnesses to say that they read the words and thought badly of the claimant.[54]

As to what kind of evidence would suffice to prove serious harm, the best kind of evidence would be from a person who had read/heard the publication and who formed a negative view of the claimant as a result. The judge's task is to evaluate the material before them and arrive at a conclusion, recognising that serious harm is an issue on which precision will rarely be possible.[55] The judge can consider the impact of the publication upon people who do not presently know the claimant but might get to know them in the future.[56] But it must be acknowledged that evidence proving serious harm would sometimes be almost impossible to obtain: the third parties to whom the communication

50 *Lachaux*, SC note 43, para 16.
51 *Sobrinho v Impresa Publishing SA* [2016] EWHC 66, per Dingemans J, paras 46 to 50.
52 Ibid, para 47. See also *Banks v Cadwalladr* [2023] EWCA Civ 219, para 52.
53 Ibid, para 48.
54 Cf. the difficulties faced in *Ames v The Spamhouse Project* [2015] EWHC 127 (QB) at para 55.
55 Ibid, para 21.
56 Ibid, para 25.

took place may be anonymous or, if known to the claimant, may be reluctant to give evidence, or may not have formed a negative opinion of the claimant as they knew the claimant and therefore knew the allegations not to be true.[57]

Because of these evidentiary difficulties, the court in *Lachaux* was careful to reserve for itself the right to make inferences from the factual matrix laid before it in evidence: 'There is no reason why inferences of fact as to the seriousness of the harm done to . . . reputation should not be drawn from considerations of this kind,' and '[a] Claimant's case 'must not necessarily fail for want of such evidence.'[58] In casu, the court held that factors such as the scale of publications (including print runs and estimated readership) and the gravity of the statements themselves (according to the meaning attributed to them) had to be considered. The Supreme Court's finding that serious harm had been proved was therefore based on a combination of the meaning of the words, the situation of the claimant, the circumstances of publication, and finally, the inherent probabilities of the words themselves.

The key aspect of the Supreme Court's decision in *Lachaux*, however, is its judgment on the meaning of the 'beguilingly simple' 23 words comprising section 1(1) which gave rise to so much debate: It clarified once and for all that it did not just raise the bar of the common law but set a new evidentiary hurdle for the libel claimant. In short, libel claims are actionable *per se* no more. The free speech significance of this decision was recognised by the defendants' barrister when she triumphantly stated: 'In a boost to free speech & the Fourth Estate the Supreme Court has come off the bench on defamation.'[59]

Nicklin J in *Riley v Murray* [2021] highlighted three further relevant principles that must be added to Lord Sumption's analysis in *Lachaux*:[60] First, in an appropriate case, a claimant can also rely upon the likely 'percolation' or 'grapevine effect' of defamatory publications, an effect that has been immeasurably enhanced by social media and modern methods of electronic communication.[61] In this regard, Bingham LJ memorably said that

> the law would part company with the realities of life if it held that the damage caused by publication of a libel began and ended with publication to the original publishee. Defamatory statements are objectionable

57 *Lachaux*, QB note 36, paras 138–140, 145.

58 *Lachaux*, SC note 43, para 21.

59 Canneti, R 'Rewriting the Defamation Act?' (2019) 169 *New Law Journal* 7845, 7. For another comment on the case see Dobson, N 'Defamation & "Serious Harm" Post Lachaux' (2019) 169 *New Law Journal* 7848, 13.

60 Nicklin J provides a helpful summary of the law on the test for serious harm, including the principles to be derived from *Lachaux* in *Riley v Murray* [2021] EWHC 3437 (QB); [2022] EMLR 8, para 34.

61 *Cairns v Modi* [2013] 1 WLR 1015, para 25 per Lord Judge LCJ.

> not least because of their propensity to percolate through underground channels and contaminate hidden springs.[62]

Secondly, the law recognises very well that a claimant may struggle to identify, or to produce evidence from, all those to whom an article was published and in whose eyes the claimant's reputation was damaged.[63] Finally, assessment of harm to reputation amounts to more than a mere 'numbers game' insofar as 'one well-directed arrow [may] hit the bull's eye of reputation' and cause more damage than indiscriminate firing,[64] and publication to a relatively small number of publishees can cause very serious harm to reputation.[65]

A number of cases were decided on the serious harm requirement following the clarification provided in *Lachaux*. They tend to show that the defamation claimant now faces a more difficult task than before the reforms of the law. In *Yavuz v Tesco Stores* [2019] the claimant sued in slander after the defendant accused him of theft.[66] The court accepted that such an allegation has an inherent tendency to cause serious harm.[67] However, on the facts of the case it was clear that only a handful of people unknown to the claimant were likely to have heard the defamatory words. Nor did the claimant provide any evidence of the 'grapevine effect.' Therefore, although the imputation was grave, there was no factual basis for drawing an inference of serious harm. Nor was there any likelihood of the imputation to spread and to potentially thereby cause serious harm.[68]

Likewise in *ZC v Royal Free London NHS Foundation Trust* [2019] a patient's libel claim against a hospital failed where, although the hospital had sent an email to four people imputing that the patient had behaved dishonestly and fraudulently, she was unable to prove as a fact that the email had caused or was likely to cause her serious harm.[69] The evidence showed that the number of publishees was very limited and there was no grapevine effect. Furthermore, two of the four recipients of the email already knew about the contents of the email beforehand, and there was no evidence that anyone thought any less of the claimant because of the email.[70] Similar reasoning was followed in another case involving emails containing allegedly defamatory statements: In *Palmer v Farmer* [2023] the court dismissed a claim based on an email falsely

62 *Slipper v British Broadcasting Corporation* [1991] 1 QB 283, 300.
63 *Doyle v Smith* [2019] EMLR 15, para 122 (iv); *Sobrinho v Impresa Publishing SA* [2016] EMLR 12, para 48; *Ames v Spamhaus* [2015] 1 WLR 3409, para 55.
64 *King v Grundon* [2012] EWHC 2719 (QB), para 40 per Sharp J.
65 *Sobrinho*, note 63, para 47; *Dhir v Sadler* [2018] EWHC 2935 (QB), para 55 (i); *Monir v Wood* [2018] EWHC 3525 (QB), para 196.
66 *Yavuz v Tesco Stores Ltd & Anor* [2019] EWHC 1971 (QB).
67 Ibid, para 59.
68 Ibid.
69 *ZC v Royal Free London NHS Foundation Trust* [2019] EWHC 2040 (QB).
70 Ibid, para 131.

stating that the claimant had been found guilty of a sex offence as not being inherently injurious, as the defamatory *tendency* of words are not, without more, now regarded as sufficient to satisfy section 1.[71] Instead, consideration of serious harm, now recognised to be concerned with impact or likely impact, requires taking account of the context of the words and circumstances of their publication.[72]

The following case illustrates facts that did indeed support a claim of serious harm to reputation. In *Al Sadik v Sadik* [2019] the defendant subsequent to a property dispute sent a WhatsApp message to 34 family members and friends alleging that her brother-in-law, the claimant, had (*inter alia*) arranged to rob his brother's house, had lied even after having sworn on the Quran to tell the truth, and had committed perjury in order to dishonestly promote his interest at the expense of his own brother.[73] Among the factors that informed the decision by the court that the section 1(1) threshold had been met were the fact that the allegations were very serious, had a religious component, and were specifically targeted to the claimant's family members. The court found that the number of publishees were not trivial and that there was evidence of further dissemination via the grapevine, even though this could not be fully quantified.[74] There was no direct evidence of adverse impact. However, given the nature of the statement, the standing of the claimant in London and abroad, the sender of the messages and the targeted nature of the publication, Knowles J regarded it as an arguable inference that there would have been be some among the population, who did not know the claimant, in whose eyes he had suffered serious reputational harm. He held that the inherent probabilities in the case were that there would have been some people who had become aware of the WhatsApp messages and concluded that the defendant would not have made such widespread and serious accusations against her sister's husband (the claimant) unless there was some substance to them.[75] In other words, the law recognised the legal equivalent of the saying that there is 'no smoke without a fire.'

Fentiman v Marsh [2019] concerned allegations against a company of which the claimant was a director and posted on various social media sites and blog entries.[76] The publications included allegations of fraudulent and criminal activity. The court held that the subject matter of the publications was grave and had an inherent tendency to cause serious harm. The number of publishees were also substantial, comprising 100 to 230 views for each post.[77] Furthermore, the court stated that even though the claimant led evidence

71 *Palmer v Farmer* [2023] EWHC 976 (KB), para 41.
72 Ibid, para 42.
73 *Al Sadik v Sadik* [2019] EWHC 2717 (QB).
74 Ibid, paras 95, 99–100.
75 Ibid, para 101.
76 *Fentiman v Marsh* [2019] EWHC 2099 (QB).
77 Ibid, para 55.

of substantial further dissemination via the grapevine, the court would have been prepared to draw such inference as such percolation typically results from allegations such as those under contention on social media. What is more, the claimant submitted evidence from staff members who had read the post, that they were troubled that the allegations against Mr Fentiman might be true, even though these publishees were persons close to the claimant and trusted and admired him.[78]

Banks v Cadwalladr [2023] is a high-profile, recent case which also illustrates the steeper uphill battle that defamation claimants now face regarding serious harm to reputation.[79] The Court of Appeal considered how, in cases of continuous/ongoing publication, impact, likely impact, context, and changed circumstances affect the 'serious harm' analysis. The claim arose from the Brexit referendum and its aftermath. Mr Banks is a millionaire businessman who funded parts of the campaign for the United Kingdom to leave the European Union (Brexit), Ms Cadwalladr a well-known journalist and vocal Brexit opponent. In order to understand the court's reasoning, it is useful to know the timeline of relevant events. In 2017 Cadwalladr published an article which had the effect of prompting an Electoral Office investigation into Mr Banks' doings, which in turn led to a criminal investigation. She then gave a TED Talk on 15 April 2019 at the TED2019 Conference in Canada in which she said: 'And I am not even going to get into the lies that Arron Banks has told about his covert relationship with the Russian Government.' Her talk was recorded and posted on the TED Talk website. Banks responded by sending her a pre-action letter complaining about the TED Talk, whereupon Cadwalladr tweeted:

> Oh Arron. This is too tragic. Nigel Farage's secret funder Arron Banks has sent me a pre-action letter this morning: he's suing me over this TED talk. If you haven't watched it please do. I say he lied about his contact with the Russian govt. Because he did.

The tweet contained a hyperlink to the TED Talk. Banks thereupon sued Cadwalladr for libel in the TED Talk and the tweet, each of which suggested that he had secretly broken the law on electoral funding by taking money from a foreign power and lied about the matter. In the midst of all this, the National Crime Agency (NCA) exonerated Banks, and in early 2020 the Electoral Commission and others including Banks himself made a joint statement publicly confirming the NCA's findings. It was now clear to all that the defendant's statements about the claimant were untrue. She abandoned her original defence of truth and apologised but denied liability and raised the defence of publication in the public interest.

78 Ibid.
79 *Banks v Cadwalladr* [2023] EWCA Civ 219.

The trial judge dismissed both claims, holding that although the initial publication of the TED Talk had caused serious harm to the claimant's reputation, it was protected by the public interest defence; whereas the later publication of the TED Talk was not protected by the public interest defences, but had not caused serious harm and was therefore not actionable. The publication of the tweet, she found, would have been protected by the public interest defence to the same extent as the TED Talk but none of it was actionable anyway as it had not caused any serious harm to the claimant's reputation.[80] Banks appealed on the following three grounds:[81] He contended that it was wrong to hold that the issue of whether or not a statement has caused or is likely to cause serious harm to a claimant's reputation needs to be determined again from the date on which the defendant's belief that it is in the public interest to publish the statement ceases to be reasonable, i.e. from where the public interest defence falls away. Secondly and thirdly, he contested the judge's finding that he had not proved that the tweet and the publication of the TED Talk caused (or was likely to cause) serious harm to his reputation.

As to the first ground of appeal, i.e. the question about what happens when an initially successful libel defence becomes inoperative, the court found that the answer lies in the 'multiple publication' rule: Lord Justice Warby, with whom the other judges concurred, started off by noting that the method which Parliament adopted to achieve the section 1 'serious harm to reputation' reform was by modifying the pre-existing common law definition of the term 'defamatory' itself. That term can no longer be applied to a statement just because the statement has the inherent qualities required by the common law – instead such a statement 'is not defamatory unless' it also satisfies the additional statutory criterion that '*its publication* has caused . . . serious harm to the reputation of the claimant' or is likely to do so (own emphasis).[82] Next, Warby LJ paused at the words 'its publication' and reiterated that the touchstone is now no longer the nature of the statement itself, but the impact of the *publication* of the statement. If, as in other jurisdictions, the 'single publication' rule was operative, the appeal would succeed. But if the common law 'multiple publication' rule was retained, the issue became more complex. Warby LJ noted in this regard that section 15 of the Act expressly provides that in the Act 'publish' and 'publication' have the meaning they have for the purposes of the law of defamation generally, i.e. the same as in the common law.[83] Once this is accepted, Warby LJ continued, there are only two available readings of section 1(1): 'Either it means that a statement is defamatory *if any publication* of that statement causes serious harm to the claimant's reputation;

80 *Banks v Cadwalladr* [2022] EWHC 1417 (QB).

81 *Banks v Cadwalladr* [2023] EWCA Civ 219, paras 36–37.

82 Ibid, para 42.

83 Ibid, para 43.

or it means the statement is defamatory *only if and to the extent* that the publication of it causes serious harm.'[84]

In the instant case, the court found that the TED Talk had harmed the claimant's reputation – but it was covered by the public interest defence. By the time the public interest defence fell away, however, the logical application of the 'multiple publication' rule meant that the claimant had to again prove serious harm to his reputation. Put another way, the claimant had to prove serious harm for publications that were not covered by the defence. This brought the court to the second ground of appeal, which entailed the approach to be taken towards the assessment of serious harm.[85]

Both courts considered that the TED Talk was 'a serious talk on a serious subject given by an award-winning journalist on an authoritative and credible international platform'[86] concerning a claimant with a prominent role in public life and business. The courts also considered the scale of publication – peaking at around one million views. In these circumstances it was allowed to infer that serious harm was caused, as a result of the inherent gravity of the allegation and its natural tendency to cause serious reputational harm. Both the TED Talk and the tweet were covered by the public interest defence for a period of ten months. After that, the court found that serious harm was made out for the continued publication of the TED Talk but not for the tweet. The reasons for this dichotomy are interesting. As to the TED Talk, even though now the number of views were significantly lower at around 100,000, they still amounted to approximately the readership of a large newspaper and were therefore significant. The subject matter remained grave. However, as far as the tweet was concerned, the court observed that it was 'trite' that Twitter works in a way that made it 'inherently improbable' that anyone in this jurisdiction read the tweet ten months after it was posted, and even more unlikely that any such person both read the tweet and followed the link to the TED Talk. Significantly, the claimant did not offer direct evidence that this happened. Engagement figures tended to support the conclusion that the harm was done at the start, when the tweet was first published, and that in the period after the public interest defence became inoperative there was no publication, or no harm, or none that was serious.[87] The grapevine effect was not raised, nor considered.

The court addressed the so-called echo chamber nature of most social media posts (i.e. akin to 'preaching to the choir'; most social media posts are usually read by followers who already agree with the poster), which was advanced by the defence as militating against an inference that the claimant's reputation was seriously harmed. In effect, the defence argued that the

84 Ibid, para 44.
85 Ibid, paras 52–70.
86 Ibid, para 67.
87 Ibid, para 70.

confirmation bias inherent in most social media posts was crucial to the serious harm inquiry. The court rejected this as being akin to the argument that no harm can be done if a statement is made to an audience who already dislike/consider the claimant as having a bad reputation:[88] The long established common law rule in *Dingle*,[89] that damage to the claimant's reputation done by earlier publications of the same matter is legally irrelevant when assessing harm to reputation, was confirmed by the Supreme Court in *Lachaux* to be equally applicable to the question arising under section 1.[90] Mr Banks' feelings about Ms Cadwalladr's audience were irrelevant to the factual question whether his reputation was harmed. The court held the TED Talk and its posting on the internet did in fact harm his reputation, whereas the tweet did not from the time the public interest defence became inoperative. These findings are important as they illustrate how the law deals with evidence on the facts regarding serious harm to reputation.

To summarise: These cases clearly illustrate the two-pronged approach to serious harm under section 1(1) of the Defamation Act 2013 as described by Lord Sumption in *Lachaux*: The courts will consider the 'inherent tendency' of the statement(s) to cause harm, and secondly their 'actual impact.'[91] It is clear that although the inherent tendency of the statement to cause harm, i.e. the gravity of the statement, is important, it would be unwise for the claimant to rely solely on this. Evidence on the facts about the actual impact on the claimant's reputation must be led. These include for instance the number and nature of publishees, whether the publication was targeted and whether the defendant intended to harm the claimant's reputation. Publication to family, friends, colleagues and the like would be viewed seriously.[92] Data analytics in the case of internet and/or social media dissemination could be submitted to prove the extent of publication.[93] The location of the likely publishees are taken into account, and the court is not averse to noting the probability of the grapevine effect, especially as an inference in social media cases.[94] Evidence should be brought that publishees thought worse of the claimant, i.e. evidence of the adverse impact of the publication, although the absence of such evidence is not fatal to the case.[95]

88 Ibid, para 70.

89 *Dingle v Associated Newspapers Ltd* [1964] AC 371.

90 *Lachaux*, SC note 43, para 24.

91 *Lachaux*, SC note 43, para 17. For a discussion of key cases on the section 1(1) requirement decided after the Supreme Court decision in *Lachaux* see Aamodt, A 'What Next for Defamation?' (2019) 169 *New Law Journal* 21–22.

92 *Al Sadik*, note 73, paras 96–98.

93 In the case of *Monroe v Hopkins* [2017] EWHC 433 (QB) data was submitted about the reach of tweets sent out by the journalist Katie Hopkins about left wing food blogger Jack Monroe, see para 84 of the judgment.

94 *Fentiman*, note 76, para 55.

95 *Lachaux*, SC note 43, para 21.

Corporate claimants

It was argued, and debated in Parliament, whether to restrict the rights of corporate claimants in defamation actions, bearing in mind that this had been done in some other jurisdictions.[96] The main contention in favour of such restriction relates to the chilling effect that the common law defamation law had on free speech. As discussed in chapter 2, the McLibel litigation is a reminder of the kind of power wielded by large corporations to silence critique. The counter-argument is that not all companies are well resourced and powerful, and there will be cases where a company ought legitimately to be able to seek judicial redress for potentially irreparable harm caused to it by a defamatory publication. In the end a compromise was enacted, with the insertion of a provision that for the serious harm threshold in section 1(2), in case of bodies trading for profit, harm is not serious unless it has caused or is likely to cause serious *financial* loss to the body.[97] As was the case for section 1(1) of the Defamation Act 2013, section 1(2) also gave rise to interpretational difficulties. Following the lead of the Appeal Court's decision in *Lachaux* upholding the common law legal inference of damage, it was not surprising that the Court in *Burki v Seventy Thirty Ltd* [2018] held that the claimant company did not need to provide evidence of serious financial loss, nor of a likelihood of such loss occurring, in order to satisfy section 1(2).[98] In the court's view, doing so would wrongly confuse 'serious financial loss' with special damage. The court then went on to infer a tendency to cause serious financial loss from broader circumstantial facts. Interpreting section 1(2) in the same way as section 1(1) in this way meant that very few corporations would be barred from being able to sue. Put another way: 'The problem [with interpreting these concurrent subsections in the same way] is that it builds a claim for a commercial claimant by stacking inferences on top of one another, creating an inferential house of cards.'[99] The Supreme Court's decision in *Lachaux*, however, toppled this 'inferential house of cards.' If the presumption of damage did not survive for section 1(1), it could not survive for section 1(2), as the latter is meant to be a narrower construct than the former.

Apart from this, section 1 does not otherwise alter the common law tests for determining whether a statement is defamatory. However, section 1 of the Act is far reaching and significant. The serious harm requirement as a substantive and substantial element of the tort is now established law, and a

96 Ministry of Justice, *Draft Defamation Bill: Consultation* (2011), paras 136–145; Ministry of Justice, *Draft Defamation Bill: Summary of Responses to Consultation* (2011), 7, 70–72; Joint Committee on the Draft Defamation Bill, *Draft Defamation Bill* (2011), paras 108–118.

97 Section 1(2).

98 *Burki v Seventy Thirty Ltd* [2018] EWHC 2151 (QB).

99 Bennett, TDC 'An Inferential House of Cards – Serious Financial Loss under Section 1(2) Defamation Act 2013: Burki v Seventy Thirty Ltd & Ors' (2019) 24(1) *Communications Law* 34–37.

marked departure from the common law. Warby LJ put it best by remarking that establishing serious harm to reputation is nowadays the very gist of a claim in the tort of defamation.[100]

Jury trials 'abolished'

Another way in which the Act now makes the defamation claimant's task much more difficult is the fact that for all practical purposes, jury trials for defamation cases have been abolished by section 11 of the Act, which directs that defamation trials are to be without a jury unless the court orders otherwise. Defamation juries were seen as notoriously sympathetic to claimants – a quick glance at the high costs awarded by juries to defamation claimants as discussed in the preceding chapter illustrate the point. By abolishing the right to a jury trial, it is submitted, the Act therefore deprived the would-be libel claimant of a traditional advantage. The result can be seen in the differing outcomes in the defamation claims the actor Johnny Depp pursued – his losing claim in the UK[101] as opposed to his victory in the US.[102] The different results in England and Virginia are hard to square with the traditional view that the former is claimant-friendly, while law in USA favours defendants, but this can be explained in part by the fact that the latter was a trial by jury whereas the case in the UK was decided by a judge alone. The differing outcomes in these two cases is discussed in more detail later in this chapter.

Abolishing juries also have an impact on costs. It was noted in earlier chapters that costs issues became an access to justice issue in defamation suits, and as such, led to the chill on free speech. In this regard it must be pointed out that *not* using a jury in itself is a cost saving measure.[103] Furthermore, one of the issues that drove libel reform was the occurrence of several high awards by juries that subsequently had to be reduced on appeal.[104] At this point, it is important to note that although the remedies in defamation include, possibly, an injunction, a published correction, an apology or statement in open court under para 6 of CPR PD 53, the main remedy remains an award of damages.[105] There are three heads of damages – general (compensatory) damages, aggravated damages, and exemplary damages. Lord Donaldson MR and Nourse LJ in their respective judgments in *Sutcliffe v Pressdram* [1990][106] analyse why

100 *Banks v Cadwalladr* [2023] EWCA Civ 219, para 61.

101 *Depp v Newsgroup Newspaper Ltd* [2020] EWHC 2911, *Depp v News Group Newspapers Ltd* [2021] EWCA Civ 423.

102 *Depp v Heard* [2022] Va. Cir. LEXIS 84.

103 Joint Committee on the Draft Defamation Bill, note 12, 3. See also Ministry of Justice, *Draft Defamation Bill. Consultation* (2011), para 95.

104 See the discussion of *John v Mirror Group Newspapers* [1996] 2 All ER 35 and *Tolstoy Miloslavsky v United Kingdom* [1996] EMLR 152 in chapter 2.

105 This was confirmed in *Cairns v Modi* [2012] EWCA Civ 1382.

106 *Sutcliffe v Pressdram* [1990] 1 All ER 269, per Lord Donaldson MR at 281.

the *quantum* of libel damages has historically been on a vastly different scale to awards made in personal injury cases: 'juries do not give reasons for their awards and it is the common experience of judges that having to give reasons is something which puts a substantial premium on ensuring that the head rules the heart.' Libel damages are now subject to a notional ceiling which rises with inflation.[107] The current ceiling is in the order of £275,000.

Libel tourism

The matter of libel tourism is addressed in section 9 of the Defamation Act 2013, in terms of which courts in England and Wales no longer have jurisdiction against defendants domiciled outside the United Kingdom, other European Union member states, Iceland, Norway, or Switzerland, unless, of all the places in which the statement complained of has been published, this jurisdiction is clearly the most appropriate place in which to bring the action. For instance, in *Craig Wright v Roger Ver* [2019][108] the High Court found it did not have jurisdiction to hear a libel claim brought against an individual who was not domiciled in the UK or a member state, as England and Wales was not the most appropriate forum, and the majority of the offending publications had been in the US. Some commentators have pointed out that the issue of libel tourism may have been overstated to start with, citing decisions not allowing claims brought by non-domiciled claimants shortly before the Act came into effect.[109] Furthermore, it is questionable whether section 9 has completely achieved the intended deterrent effect. The courts of England and Wales remain a popular choice, and there have been a number of high-profile claims where neither claimant nor defendant resided in this jurisdiction – although in these instances the courts did not hesitate to apply section 9 restrictively.[110]

The Defamation Act 2013: defences

From the preceding discussion it is clear that the Act did not make major structural changes to the law of defamation. Granted, the claimant now faces

107 Civil Procedure Rules 1998/3132, Practice Direction 53, para 6.1.

108 *Craig Wright v Roger Ver* [2019] EWHC 2094 (QB).

109 These include *Subotic v Knezevic* [2013] EWHC 3011 (QB) (QBD) and *Karpov v Browder* [2013] EWHC 3071 (QB). See Rudkin, T and Pearce, C 'Forum Shopping in the 21st Century' (2014) 25 *Entertainment Law Review* 73.

110 To name a few: *Ahuja v Politika Novine I Magazini Doo* [2015] EWHC 3380 (QB); *Euro-eco Fuels (Poland) Ltd v Szczecin and Swinoujscie Seaports Authority SA* [2018] EWHC 1081 (QB); *Sobrinho v Impresa Publishing SA* [2016] EWHC 66 (QB) and *Sloutsker v Romanova* [2015] EWHC 545 (QB). For recent discussions of forum choice see Baker, PB 'Legal Update: Media: Libel Actions – Here or the United States?' (2018) 39 *Law Society Gazette* 28; Hooper, D 'How the Court Will Interpret Whether England is the Most Appropriate Place to Bring a Libel Action' (2016) *Entertainment Law Review* 102; and Rudkin and Pearce, note 109.

the major hurdle of proving serious harm to their reputation, but once this is done, the heavy lifting shifts to the defendant. The burden of proof still lies mostly with the defendant, and in fact the larger part of the Act deals with defences, reflecting the common law position. Having examined the Act from the perspective of the claimant, we now turn to that of the defendant and ask whether and to what extent the changes to defences wrought by the Defamation Act 2013 succeed in levelling the playing field between defamation claimants and defendants, and to what extent, if any, they redress the balance in favour of the robust exercise of free speech.

Although the Act states that it 'abolished' the three main common law defences (justification, fair comment, and privilege), in reality it did no more than repackaging each of them with a statutory variant that amended the defences to varying degrees.

Truth

The common law name for this defence was 'justification,' and its successor remains the most powerful and complete defence against a claim in defamation. At common law, justification was made out when the defendant could show on a balance of probabilities that the imputation conveyed by a defamatory statement was substantially true. Added to this was a statutory defence of contextual justification: A defendant could still succeed where a defamatory statement contained two or more distinct imputations, not all of which were substantially true.[111] Section 2 of the Act abolished these defences but for the most part their replacement, the defence of truth, is a faithful codification of the prior position. Again, the defence succeeds should the defendant be able to show that the imputation conveyed by the statement complained of is *substantially* true. Thus, a defence of truth can succeed if the defendant proves the essential or substantial truth of the 'sting' of the libel. Warby J noted in this regard that proof of every detail is not required and peripheral inaccuracies, even extensive ones, should not distract the court.[112] If the imputation consists of two or more statements, of which some are true and some untrue, the Act directs the court in section 2(3) to allow the defence provided the untrue imputations do not seriously harm the claimant's reputation. This does provide some 'benefit of the doubt' to the defamation defendant.

Nevertheless, the same critique levelled against the common law defence of justification remains against the statutory version of the defence – namely, why the burden should be on the defendant to prove this matter. Why not require that the defamation claimant prove that the statement complained of is false? Surely the claimant would be best placed to prove this, and

111 Defamation Act 1952, section 5, repealed by S3(8) Defamation Act 2013.

112 *Riley v Murray*, note 25, para 32, paraphrasing Nicklin J.

cross-examination of the defendant should also assist. Moreover, as will be clear from the discussion of the US law in chapter 4, this is an entirely workable solution.

Honest opinion

Section 3 of the Act replaces the common law defence of 'fair comment' (or 'honest comment'),[113] which protected the non-malicious publication of an objectively fair opinion relating to a matter of public interest. The opinion had to be based on true or privileged facts, and the facts had to be generally indicated, at the least implicitly. Section 3 is perhaps most clearly intended to promote vigorous free speech – the explanatory notes to the Act acknowledge that the common law predecessor to this defence was complex and not clear or user friendly. 'Fair comment' as a common law defence was seen as being weighed down by 'complex case law limiting [its] practical value.'[114] Revising the defence was aimed at making the defence more user-friendly by removing unnecessary technical difficulties and clearly stating the elements of the defence. The reformulation aimed to update and simplify the defence. The new defence reads as follows:

> (1) It is a defence to an action for defamation for the defendant to show that the following conditions are met.
> (2) The first condition is that the statement complained of was a statement of opinion.
> (3) The second condition is that the statement complained of indicated, whether in general or specific terms, the basis of the opinion.
> (4) The third condition is that an honest person could have held the opinion on the basis of –
>
> > (a) any fact which existed at the time the statement complained of was published;
> > (b) anything asserted to be a fact in a privileged statement published before the statement complained of.
>
> (5) The defence is defeated if the claimant shows that the defendant did not hold the opinion.
> (6) Subsection (5) does not apply in a case where the statement complained of was published by the defendant but made by another person ('the author'); and in such a case the defence is defeated if the claimant shows that the defendant knew or ought to have known that the author did not hold the opinion.

113 As it was known since a direction from the House of Lords in *Joseph v Spiller* [2010] UKSC 53.
114 *Explanatory Notes to the Lester Bill*, para 62. Joint Committee on the Defamation Bill; *First Report: Draft Defamation Bill* [2010–12] HL Paper 203/HC930, para 62.

Subsections (2), (3), (4), and (5) reflect the previous common law to the extent that the statement must be one of opinion rather than fact; it must indicate its basis in some way, and there must be some fact on the basis of which an honest person could have held the opinion, but satisfaction of these conditions will not be enough if the claimant proves as a fact that the defendant did not hold the opinion they expressed – i.e. dishonesty disqualifies the defence.

When a statement is couched as reflecting the facts, it is presented as the truth, and readers are not invited to disagree. But when statements are made not as reports of fact, but as opinion or commentary, the law accords these with more protection than those of fact, as the former allows for the reader to differ, disagree, or come to a different conclusion. This, in theory, encourages vigorous public debate and hence deserves protection of even factually incorrect statements. This defence is therefore clearly important in terms of freedom of speech. In essence it allows a defence that the statement was a piece of criticism or opinion based upon factual statements.

Section 3 differs from the common law in three respects, which also indicate a significant liberalisation of the defence:[115] First, it does not require the opinion to be on a matter of public interest. Second, by section 3(4) (b) the opinion could be based on a 'privileged statement,' i.e. statements that would have a section 4 defence and not only on facts, as was the position previously. Third, it is now an almost entirely objective defence: The defendant can rely on any fact objectively existing at the time of publication, not necessarily facts of which the defendant was apprised at the time of the statement.

Honest opinion as a defence relates mostly to editorial comments and the like. It must be an opinion, and not a statement of fact, and must indicate in either general or specific terms, what the basis for the opinion is. Further, it must be an opinion that is capable of being held by an honest person. Under the common law this defence is defeated if the claimant can show that the defendant was acting with malice – section 3(5) instead states that the defence is defeated if it can be shown that the defendant did not actually hold the opinion.

Privilege

The defence of privilege protects the makers of certain defamatory statements because the law considers that in the circumstances covered by this defence, free expression is more important than protection of reputation. In other words, these are occasions where it is important that people are allowed to say what they think without fear of legal action. In some instances, the protection is absolute and in others qualified by certain conditions (such as that the maker of the statement should actually hold the opinion they utter). Both

115 Mullis, A and Scott, A 'Tilting at Windmills: The Defamation Act 2013' (2014) 77(1) *Modern Law Review* 92–95.

absolute and qualified privilege were mostly codified in the Defamation Act 1996, which is still in operation. The Defamation Act 2013 extends and significantly liberalised the protection given by the 1996 Act in section 7.

The law gives some statements absolute privilege, which means that it is impossible to sue the person who makes that statement – the statement cannot be used in a court of law. The most important instance of absolute privilege relates to statements made in Parliament or in any parliamentary report. Free speech in Parliament is an ancient right. Article 9 of the Bill of Rights 1688 declares:

> That the Freedom of Speech and Debates or Proceedings in Parlyament ought not to be impeached or questioned in any Court or Place out of Parlyament.

Other examples of absolute privileged statements include those made in the course of proceedings before any court or tribunal; fair and accurate media reports of such public judicial proceedings and any statement made by one spouse to another. Section 7 extends absolute privilege to contemporaneously published fair and accurate reports of proceedings in public before courts established by law anywhere in the world and to international courts and tribunals established by international agreement.

Qualified privilege is a more limited form of privilege, but it has the same effect as absolute privilege: It means that the statement cannot be used in a court of law. At common law, the traditional statement of when qualified privilege will apply comes from Lord Atkinson in *Adam v Ward* (1917):[116]

> A privileged occasion is . . . an occasion where the person who makes the communication has an interest or a duty, legal, social or moral, to make it to the person to whom it is made, and the person to whom it is so made has a corresponding interest or duty to receive it. This reciprocity is essential.

A good example of qualified privilege would be when an employment reference is given. Qualified privilege continues to be subject to one important restriction: It does not cover statements made with malice or with a bad motive, or if the person making it did not honestly believe it was true, or both. The 2013 Act extended the categories of statutory qualified privilege in three significant categories – peer-reviewed academic publications, public proceedings, and website operators.

One of the most serious points of criticism against the common law of defamation was that it stifled academic and scientific debate. One example of the way in which powerful organisations attempted to stifle critique is the case of

116 *Adam v Ward* [1917] AC 309.

Simon Singh, who were found at first instance[117] to have defamed the British Chiropractic Association (BCA) by an article he wrote for the edition of the *Guardian* of 19 April 2008 published on the paper's 'Comment and Debate' page and which stated that 'there is not a jot of evidence' for the claims made by the BCA regarding its treatments' Dr Singh successfully appealed against this decision, with the Court of Appeal agreeing that his commentary amounted to an expression of an opinion rather than a statement of fact, and so was covered by the defence of fair comment, which, in the court's view, was 'backed by reasons'[118] (as it had to be, under the common law defence of fair comment; see the discussion of this defence and its successor above). The point here is not the fact that Dr Singh was vindicated in the end, but that the process through which he had to defend his scientific opinion was expensive, protracted and very difficult, and that this was used as a deterrent by powerful lobbies such as the BCA to stifle criticism.[119] It is therefore a very welcome development that the 2013 by section 6 introduced a defence for the publication of peer-reviewed statements, and reviews of such statements, in scientific or academic journals. This in effect created a new defence of qualified privilege for peer-reviewed material in scientific or academic journals and reflected a core concern underlying reasons for reforming the law – namely, to protect scientific and academic debate from the threat of unjustified libel proceedings. As such, it is intended to encourage open and robust scientific and academic debate. To date no major cases relying on this defence had been reported. This could be interpreted as a sign of success for the inclusion of this defence, as the fact that such cases are not being brought may well be the very sign of success of the defence.

Section 7 extended the categories of instances protected by qualified privilege in section 15 of the Defamation Act 1996, to include fair and accurate reports of 'proceedings in public,' which include, amongst others, proceedings of legislatures, courts, public inquiries, international organisations or conferences, publicly listed companies, etc. An important caveat to section 15 is that the matter reported must be of public interest – which brings us to the next defence which could very well be the heart of the Act.

Publication on matter of public interest: successor to the Reynolds defence

In order to analyse this defence, it is necessary to first examine its common law predecessor. A specialised 'responsible journalism' defence developed, under

117 *British Chiropractic Association v Singh* [2009] EWHC 1101 (QB).

118 *British Chiropractic Association v Singh* [2010] EWCA Civ 350, para 33.

119 For a first-hand account of Dr Singh's experience of the censoring effect of libel actions, see Singh, H 'The Libel Survivor' (2011) 13(32) *Legal Week* 20–21. See also Barendt, E 'Science Commentary and the Defence of Fair Comment to Libel Proceedings' (2010) 2(1) *Journal of Media Law* 43–47.

the common law, out of qualified privilege into a defence in its own right. The defence, commonly known as the Reynolds defence, arose from the eponymous case[120] and concerned a defamation claim by a politician against a newspaper. The question was raised whether there should be a generic category for media reports covering political information and debate. The House of Lords emphasised the importance of freedom of expression and acknowledged the importance of the role played by the media to inform the public at large of political matters. Lord Nicholls provided a list of factors to consider in determining whether a journalistic piece should be accorded qualified privilege:

> 1. The seriousness of the allegation. The more serious the charge, the more the public is misinformed and the individual harmed, if the allegation is not true. 2. The nature of the information, and the extent to which the subject-matter is a matter of public concern. 3. The source of the information. Some informants have no direct knowledge of the events. Some have their own axe to grind, or are being paid for their stories. 4. The steps taken to verify the information. 5. The status of the information. The allegation may already have been the subject of an investigation which commands respect. 6. The urgency of the matter. News is often a perishable commodity. 7. Whether comment was sought from the plaintiff. He may have information which others do not possess or have not disclosed. 8. Whether the article contained the gist of the plaintiff's side of the story. 9. The tone of the article. A newspaper can raise queries or call for an investigation. It need not adopt allegations as statements of fact. 10. The circumstances of the publication, including the timing.[121]

He further noted that

> it should always be remembered that journalists act without the benefit of the clear light of hindsight. Matters that are obvious in retrospect may have been far from clear in heat of the moment. Above all, the court should have particular regard to the importance of freedom of expression. The press discharges vital functions as a bloodhound as well as a watchdog. The court should be slow to conclude that a publication was not in the public interest and, therefore, the public had no right to know, especially when the information is in the field of political discussion. Any lingering doubts should be resolved in favour of publication.[122]

120 *Reynolds v Times Newspapers Ltd* [1999] 4 All ER 609 (hereafter 'Reynolds').
121 Ibid, paras 204 to 205C.
122 Ibid.

In the subsequent case of *Jameel v Wall Street Journal SPRL (No. 3)* [2006][123] Lord Hoffmann set out a two-stage test for determining whether the Reynolds defence applied in a given case. The first stage determined whether the publication was in the public interest. By this was meant the article as a whole, including the allegedly defamatory statement. If the publication passed the public interest test, the second stage asked whether the steps taken to gather and publish the information were responsible and fair.[124] It must be pointed out that Lord Hoffmann identified both of these tests as being objective and, furthermore, that the non-exhaustive list of ten matters to be considered were to be considered in a flexible manner and with regard to practical realities.[125] Lord Nicholls summarised what Reynolds privilege was concerned with in *Bonnick* [2002], where he opined that, in short, the Reynolds privilege is concerned to provide a proper degree of protection for responsible journalism when reporting matters of public concern. He characterised 'responsible journalism' as forming the point at which a fair balance is held between freedom of expression on matters of public concern and the reputations of individuals. He further noted that it is in the public interest and in the interests of those whose reputations are involved to maintain this standard. Adhering to this standard, he concluded, can be regarded as the price journalists pay in return for the privilege.[126]

The defence was further developed in *Flood*.[127] In this case the defendant published an article containing a false allegation that there were reasonable grounds to suspect the claimant, a police officer, of bribery and corruption. The court held that the defendant nevertheless had a valid defence of public interest publication. It also clearly distinguished the defence as separate from privilege.[128] Lord Brown chose to encapsulate the defence in a single question:

> Could whoever published the defamation, given whatever they knew (and did not know) and whatever they had done (and had not done) to guard so far as possible against the publication of untrue defamatory material, properly have considered the publication in question to be in the public interest?[129]

123 *Jameel v Wall Street Journal SPRL (No. 3)* [2006] UKHL 44; [2007] 1 AC 359, paras 48–49.
124 Ibid, para 55.
125 Ibid, para 56.
126 *Bonnick v Morris* [2002] UKPC 31 [2003], 1 AC 300, para 23.
127 *Flood v Times Newspapers Ltd* [2012] UKSC 11.
128 Ibid, para 27.
129 Ibid, para 113.

Lord Mance stressed the importance of giving respect, within reason, to editorial judgement in relation not only to the steps to be taken by way of verification prior to publication but also to what it would be in the public interest to publish.[130] It was also expressly stated that the public interest defence had been developed under the influence of the principles laid down in the European Court of Human Rights.

In the 2011 government proposals for reform of the law of defamation the Lord Chancellor explained that concerns had been expressed about the complexity of the Reynolds defence and about its application outside the context of mainstream journalism. The government proposed that it be replaced with an expanded and more user-friendly statutory defence which would not be seen, as the Reynolds criteria so often were, as a checklist or set of hurdles for defendants to overcome.

The legislative reform of this part of the common law therefore aimed to go much further – including but not limited to fostering responsible journalism. Section 4 of the 2013 Act, 'Publication on a matter of public interest,' is clearly based on but abolishes the Reynolds defence. However, from what follows, it seems that there was initial confusion in the courts as to whether the principles from *Reynolds* continued to apply.[131] Since section 4 purports to abolish and replace a very important common law defence, it is necessary to examine the section and its application in some detail. The defence states:

4 Publication on matter of public interest

(1) It is a defence to an action for defamation for the defendant to show that –

(a) the statement complained of was, or formed part of, a statement on a matter of public interest; and
(b) the defendant reasonably believed that publishing the statement complained of was in the public interest.

(2) Subject to subsections (3) and (4), in determining whether the defendant has shown the matters mentioned in subsection (1), the court must have regard to all the circumstances of the case.
(3) If the statement complained of was, or formed part of, an accurate and impartial account of a dispute to which the claimant was a party, the court must in determining whether it was reasonable for the defendant to believe that publishing the statement was in the public

130 Ibid, para 137.
131 Barendt, E 'Reynolds Revived and Replaced' (2017) 9(1) *Journal of Media Law* 1–13 on the public interest qualified privilege defence to libel.

interest disregard any omission of the defendant to take steps to verify the truth of the imputation conveyed by it.

(4) In determining whether it was reasonable for the defendant to believe that publishing the statement complained of was in the public interest, the court must make such allowance for editorial judgement as it considers appropriate.

(5) For the avoidance of doubt, the defence under this section may be relied upon irrespective of whether the statement complained of is a statement of fact or a statement of opinion.

(6) The common law defence known as the Reynolds defence is abolished.

In effect replacing the 'responsible journalism' criterion (as measured by the ten factors outlined in *Reynolds*) with that of 'reasonableness of belief,' the question was whether this entailed any substantive change. The answer, in the light of initial case law, seemed to be both yes and no.[132] The answer is yes in the sense that it seems as if this section is an attempt to widen the scope of the 'responsible journalism' defence which focused mainly on traditional media, to encompass the reality of 'citizen journalists' who in turn reflect the hyper-connected reality of modern life. In this way the defence protects a wider range of defendants. But the answer is also no because on the other hand it seemed at first as if the criteria from *Reynolds* remained firmly entrenched in the courts' methodology in applying the section. This was evident from both the first instance and appeal cases of *Economou v de Freitas*[133](discussed below).

Subsection 2 does not help: In what is clearly an attempt to reformulate the ten factors listed in *Reynolds*, it merely states that in this enquiry, the court 'must have regard to all the circumstances of the case.' In effect, although section 4 of the 2013 Act as it says at subsection (6), abolished and replaced the common law defence identified by the House of Lords in *Reynolds*, it is clear that parties to defamation suits and courts adjudicating these matters, continue to use the factors listed in *Reynolds*. Lady Justice Sharp in the Appeal Court decision in *Economou*[134] stated that the correct approach is to 'proceeded on the footing that the common law principles identified in *Reynolds* as interpreted or applied in subsequent cases . . . [are] of relevance to the interpretation of section 4.'[135]

132 Barendt, note 131, 13.

133 *Economou v de Freitas* [2018] EWCA Civ 2591 per Lady Justice Sharp, summarising the court a quo's findings (*Economou v de Freitas* [2016] EWHC 1853 (QB)) in para 76: '[T]he judge and the parties proceeded on the footing that the common law principles identified in *Reynolds* as interpreted or applied in subsequent cases . . . were of relevance to the interpretation of section 4 . . . [I]n my view, this is the correct approach.'

134 Ibid, para 75.

135 Ibid. The cases referred to are: *Bonnick v Morris* [2002] UKPC 31 [2003], 1 AC 300, *Jameel (Mohammed) v Wall Street Journal Europe Sprl* [2006] UKHL 44, [2007] 1 AC 359 and *Flood v Times Newspapers Ltd* [2012] UKSC 11.

Subsection (5) states: 'For the avoidance of doubt, the defence under this section may be relied upon irrespective of whether the statement complained of is a statement of fact or a statement of opinion.' This, in the opinion of Mullis and Scott, muddies the waters considerably as it mingles the public interest defence with the defence of honest opinion.[136] They point out that in *Reynolds*, both Lords Nicholls and Hobhouse stressed that if statements of opinion were to be protected, this should be done by means of the defence of fair comment only.[137] Going further than that and protecting it in the expanded 'responsible journalism' section 4 also, means that in theory editors of newspapers can defend serious allegations without evidence of fact by citing 'editorial freedom.' Mullis and Scott therefore state that 'circumspection in the levelling of allegations made is a marker of responsibility.'[138] They are of the opinion that section 4 does not draw appropriate distinction between opinion, fact, allegation, or suspicion and therefore does not correctly address the *Chase* levels of meaning.[139] From subsequent case law, however, it seems to have proven to be an unfounded fear, as due weight seems to be given to the 'other factors' to be taken into consideration to determine whether it was reasonable to believe that publication was in the public interest. The issue is far from clear, however, but at least it can be argued to be a clear nod in the direction of freedom of expression and particularly of the press and non-journalist commentators.

Economou v de Freitas

A closer look at *Economou* is useful as this illustrates how the successor to the Reynolds defence widened the scope to provide a robust defence to non-journalists. Alexander Economou's appeal against David de Freitas stemmed from two events – a serious allegation of criminality against the claimant, namely, an allegation of rape made to the police in 2013, and a truly dreadful tragedy for the defendant, the suicide of his daughter, Ms Eleanor de Freitas. In both courts it was agreed that 'there has been no monopoly of misery in relation to these events or their outcome.'[140] The facts of the case were as follows:[141] After having spent a night in custody following an allegation of rape by the defendant's daughter, the claimant was released with no charge. He thereupon complained to the police, alleging that he'd been falsely accused of rape. The police declined to take the matter further, but Mr de Freitas then instituted a private prosecution against Ms Economou for

136 Mullis and Scott, note 115, 95.
137 *Reynolds*, note 120, 201 and 193–195, per Lord Nicholls, and 237–238, per Lord Hobhouse.
138 Mullis and Scott, note 115, 96.
139 *Chase v News Group Newspapers Ltd* [2002] EWCA Civ 1772 – see Ch 2 on Defamatory meaning.
140 *Economou*, Appeal note 133, para 3.
141 Ibid, paras 2 to 8.

perverting the course of justice, which upon review was taken over by the Crown Prosecution Service (CPS). Before the matter could come to trial, Ms Economou, who suffered from bipolar disorder, committed suicide. In seven subsequent news publications Mr Economou was highly critical of the CPS and their decision to prosecute his daughter. Although the claimant was not directly named, it was relatively easy to identify him as the person who'd been accused of the alleged rape.

Two main issues fell to be decided – the statement's meaning and the defence in section 4. The claimant alleged that the statement's meaning was that he had prosecuted Ms de Freitas for perverting the course of justice on a false basis and was guilty of her rape, or there were strong grounds for suspecting that he was. The defendant relied upon the public interest defence under section 4. The case is especially interesting as the defendant was not a journalist but was interviewed by professional journalists. In other words, the court in particular clarified the status of contributors and their reliance upon the conduct of the media organisation they contributed to in advancing a public interest defence.[142]

In dismissing the appeal, the court found that the well-versed Reynolds criteria were applicable here subject to a holistic approach which considered all the facts of the case. In relation to *mere contributors* to publications, it was held that their standard of conduct need not reach that of professional journalists to qualify for the absolute public interest defence. Further guidance will no doubt clarify this fact-sensitive issue, building upon this significant precedent to give certainty to amateur journalists, bloggers, and freelancers. The statutory formulation in section 4(1) obviously directs attention to the publisher's belief that publishing the statement complained of is in the public interest, whereas the Reynolds defence focused on the responsibility of the publisher's conduct. This is significant as the latter entails an objective test, whereas the new defence introduces a subjective element.

As opposed to the two-stage objective approach formulated by Lord Hoffmann in *Reynolds*, viz. (1) if the publication is in the public interest and (2) if the steps taken to gather and publish the information were responsible and fair,[143] according to the interpretation by the Court of Appeal in *Economou*, section 4 now requires a three-stage enquiry comprising both an objective and subjective element. These questions are as follows: (1) Was the statement complained of, or did it form part of, a statement on a matter of public interest? (2) If so, did the defendant believe that publishing the statement complained of was in the public interest? (3) If so, was that belief reasonable?[144] Clearly, the second question adds a subjective element.

142 Warby J listed 12 grounds for his conclusion that de Freitas had a reasonable belief it was in the public interest to publish the statements: *Economou*, note 133, para 249.

143 *Reynolds*, note 120, para 55.

144 *Economou*, Appeal note 133, para 87.

Opinion was therefore divided as to whether the section 4 defence constituted a simplification and improvement of the Reynolds defence. Following the decision in *Economou* Barendt opined that although the case did not resolve every question about the scope of the defence, it did show a high regard for the concerns of defendants who raise the public interest defence in libel cases.[145] More clarity was provided by the Supreme Court in the extraordinary saga of *Serafin v Malkiewicz*.

Serafin v Malkiewicz

The public interest defence was a core issue in this case. The claim was about an article containing serious allegations against the claimant concerning his charitable work at a Polish cultural organisation and a care home for elderly Polish people and about his business dealings. The defendants did not approach the claimant for comment before the article's publication. Mr Serafin represented himself throughout – he had a little help from a McKenzie friend at times, but for the most part he was on his own – and he came up against a leading QC representing the defendants in court.[146] At first instance, Judge Jay rejected his claims – some of the statements, he held, did not meet the serious harm requirement of section 1(1), whereas for the others he upheld the defences of substantial truth and the section 4 public interest defence.[147] The claimant successfully appealed, but it became clear that there would have to be a re-trial, because the conduct of the trial judge had been utterly unacceptable. The Court of Appeal found the trial to have been unfair, and observed: 'One is left with the regrettable impression of a judge who, if not partisan, developed an *animus* toward the claimant.'[148] The matter should have been referred back, without more, for a retrial, but the Court of Appeal addressed the substance of the law, and against these findings the defendants appealed to the Supreme Court. The Supreme Court was less restrained in its criticism of the trial judge's treatment of Mr Serafin as a litigant in person:

> [W]hen one considers the barrage of hostility towards the claimant's case, and towards the claimant himself acting in person, fired by the judge in immoderate, ill-tempered and at times offensive language at many different points during the long hearing, one is driven, with profound regret, to uphold the Court of Appeal's conclusion that he did not allow the claim to be properly presented; that therefore he could not fairly appraise it; and, that, in short, the trial was unfair.[149]

145 Barendt, note 131.
146 *Serafin v Malkiewicz & Ors* [2020] UKSC 23 (*Serafin* SC), para 3.
147 *Serafin v Malkiewiçz & Ors* [2017] EWHC 2992 (QB).
148 *Serafin v Malkiewicz & Ors* [2019] EWCA Civ 852 (*Serafin* Appeal), para 114.
149 *Serafin*, SC note 146, para 48.

The Supreme Court judgment includes a schedule of extracts from the trial which make for sobering reading. Irritation, foul language, and clear infringements of the Bench Book are evident throughout, with the following a typical example of the judge's interjections aimed at the claimant:

> J: . . . I am not going to take your word for it, ok? I need you to prove it to me. A bunch of assertions is not going to cut any ice. I need proof. Strictly speaking, the burden of proof is on the defendant to prove that under the Defamation Act, but it is not going to work like that in the sense that I will draw inferences.[150]

One cannot help but wonder whether a measure of sympathy with the claimant, after his treatment at trial, perhaps influenced the Appeal Court to reverse the judgment upholding the defence of publication in the public interest. It gave an extensive judgment focusing on the section 4 defence. However, the fact is that this should not have happened – the matter should have been referred back to trial. The Appeal Court comments, as well as, for that matter, those of the Supreme Court, must therefore surely be obiter.[151] Lord Wilson in handing down the Supreme Court judgment was therefore 'driven, with a degree of embarrassment in relation to respected colleagues, to suggest that the new judge should determine the availability of the public interest defence' without reference to the Court of Appeal's reasoning.[152] Nevertheless, the Supreme Court's commentary on section 4 must certainly be highly persuasive, and therefore, it is worthwhile examining it in some detail. The Supreme Court felt duty-bound to address the Court of Appeal's analysis of the defence of public interest under section 4, as it is clear that the Supreme Court fundamentally disagreed with the Appeal Court's interpretation of section 4 as a kind of continuation of the Reynolds defence. The Supreme Court held that the new defence should not be interpreted as essentially the same or even closely analogous to *Reynolds*. It responded to the Appeal Court's discussion of section 4 point by point:

The Court of Appeal in *Serafin* held that *Reynolds* continued to be relevant and applicable.[153] For instance, it mentioned: 'In *Reynolds*, Lord Nicholls set out a well-known check list for use when determining whether the defendant reasonably believed that publishing the statement complained of was in the public interest'[154] – but Lord Wilson pointed out in the Supreme Court

150 *Serafin*, SC Schedule.

151 See Rozenberg, J 'A Bad Day for Jay J' *Law Society Gazette* (15 June 2020), <www.lawgazette.co.uk/commentary-and-opinion/a-bad-day-for-jay-j/5104585.article> accessed 30 October 2023.

152 *Serafin*, SC, para 78.

153 Weinert, E 'Serafin v Malkiewicz – Guidance on Responsible Journalism' (2019) 30(7) *Entertainment Law Review* 228–231.

154 *Serafin*, Appeal, para 36.

that the inquiry which the Court of Appeal there described is the inquiry mandated by section 4(1)(b) rather than that suggested in the *Reynolds* case.[155]

Whereas the Court of Appeal understood *Economou* to confirm that the *Reynolds* 'public interest' defence was not materially different to the section 4 'public interest' defence, the Supreme Court held that what the Court of Appeal said in the *Economou* case was that the *rationale* for each of the tests was not materially different. It is therefore wrong to consider that the elements of the statutory defence can be conflated with those of the Reynolds defence.[156] Nor was the defence, as the Court of Appeal averred, a form of qualified privilege. Lord Wilson was adamant: 'The concept of qualified privilege is laden with baggage which, on any view, does not burden the statutory defence.'[157]

As to the meaning of 'on a matter of public interest,' in its judgment the Court of Appeal said that when determining the issue whether defamatory material is published in the 'public interest' under section 4, the public interest in publication is to be balanced with the fact that an individual's article 8 right to reputation will be breached by the publication of unproven allegations without a remedy. The section 4 defence, in the Court of Appeal's opinion, therefore, needed to be confined to the circumstances *necessary* to protect article 10 rights. The Supreme Court pointed out that the section required, not whether the statement 'is published in the public interest' but whether it is '*on* a matter of public interest,' and that, with respect, it is important to adhere to the statutory wording. As to the Appeal Court's reference to human rights under the European Convention, Lord Wilson pointed out that just as the common law defence was developed under the influence of Convention principles, so was the statutory defence:

> Its three requirements that the statement should have been on a matter of public interest, that the defendant should have believed that publication of it was in the public interest and that the belief should have been reasonable, all of which have to be established by the defendant, are intended, and may generally be assumed, to ensure that operation of the section generates no violation either of the claimant's right under article 8, or of the defendant's right under article 10.[158]

Should a court decide to consult Convention case law whilst mulling section 4, Lord Wilson continued, they are likely to find that the word 'reasonably' in subsection (1)(b) is sufficiently elastic to enable the section to be given

155 *Serafin*, SC, para 71.
156 *Serafin*, SC, para 72.
157 *Serafin*, SC, para 73.
158 *Serafin*, SC, para 74.

effect in a way which is compatible with Convention rights. In other words, the section is a self-contained system.

Furthermore, the Supreme Court disagreed with the Court of Appeal's assertion that it is a core *Reynolds* requirement of fairness and responsible journalism that a person who is going to publish a story without being required to show that it is true should give the person who is the subject of the story the opportunity to put his side of the story.[159] Lord Wilson pointed out that such a prior invitation to comment, although forming a subject of consideration under section 4(1)(b), was never a requirement of the common law defence and neither is it a requirement under section 4.[160] The court also made short shrift of the 'checklist' approach commonly followed in *Reynolds* interpretation, including by the Court of Appeal when it said in para 83 of its judgment: 'Finally, by way of a checklist, it is useful to consider the *Reynolds* factors *seriatim*.' This was not intended by Parliament, nor does that follow from a correct interpretation of *Economou*.[161]

Even though all 78 paragraphs of its judgment must, under the circumstances, be obiter, they do provide clear guidance by the Supreme Court and should surely suffice to lay to rest the ghost of *Reynolds*: Section 4 is a new defence, not a mere development of the common law defence. The *Serafin* litigation and its core issue namely the meaning of the section 4 public interest publication defence mirrors, to an extent, the development of the section 1 'serious harm' issue in *Lachaux*: After an initial interpretation by the lower courts and the Appeal Court, the Supreme Court clarified that the principle did not merely further develop or mirror or extend the common law; it went much further. The serious harm requirement was held to be not a mere raising of a common law threshold; it was a new, substantive element to the tort of defamation. Likewise, section 4 publication on a matter of public interest is not an extension or further development of the common law: It is wider in scope than *Reynolds* and its interpretation by the Supreme Court in *Serafin* tilt distinctly in favour of the defamation defendant and, therefore, free speech.

Claims against persons who are not the primary publisher of the defamatory statement

This used to be known in the common law as 'innocent publication' and aims to protect those who do not have any editorial control over the material they handle. The defence extends to those who provide access to information on the internet where the information is provided by a person over whom the service provider has no control.

159 *Serafin*, Appeal, para 66.
160 *Serafin*, SC, para 76.
161 *Serafin*, SC, paras 69 and 77.

Section 5 of the Defamation Act 2013 introduced a new defence to actions that are brought in defamation against operators of websites in respect of a statement posted on the website. In such an instance, the operator can raise as a defence that it was not the operator who posted the statement. If the real author cannot be identified (and therefore sued) by the claimant, however, the claimant will be entitled to complain to the operator, and if the operator does not respond to the complaint, it may be sued in defamation. The important caveat here is that this defence is intended for the protection of facilitators of publication of defamatory statements not created by the operator itself. Malice defeats the defence, as would failure to respond to notices of complaint in accordance with the procedure set out in the Defamation (Operators of Websites) Regulations 2013.[162] The law around internet defamation is complex and evolving, and this is reflected in the fact that the regulations drafted to flesh out section 5 are themselves complex and cumbersome.[163]

Section 10 deals with more 'traditional' publishers but provide essentially the same defence as it relates to defendants who do not exercise editorial control. Section 10 changes the common law significantly by removing the jurisdiction of courts in England and Wales to hear defamation actions against secondary publishers of defamatory statements (in most cases, at least). The section states:

> (1) A court does not have jurisdiction to hear and determine an action for defamation brought against a person who was not the author, editor or publisher of the statement complained of *unless the court is satisfied that it is not reasonably practicable for an action to be brought against the author, editor or publisher*. [Own emphasis]
> (2) In this section 'author,' 'editor' and 'publisher' have the same meaning as in section 1 of the Defamation Act 1996.

By section 1(3)(a) of the Defamation Act 1996, persons who are involved only in printing, producing, distributing, or selling printed material containing a defamatory statement are not to be treated as authors, editors, or publishers of the statement. This means that, read with the 2013 Act, courts in England and Wales no longer have jurisdiction to determine a defamation action brought against such person, for causes of action accruing after the Act's commencement, unless it is satisfied that it is not reasonably practicable for an action to be brought against the author, editor, or publisher of the statement.[164]

162 SI 2013/3028.

163 Ibid.

164 For an application of this section, see *Richardson v Facebook* [2015] EWHC 3154 (QB). However see *Monir v Wood* [2018] EWHC 3525 (QB); [2018] 12 WLUK 367 and the reasoning as to why the chairman of a local branch of a political party was held liable for a libellous tweet sent by a branch member through the branch's Twitter account.

The significance of this change is that it protects secondary publishers such as wholesale and retail newspaper and magazine vendors and distributors, commercial printers, libraries, and book distributors, who at common law, were deemed to be publishers and, as such, potentially liable. The question is, when will it be deemed to be 'not reasonably practicable' to sue the author, editor, or publisher? Within the meaning of section 10(1) of the 2013 Act, this answer will be fact-sensitive. Some instances could include, for example, where the claimant, despite making reasonable attempts, has not been able to identify or locate the author, editor, or publisher or where the latter could not be made to submit to the jurisdiction of the court or could not be sued for some other reason such as death or bankruptcy.[165]

How does all of this amend the common law position? A bit of history helps us here. In *Byrne v Dean* [1937][166] the Court of Appeal held that the proprietors of a golf club who failed to remove an allegedly defamatory notice from the club's notice board had taken part in the publication of the notice by allowing it to rest on the wall, even though the notice had been placed on the wall without the consent of the proprietors. It is likely that *Byrne v Dean* [1937] would be decided differently, if it were to come before the courts today, as section 10 of the 2013 Act would preclude jurisdiction to hear a defamation action against the proprietors of the club, other than where it was not reasonably practicable for an action to be brought against the author of the notice. Although the same applies to more recent internet cases such as *Tamiz v Google Inc* [2013][167] and jurisdiction would be denied at first, given that the author could not be identified, the result under the common law and the 2013 Act regime would for all intents and purposes be the same: The ISP could be held liable provided it had been placed on notice.

Should the court allow a secondary publisher to be sued, the following defences are the most likely (depending on their nature and the role they played in publication) – the defence for operators of websites in section 5 of the 2013 Act, the defences for internet intermediaries in regulations 17–19 of the Electronic Commerce Regulations, and the statutory[168] or common law defences of innocent dissemination.[169] However, here it must be noted

165 See Araromi, MA 'Determining the Liabilities of Internet Service Providers in Cyber Defamation: A Comparative Study' (2016) *Computer and Telecommunications Law Review* 123.

166 *Byrne v Dean* [1937] 1 KB 818 (CA).

167 *Tamiz v Google Inc* [2013] EWCA Civ 68.

168 Defamation Act 1996, section 1.

169 The common law defence of innocent dissemination operates as an alternative to its statutory counterpart in section 1, Defamation Act 1996, *Metropolitan International Schools Ltd v Designtechnica Corp* [2009] EWHC 1765 (QB), para 70. It relieves defendants who are secondary publishers/distributors of defamatory publications upon proof that they did not know that the publication contained a libel or was likely to contain a libel, and the absence of knowledge was not due to any negligence on their part. See *Emmens v Pottle* [1885] 16 QBD 354 (CA); *Vizetelly v Mudie's Select Library Ltd* [1900] 2 QB 170 (CA) and *Goldsmith v Sperring* [1977] 1 WLR 478 (CA).

that it seems as if free speech advocates in the UK are playing a long game of legislative Whack-a-Mole – no sooner have they achieved a victory in reforming a law to be less chilling of free speech than another pops up to restrict freedom of speech in another area: Draconian provisions and amendments in the areas of new anti-terror legislation,[170] rapidly expanding privacy and data protection,[171] and the ever-expanding regulation of 'hate speech'[172] all have a direct impact on the ability to speak freely and to communicate ideas. To this must be added the draconian provisions contained in the Online Safety Act 2023, briefly discussed in chapter 1.[173]

It is therefore submitted that although the defence is now formalised and stated more clearly, the result for free speech is unchanged or may actually be worse, as ISPs instead of engaging with the merits of the notice, may just take the path of least resistance and remove all statements complained of without any investigation.

Analysis

Overall, the 2013 reforms go far towards levelling the playing field between defamation claimants and defendants and redressing the balance in favour of free speech. But does it go far enough? Is the playing field levelled or is it still uneven? If one compares the outcomes of virtually the same complaint by the actor Johnny Depp in the UK and in the US, one might be forgiven to think that the law now tilts too far *against* the defamation claimant. The Depp litigation, therefore, makes an interesting case study showing how far the pendulum has swung in English defamation law due to the 2013 reforms.

The Depp cases

The actor Johnny Depp brought a libel action against *The Sun*'s publisher (and the newspaper's executive editor, Dan Wootton) in respect of a 2018 article which was first published online under the headline: 'GONE POTTY: How can JK Rowling be "genuinely happy" casting wife beater Johnny Depp in the new Fantastic Beasts film?' Depp sued in defamation, contending that

170 For an in-depth discussion of the far-reaching free speech implications of the UK's Counter-Terrorism and Border Security Act 2019 and its amendment of the Terrorism Act 200, *see* Bechtold, E and Phillipson, G 'Glorifying Censorship? Anti-Terror Law, Speech and Online Regulation,' in Stone, A and Schauer, F (eds), *The Oxford Handbook of Freedom of Speech* (2021), chapter 28.

171 On the proliferation of privacy and data protection suits, *see* Goutzamanis, Y 'Closing the Floodgates on Privacy Class Actions: Lloyd v Google LLC' (2023) 86(1) MLR 249–262.

172 Law Commission, *Hate Crime Laws Law Com No. 402*, 2021, paras 1.35–1.37, 1.49, 4.220. *See* also Law Commission, *Modernising Communications Offences Law Com No. 399*, 2021.

173 See Jones, M 'Regulation of Online Speech in the UK' (2024) 55(2) *University of the Pacific Law Review* 261 for a discussion of the Online Safety Act.

the article's meaning conveyed the allegation that he was guilty of serious domestic violence against his former wife and was therefore defamatory. Nicol J acknowledged that Depp had proved defamation, including that his reputation had been seriously damaged.[174] However, the court then upheld a defence of truth stating that 'the defendants have shown that what they published in the meaning which I have held the words to bear was substantially true.'[175]

In short, Mr Depp's defamation case in the UK was completely defeated. His attempt to take the matter on appeal likewise failed. The Court of Appeal could see no possible error of approach or mistake of law in Justice Nicol's reasoning, and it emphasised that it is not easy to persuade the court to overturn the findings of a trial judge on purely factual questions.[176]

Mr Depp was determined to clear his name and took what many would have thought to be an equally if not higher risk by pursuing a defamation claim in the US. As will be seen from the discussion of the US law in chapter 4, it is much more difficult to succeed with a defamation claim in that jurisdiction, especially where, as here, the parties are 'public figures.' The claimant has to prove not only fault on the part of the defendant but also falsity and that the statement complained of was made with actual malice, and before the claimant gets to this stage, there are procedural difficulties which prevent many cases to even get to trial in the first place.[177] Nevertheless, Mr Depp went ahead and sued his ex-wife Ms Heard in defamation for her 2018 *Washington Post* op-ed[178] in which she said that she was the victim of domestic abuse. On 1 June 2022, in a Virginia court, the seven-person jury unanimously ruled in favour of Depp. The court awarded Depp $15 million for the three counts of defamation that Depp claimed were inflicted on him by Heard in her *Washington Post* article; however, that number was reduced to $10.35 million due to Virginia law. Heard won on one counterclaim, with jurors awarding the actress $2 million in damages.[179]

In comparing the two cases and outcomes, a few points must be kept in mind, but perhaps we can also draw some conclusions as to the defamation reform in the UK. First, in both jurisdictions Mr Depp proved that he was, in fact, defamed. The serious harm requirement made his job in this regard a bit more difficult than it would have been, say, in 2010. But it still pales in comparison to the elements of fault, falsity, and actual malice he had to prove in the US. It is clear that he was well and truly defamed, in the sense of having suffered severe reputational damage. The key difference is that in the UK, the

174 *Depp v Newsgroup Newspaper Ltd* [2020] EWHC 2911 (QB) [585].

175 Ibid, para 583.

176 *Depp v News Group Newspapers Ltd* [2021] EWCA Civ 423.

177 See chapter 4 for a full discussion of the federal law on defamation in the United States.

178 Opinion, 'Amber Heard: I Spoke Up Against Sexual Violence – and Faced Our Culture's Wrath. That Has to Change' *The Washington Post* (18th December 2018).

179 *Depp v Heard* [2022] Va. Cir. LEXIS 84.

defence of truth was accepted. In Virginia, there was found to be no truth to the allegations. In fact, not only were the allegations found to be not true but also that they were made intentionally and with actual malice.

This brings us to another difference between the two cases. In the UK, Ms Heard was not a party to the suit; the defendants were a newspaper and its editor. Nicol J commented that there had been several allegations of unfairness to Mr Depp as his effective opponent was Ms Heard, who was not a party to the proceedings. But the judge was not convinced by this allegation of unfairness, noting that Ms Heard was under no obligations of disclosure. Third parties can only be ordered to make disclosure if very stringent conditions are satisfied,[180] and the claimant did not succeed in obtaining such disclosure. The judge stated:

> Mr Depp has not been short of legal advice. He would, I can assume, have been advised as to the consequence of suing the Defendants against whom the claim is brought, but not Ms Heard. It was a matter for him, with the benefit of that advice to decide, if he wished to pursue the claim against these defendants. The consequences of him doing so, are that they (and not Ms Heard) are subject to the obligations of a party to make disclosure. There has been no suggestion that the defendants have failed in that duty.[181]

Nevertheless, despite the limited disclosure of evidence this implied, the newspaper's defence of truth depended almost entirely on events and statements related by Ms Heard, and the judge accepted these statements as substantially true.

As to the question why Mr Depp did not sue Ms Heard in the UK, the 2013 reforms aimed at preventing libel tourism (discussed earlier) must surely have played a part – he would have had to sue her based on a publication she herself authored, and even so, it would have been subject to the section 9 domicile requirements.

A key difference between the cases is the fact that the matter was heard by a judge alone in the UK, whereas it was heard before a jury in Virginia. In other words, one person had to be convinced about the truth of the facts in the UK. In Virginia, it was seven. Does this prove the belief that defamation juries are inherently sympathetic to claimants? It would be glib to jump to that conclusion, and one has to bear in mind that the jury in Virginia upheld the defendant's counterclaim in defamation as well.

What is clear is that this case illustrates that the Defamation Act 2013 reforms have had a significant impact. English defamation courts can most certainly not be termed the most claimant friendly in the world any longer.

180 See Civil Procedure Rules r.31.17.
181 *Depp v Heard*, para 576.

A defamation lawyer commented afterward on the changed landscape for defamation claimants in the UK:

> The number of high-profile libel claims making it to trial has declined over the years, and Mr Depp's decision to go against the grain in a high-risk strategy to clear his name in court has backfired. The case played out before the world's media and necessitated the very public dissection of Mr Depp's private life, which was put on show for all to see. The decision was a high-stakes case for the defendants and is a welcome victory for the press, serving as a reminder of the importance of free speech and the media's right to publish on stories of global interest.[182]

Miscellaneous

Related to the matter of complexity, it is not clear that the Act is sufficiently holistic: It does not seem to be joining the dots with other areas of the law. For example, pre-legislative questions as to why the tort is not run more along the lines of personal injury matters as in the law of negligence remain. The contention is that in enlarging protection for free speech, the standard for liability has more closely approximated that of negligence.[183] It is also argued that, as far as the chilling of free speech is concerned, the drafters of the legislation should have taken into account the impact of privacy law and data protection law[184] as well as areas such as the law on public interest disclosures, or 'whistleblowing.'[185] Concerns are also raised that the Defamation Act 2013 lags behind developments in information technology and the concomitant speech implications of, for example, user-generated platforms. Only section 5 of the Act touches on this issue, and for the rest the common law is trusted to develop this highly contemporary area.[186]

Cost and complexity

It was seen that the Act brought about significant costs savings by effectively abolishing jury trials, but it arguably could have further addressed costs in

182 Wiggin, E 'Reputational Risks: Depp Loses High-Stakes Libel Trial' (2021) 32(2) *Entertainment Law Review* 52–63.

183 For example, Descheemaeker, E 'Protecting Reputation: Defamation and Negligence' (2009) 29 *Oxford Journal of Legal Studies* 603–641: 'the fact of the matter is that it is less and less true that defamation is not negligence-based.'

184 Jones, note 173.

185 Lewis, D 'Whistleblowing and the Law of Defamation: Does the Law Strike a Fair Balance Between the Rights of Whistleblowers, the Media, and Alleged Wrongdoers?' (2018) *Industrial Law Journal* 339.

186 This is in contrast to other legal disciplines which deal with these issues more robustly: regarding employment law, see Mangan, D 'Social Media in the Workplace,' in Mangan, D and Gillies, LE (eds), *The Legal Challenges of Social Media* (Edward Elgar, Cheltenham, 2017), chapter 10.

other ways as well. Mullis and Scott argued that the core problem with the common law of libel was that it juridified and over-complicated disputes that properly belong in the public sphere, with the result of making the cost of legal proceedings excessive.[187] Since the reforms did not change the nature and classification of defamation as falling under private law, it comes as no surprise that cost and complexity remain issues vexing this area of law. The excessive cost aspect, of course, also fed into the skewed balance of power between claimants with deep pockets and impecunious defendants which in turn added to the claimant friendly view of English libel law. The 2013 Act does not address this problem sufficiently, in fact it barely touches it, and this surely is, to again quote Mullis and Scott, 'to the benefit of no-one bar tyrants and lawyers.'[188]

In order to understand the problem with costs in defamation actions, it is necessary to examine the role of conditional fee agreements (CFA) and after-the-event insurance (ATE).[189] CFAs provide for success fees as percentage uplift (up to 100%) on base costs, payable to a litigant's lawyers in the event that the claim is successful. ATE insurance premiums are sums paid by a litigant to insure them against, amongst others, potential costs liability. In the context of defamation, both are problematic. The following case is illustrative.

In the 2017 Supreme Court case *Times Newspapers Ltd v Flood*,[190] the central question was whether the claimants were entitled to recover their entire costs which far outstripped their damages awards and, in two instances, were awarded even though the defendants had largely succeeded with their respective defences. The appeals involved a challenge to an order for costs made by a High Court judge against a newspaper publisher after a trial. In two of the appeals, the trial involved an allegation that the newspaper had libelled the claimant; the third appeal involved allegations that the newspaper had unlawfully gathered private information about the claimants by hacking into their phone messages. In each case, the newspaper publisher lost and was ordered to pay the claimants' costs, and in each case the newspaper publisher contended that the costs order infringed its rights under article 10 of the ECHR.[191]

The claimant was awarded £60,000 damages and his entire costs of the action, with the result that his base costs and the additional liabilities by way of success fee and ATE premium totalled some £1.6million.[192] Here we should

187 Mullis and Scott, note 115, 87.

188 Ibid, 88.

189 CFAs are recoverable by the provisions of Part II of the Access to Justice Act 1999. The 1999 Act regime, *inter alia*, inserted section 58A(6) into the Courts and Legal Services Act 1990 allowing for the recovery of CFA success fees and, by section 29 of the 1999 Act, allowed for after-the-event (ATE) insurance premiums also to be treated as a recoverable cost.

190 *Times Newspapers Ltd v Flood* [2017] UKSC 33.

191 Ibid, 1421, para 1.

192 Ibid, 1415.

note that in September 2013 the government released for public consultation proposals for costs protection in defamation and privacy claims. The proposed changes were 'designed to help people and organisations of modest means to be able to bring and defend defamation and privacy claims without the fear of having to pay unaffordable legal costs to the other side if they lose.'[193] The consultation proposed that those of substantial means (whether individuals or organisations) would be excluded from the costs protection regime, while those of less modest means might have to pay something towards the legal costs of the other side if they lose.[194] These proposals were to give effect to Lord Justice Jackson's recommendations on civil litigation funding and costs[195] and to try and achieve at least some measure of parity with the implementation of qualified one way costs shifting (QOCS) which were introduced for personal injury claims from 1 April 2013 following the coming into force of the Legal Aid, Punishment and Sentencing of Offenders Act 2012 (LASPO).

However, by the time that *Flood* reached the Supreme Court, these proposals had not reached any concrete resolution. The case therefore had to be decided on the law as it stood. While part 2 of LASPO ended the recovery of CFA and ATE insurance sums from opponents, a transitional order preserved the pre-LASPO position in specific categories of litigation, including publication cases such as privacy and defamation cases. As stated, this was pending the introduction of a new cost regime for publication cases.

Lord Neuberger delivered the judgment in *Flood* on behalf of all members of the court. The Strasbourg Court's decision in *MGN v UK* (2011)[196] was given careful consideration. This case followed from the House of Lords' decision in *Campbell (No. 2)* [2005],[197] and the court decided that MGN's article 10 rights were infringed by having to reimburse the claimant the very large success fee and the ATE premium which Ms Campbell had incurred.[198] This decision was reached on the basis of the 1999 Act regime and considered the wide margin of appreciation granted to the UK. Lord Neuberger interpreted the *MGN* case as in effect meaning that, although 'Article 10 is [not] automatically infringed in every case,'[199] 'where a claim involves restricting a defendant's freedom of expression, it would normally be a breach of its Article

193 Ministry of Justice, *Costs Protection in Defamation and Privacy Claims: The Government's Proposals* (2013), 4.

194 Ibid, 7, para 42 'Summary of proposals.'

195 Jackson, Sir R *Review of Civil Litigation Costs: Final Report* (The Stationery Office, London, 2010).

196 *MGN v UK* [2011] 53 EHRR 5. See the discussion of this case in chapter 6.

197 *Campbell v MGN Limited (No. 2)* [2005] UKHL 61.

198 Ibid. Ms Campbell had funded her own litigation in the lower courts, but in the House of Lords hearing she retained solicitors and counsel pursuant to a CFA which provided for her solicitors and counsel to be entitled to success fees of 95% and 100%, respectively. The success fee MGN was liable to pay amounted to £279,981.35, which brought total liability for legal costs to £1,086,295.47.

199 *Times Newspapers Ltd v Flood*, note 190, para 34.

10 rights to require it to reimburse the claimant any success fee or ATE premium which he would be liable to pay.'[200]

Lord Neuberger then proceeded on the basis that it would *normally* breach a publisher's article 10 rights to require it to reimburse any success fee or ATE premium, and therefore the starting point was that, in the absence of a good reason to the contrary, the appellant would be entitled to have the costs orders amended to remove the additional liabilities.[201] However, the court found that on the facts it would undermine the rule of law if the additional liabilities could not be claimed – Parliament had decided that post-LASPO, the 1999 Act would not be dis-applied retrospectively, in cases where additional liabilities were no longer recoverable.[202] It also found that amending the costs order would infringe another Convention right – namely, the right to property under article 1 of the First Protocol to the Convention. Lord Neuberger accepted that it was therefore inevitable that one side's Convention rights would be infringed. He reasoned that allowing the appeal would involve a graver infringement of the rights of the respondents than the infringement of the appellant publishers' article 10 rights that would result from permitting the cost orders to stand.[203] This decision did not provide the clarity on the recoverability of additional liabilities which might have been hoped for. In fact, it reflected the uneasy situation with the continuing application of the 1999 Act regime,[204] permitting the recovery of additional liabilities in publication cases.[205]

In the meantime, what happened to the government proposals regarding costs? In the end, following the consultation, the government decided not to proceed fully with the costs protection proposals as set out in the consultation. Part 2 of the LASPO contains CFA reforms relevant to defamation and privacy cases. These 'success fees' are from 6 April 2019, non-recoverable for new cases. This certainly impacts the costs of these cases and also gives effect to the UK's legal obligations under *MGN v UK*. However, this is as far as it goes. The government decided to keep the existing arrangements in place beyond the success fee reforms coming into force on 6 April 2019.[206] Therefore, at least for the time being, the existing costs protection regime is retained, which

200 Ibid, para 42.
201 Ibid, paras 42 and 45.
202 Ibid, paras 46–48.
203 Ibid, paras 54 and 56.
204 by operation of the LASPO (Commencement No. 5 and Saving Provision) Order 2013.
205 See the discussion of this case on the INFORRM blog: Wills, A *Flood v Times Newspapers, CFA Appeals Dismissed, Future of the Scheme Left Open* (20 April 2017), <https://inforrm.org/2017/04/20/case-law-flood-v-times-newspapers-cfa-appeals-dismissed-future-of-the-scheme-left-open-aidan-wills/> accessed 4 April 2019.
206 Ministry of Justice, 'Costs Protection in Defamation and Privacy Claims: The Government's Proposals' *The Government Response* (29 November 2018), <https://consult.justice.gov.uk/digital-communications/costs-protection-in-defamation-and-privacy-claims/> accessed 18 October 2023.

means that ATE insurance premiums will remain recoverable. The rationale is that this will enable parties with a good case to litigate and discharge their article 10 rights without the fear of having to pay potentially ruinous legal costs if their case fails. The government hoped that this approach would control costs but protect access to justice, since parties with good cases can still benefit from recoverable ATE insurance in respect of adverse costs.

Overall, the procedure in defamation cases (as in all civil litigation) has been streamlined and clarified, and with the abolition of jury trials, simplified to a large extent. However, the procedure is still complicated and it is a pity that the alternative dispute proposals mooted prior to the 2013 Act never got any serious consideration.[207] As to costs, the effect of the demise of CFA's may be interesting to explore. This, coupled with the encouragement in the 2013 Act to use alternative remedies to damages awards, may well have a significant impact on the costs associated with defamation suits. For example, section 11 provides as a remedy, where the court gave judgment for the claimant, that it could order the defendant to publish a summary of the judgment. There is also, of course, the order to remove the offending statement or cease its distribution, among other provisions, contained in section 12.

Strict liability and the reverse burden of proof retained

When the Defamation Act 1996 was being debated, it was suggested that the burden of proof be altered along the lines of this proposed amendment: 'In an action for defamation, the burden shall be upon the plaintiff to prove that the defamatory words of which he complains are false.' This amendment was not passed,[208] nor did the idea of abolishing no-fault liability for defamation find any traction in the 2013 reforms. The Ministry of Justice refused to make this change in the Defamation Bill because 'proving a negative is always difficult.'[209] But commentators have taken issue with this assumption, pointing out that all that would be required of the claimant is to go into the witness box and aver that the story is false and to submit to cross-examination. If the claimant survives this, they prove their case on the balance of probabilities, like any other civil litigation claimant.[210] Placing the burden of proof on the claimant would have meant that the press, and others would be free to raise questions about the conduct of people such as Jimmy Savile, for whom cross-examination may well have been too much of a risk.

207 Webb, S 'Double Trouble? How ADR Can Help Resolve Libel Disputes' (2010) 160 *New Law Journal* 989.

208 *Hansard* HL Deb Col 242 (2 April 1996).

209 Ministry of Justice, *Draft Defamation Bill Consultation Paper CP3/11* (March 2011), para 144.

210 Robertson, G 'Put Burden of Libel Proof on Claimants' *The Guardian* (25 February 2013), <www.theguardian.com/law/2013/feb/25/libel-laws-speech-uk-expensive> accessed 2 April 2019.

It is a pity that the legislator did not see fit to fundamentally transform the law of defamation in this way nor to go much further and require an element of fault. However, it is interesting to note that it could be argued that fault, or at least fault-adjacent thinking, may be making a little bit of headway in the reformed law – notably in the new 'public interest publication' defence. The language used is also reminiscent of fault-based torts: In a test similar to the 'reasonable man test' used to determine fault in negligence, the judge now makes extensive use of the 'hypothetical ordinary reasonable reader' test to determine the meaning of the words complained of.

The presumption of falsity retained

Unfortunately, the Act does not alter the common law presumption that a defamatory statement is false. It was a fundamental tenet of libel at common law that a defamatory imputation was presumed to be false, and that the burden was therefore on the defendant to prove that it was substantially true, or failing that, covered by another defence. The inclusion of truth, the successor to the common law defence of justification, as a defence in section 2 of the Act means that this principle has now been enshrined by statute.[211] The remarks in chapter 2 concerning the lack of judicial and legislative will to reform this presumption can therefore be repeated here without much further comment.

It is clear that the serious harm requirement introduced by section 1 of the Act substantially addresses one of the three main structural issues that Milo identified as being problematic in the common law of defamation. But the other two remain fundamentally unaltered: Defamation remains a strict liability tort in which the claimant is aided by the legal presumption of falsity. The lack of more significant structural change to the law may well be a golden opportunity missed, given that alternatives are available – as will be seen from the discussion of the other jurisdictions in this book.

This brings us back to the question whether the changes wrought by the Act are far reaching enough to address the issues that led to its enactment. Certain societal/qualitative effects may be very difficult to gauge, such as the impact on freedom of speech. Others may be easier as relevant empirical databases expand, such as analysis of the number of foreign claimants pursuing claims in England and Wales, to gauge the effect of the Act's reforms on the occurrence of libel tourism. A good starting place is the annual Ministry of Justice Royal Courts of Justice Tables.[212] Their 2022 figures suggest that there has been a substantial decline in the number of defamation claims issued in London, with a 60% decrease from the 2021 figure.

211 *Serafin v Malkiewicz & Ors* [2019] EWCA Civ 852 H16 (9).

212 Ministry of Justice, *Civil Justice Statistics Quarterly*, <www.gov.uk/government/statistics/civil-justice-statistics-quarterly-january-to-march-2022> accessed 31 October 2023.

This figure may be even lower, if figures from the courts' e-filing systems instead are considered.[213]

Summary

Having examined relevant parts of the Defamation Act 2013, related statutory instruments and procedural rule amendments, and key case law, a picture emerges about the effect of the reforms enacted. This chapter set out to do two things – to make an attempt at gauging whether the Defamation Act 2013 delivers on solving the problems with the common law of defamation that led to its enactment and whether benefits of the change are apparent.

The benchmarks against which this exercise was done include whether the playing field between defamation claimants (who, it was argued, were unfairly advantaged) and defendants has been levelled. If the common law was too claimant-friendly, can the same be said of the new statutory regime? Further benchmarks included the issues of libel tourism and the chilling of free speech.

The changes made by the 2013 Act as they impact defamation defendants can be summarised as shrinking the potential pool of defendants (sections 9 and 10) and reducing costs both in terms of potential damages awards and legal costs. The absence of legal aid (save for natural persons defending a suit brought by a multinational corporation) remains problematic in terms of access to justice. Moreover, the procedure faced by parties to a claim of defamation, although streamlined and slimmed down, still remain a daunting prospect. Most significantly, however, the core characteristics of the common law which made it problematic for defendants remain unchanged. Defamation is still a strict liability tort, subject to a presumption of falsity and with the burden of proof still largely on the defendant. The structure of the common law as far as defamation in England and Wales is concerned survived the reforms more or less intact. The Act's reforms go far, but for free speech they do not go the distance. It is submitted that a golden opportunity was therefore missed to fundamentally change the nature of defamation law and that a fundamental change was indeed necessary. An alternative structure is possible – that is clear from jurisdictions such as the US, as will be seen from the discussion in chapter 4.

Moving on to the changes that the Act did in fact make, the most fundamental change is wrought by section 1, dealing with the serious harm requirement. The scope of this section was decisively clarified by the Supreme Court in *Lachaux* where it was held that the section entails more than a threshold as per the *Jameel* exception. The defamation claimant now carries an evidentiary

213 Inforrm blog, 'Judicial Statistics, 2022: A 60% decrease in issued defamation claims but doubts remain over the reliability of the figures' 21 June 2023 at <https://inforrm.org/2023/06/21/judicial-statistics-2022-a-60-decrease-in-issued-defamation-claims-but-doubts-remain-over-the-reliability-of-the-figures/> accessed 31 October 2023.

burden of proving to the court that their reputation is in fact or is likely to be seriously harmed. The claimant also now needs to prove causation of their harm. Since the common law libel action was actionable *per se*, no damage needed to be proved and thus causation did not come into the equation. In fact, the presumption of harm assisted the claimant. Now that assistance is taken away and an extra factor to prove is added. In this sense the defamation claimant's burden of proof is more onerous under the Act than it was under the common law. Although the defendant's intention in publishing the aggrieving statement may be relevant to prove serious harm to reputation, the tort of defamation remains one of strict liability.

There are other welcome innovations and changes in the reforms. The scrapping of the jury trial is not to be regretted. Expanding the defence of publication in the public interest and of protecting opinion is to be welcomed by free speech advocates, as is the inclusion of protection for academic and scientific publications and internet intermediaries. But in the final analysis it remains unclear to what extent the vexing issue of balancing freedom of speech with the protection of an individual's reputation is really addressed. So although much progress has been made, most notably the final and welcome demise of conditional fee arrangements, the issue of costs and complexity could have been addressed in much more detail.

The focus now shifts in the following chapters to analogous law in three relevant jurisdictions, starting with the US as the state with arguably the most stringent protection of free speech in the world.

4 Defamation in the United States of America

Introduction

No other country protects freedom of speech to the same extent as the United States of America (US). In an analysis of the UK Defamation Act 2013, largely informed by the debates around free speech, it is therefore useful to examine the US as a jurisdiction that accords the highest protection to free speech in defamation claims.

The US Constitution values free speech very highly, prioritising it over other rights. This in turn is reflected in the US law of defamation, which had undergone a profound transformation in the latter half of the 20th century. For common law scholars, making sense of the way the US Supreme Court[1] reshaped defamation law is impossible without understanding the key position accorded to the First Amendment to the Constitution, guaranteeing free speech in the US. Any discussion of US defamation law thus needs to include an exposition of the role and influence of the constitutional protection of free speech.

Further, in any discussion of US law deference must be paid to the fact that we are dealing with a federal system, where much of the law of defamation remains the creature of state tort law. These laws are in their turn descended from the common law and therefore suffer from the same convoluted history and haphazard evolution as that of the other common law jurisdictions across the globe.[2] However, the most significant development on a federal, i.e. State-wide level, occurred in 1964 when the Supreme Court in *New York Times Co. v Sullivan* (1964)[3] 'constitutionalised' a substantial portion of the law of defamation by holding that the First Amendment places limitations on the defamation rules created by the states.

Thus, from initially closely mirroring the English common law tradition, in most important respects US defamation law has now devolved to its opposite.

1 In this chapter, all references to the Supreme Court are to the federal US Supreme Court, unless otherwise stated.

2 Keeton, WP, Dobbs, DB, Keeton RE *et al. Prosser & Keeton on the Law of Torts* (5th edn, West Group Publishing, St. Paul, MN, 1984), 772.

3 *New York Times Co. v Sullivan*, 376 US 254, 270 (1964).

DOI: 10.4324/9781003416005-5

In particular, US defamation law is fault based, there is no reverse burden of proof, and the tort is generally not actionable *per se*. It could be argued that where the English common law of defamation favoured the claimant, the opposite was the case in the US. The defamation claimant in the US under most circumstances face a very uphill battle. In what follows we examine how the US law of defamation's move away from the English common law took place and compare the relative advantages and disadvantages of this highly contrasting way of approaching defamation law.

Constitutional protection of freedom of speech

The Constitution of the United States of America guarantees and protects freedom of speech. The First Amendment to the Constitution states:

> Congress shall make no law respecting an establishment of religion, or prohibiting the free exercise thereof; or abridging the freedom of speech, or of the press; or the right of the people peaceably to assemble, and to petition the government for a redress of grievances.

It is important to note that the First Amendment and the free speech protection it offers are binding only on the *state*. The Supreme Court stated that as 'a general matter, the First Amendment means that government has no power to restrict expression because of its message, its ideas, its subject matter, or its content.'[4] Freedom of speech in the US, then, is first and foremost protected from infringement by government. As to the reasons that this is so, a brief historical detour is useful.

The United States can be seen as a prime example of a liberal democratic republic:[5] It is *liberal* in that it protects civil liberties and political freedom by means of the rule of law and constitutional limitation, *democratic* as American citizens elect their leaders, and *republican* because policy decisions are primarily made by elected leaders.[6] McCanse Wright points out that one of the essential features of the American political scheme is civil society, which presupposes a social sphere, separate from government but at the same time necessary as forming the basis of legitimate government (i.e. the consent of the governed) as well as the building blocks of democratic self-government (i.e. empowered citizens).[7] Here historical and constitutional analysis should be complemented by civil society theory. In this context questions arise as to what kind of citizen

4 *Ashcroft v American Civil Liberties Union*, 535 US 564, 573 (2002). *See also United States v Alvarez*, 567 US 709 (2012); *Brown v Entertainment Merchants Ass'n*, 564 US 756 (2011).

5 See in general, Dworkin, R *A Matter of Principle* (Harvard University Press, Cambridge, MA, 1985).

6 McCanse Wright, A 'Civil Society and Cybersurveillance' (2017) 70(3) *Arkansas Law Review* 745–768.

7 Ibid, 746.

a liberal democracy needs, what zone of autonomy is necessary to build that kind of citizen, and what space is required to build the political culture necessary for government by the people.[8] In the US, the presupposition seems to be that democracy only functions fully when citizens can freely speak their mind.

Thomas Jefferson famously stated that freedom of expression 'cannot be limited without being lost.'[9] To this day, a debate continues between free speech absolutists, who claim that the US government and the states have no power to regulate or limit speech, and those who believe that restrictions are appropriate.[10] Justice Black, a vocal absolutist, argued that the First Amendment should be taken at face value: '[T]he unequivocal command that there shall be no abridgment of the rights of free speech and assembly shows that those who drafted our Bill of Rights did all the "balancing" that was to be done in this field.'[11] He went on to emphasise that the very object of adopting the First Amendment was to put the freedoms protected there completely out of congressional control.[12] As stated in chapter 1, the reasons for protecting free speech are indisputably important and could even be argued to be eternally valid for liberal democracies.[13] The reasons for protecting speech included finding the truth, the individual's right to autonomy and self-expression, and meaningful citizen participation in democracy. Howard argues that it is for this latter reason that the US accords such high protection to free speech, more than in virtually any other liberal democracy: If citizens do not feel free to express themselves fully there can be no meaningful public debate and the state loses legitimacy.[14]

Given this, it comes as no surprise that freedom of expression has been accorded a preferred position in the US constitutional hierarchy. Free speech frequently prevails over other countervailing interests. Bar a few exceptions, the US and state governments are given only limited authority to regulate or control speech, regardless of whether the dispute is about the content or opinion expressed in the speech.[15] The right to free speech is regarded as so important that even 'the most noxious forms of extreme speech imaginable' are protected.[16]

8 Ibid.
9 Letter to James Currie, 28 January 1786, Library of Congress.
10 *Konigsberg v State Bar of California*, 366 US 36, 60–61 (1961) (Black, J dissenting).
11 Ibid.
12 Ibid.
13 Chapter 1, para 6.1.
14 Howard, E *Freedom of Expression and Religious Hate Speech in Europe* (Routledge, London, 2018), 113.
15 *R.A.V. v City of St. Paul*, 505 US 377 (1992).
16 Weinstein, J 'An Overview of American Free Speech Doctrine and its Application to Extreme Speech,' in Hare, I and Weinstein, J (eds), *Extreme Speech and Democracy* (OUP, Oxford, 2009), 81. For a detailed discussion of the protection of extreme speech in the US see Howard, note 14, 112–120.

A prohibition on any laws prohibiting freedom of speech in the US at first glance may seem absolute. But in reality, this does not mean that the right to freedom of expression trumps all other fundamental rights in the US. Even from a purely practical point of view it seems as if this absolutist position is impossible to sustain, and an examination of case law shows that the US courts, including the federal Supreme Court, do indeed depart from a literal or absolute interpretation of the First Amendment. Many cases can be quoted as examples where free speech was restricted – a select sample would include the 'prior restraint' cases, of which the prime example is the famous *Pentagon Papers* case.[17] But perhaps Holmes J put it best in *Schenk v US* (1919), a landmark decision on the First Amendment: 'The most stringent protection of free speech would not protect a man falsely shouting fire in a theatre and causing a panic.'[18] At its simplest, freedom of speech sometimes needs to be restricted in order to enable others to exercise their own right to freedom of speech.

Barendt thus points out that in the US, freedom of speech is not regarded as an undifferentiated monolith. Various forms of speech are given differing levels of protection with particularly strong protection being accorded to political speech as opposed to, for example, commercial speech or advertising.[19] Whilst the courts perform a balancing exercise when free speech conflicts with other rights, as courts do in other jurisdictions, in the US there is a strong presumption in favour of free speech. More specifically, the courts take a strong position that the government's ability to limit or control speech should be limited, both as far as content of speech (except for certain limited categories of speech) as well as opinions expressed in that speech are concerned.[20] The reason for this goes back to the very notion of liberal democracy; the conviction that the power to govern derives from the consent of the governed.[21] And if the power to govern derives from the consent of the governed, then freedom of expression is not simply a luxury but must be regarded as a cornerstone of the governmental system. The courts' view is that the First Amendment reflects 'a profound national commitment to the principle that debate on public issues should be uninhibited, robust, and wide-open.'[22] The Supreme Court has stated that speech concerning public affairs is more than self-expression; it is the essence of self-government.[23] Indeed, it is regarded as essential to the maintenance of democratic institutions.[24]

17 *New York Times v US*, 403 US 713 (1971).
18 *Schenk v US*, 249 US 47, 52 (1919).
19 Barendt, E *Freedom of Speech* (2ndedn, OUP, Oxford, 2005), 48.
20 *R.A.V. v City of St. Paul*, note 15.
21 US Declaration of Independence (4 July 1776).
22 See *Garrison v Louisiana*, 379 US 64, 74–75 (1964); *Snyder v Phelps*, 131 S. Ct. 1207, 1215 (2010) (citing *New York Times Co. v Sullivan*, note 3).
23 Ibid; Weaver, RL, Hancock, C and Knecthle, J *The First Amendment: Cases, Materials & Problems* (5th edn, Carolina Academic Press, Durham, NC, 2017).
24 *McDonald v City of Chicago*, 561 US 742 (2010).

It is therefore not surprising that the Supreme Court has specifically formulated principles intended to guard against the danger of according the First Amendment right to freedom of speech less protection than it should enjoy, i.e. to guard against it being ranked as just another issue to consider in combination with other factors in a constitutional democracy. These guiding principles have clearly set the threshold to infringe free speech very high.

Permissible limitation of freedom of expression in the United States

Clear and present danger (of imminent lawless action)

Foremost among the instances where speech may be curtailed is the 'clear and present danger' test: Free speech is allowed unless it can be shown that allowing it presents a clear and present danger, or put another way, when it is intended to, and likely to, produce imminent lawless behaviour.[25] This test was first formulated by Justice Holmes in *Schenk v United States* (1919) as follows:

> The question in every case is whether the words used are used in such circumstances and are of such a nature as to create a clear and present danger that they will bring about the substantive evils that Congress has a right to prevent.[26]

The Supreme Court further explained this test in *Brandenburg v Ohio* (1969) as meaning that speech calling for violence or other illegal acts may be restricted only if it 'is directed to inciting or producing imminent lawless action and is likely to incite such action.'[27]

If one compares the use of this test to the practice in other common law jurisdictions, including England and Wales, insulting and inflammatory speech that would almost certainly fall foul of contempt of court proceedings in these jurisdictions would be protected under the First Amendment in the US.[28] A proper appreciation of the extent to which free speech is protected in the US is crucial for understanding the US law of defamation.

Prohibition against prior constraint

The courts are extremely reluctant to issue prior restraints, i.e. prohibitive injunctive relief before publication, against speech, as this is mostly regarded

25 *Brandenburg v Ohio*, 395 US 444 (1969).
26 *Schenk*, note 18.
27 *Brandenburg v Ohio*, note 25.
28 Barendt, note 19, chapter IX.

as being a form of censorship. The following case is a good example. In *Near v Minnesota* (1931)[29] a local newspaper published a series of articles alleging, amongst other things, that a Jewish gangster had controlled gambling, bootlegging, and racketeering in Minneapolis and that law enforcement officers and agencies were not energetically performing their duties. Prior to publication, the county attorney sought an injunction against publication of the articles, alleging them to be defamatory.[30] The court held that an injunction would constitute an unconstitutional prior restraint on speech.[31] The court's view was that any injunction would be censorship which interfered with a person's 'right to lay what sentiments he pleases before the public; to forbid this, is to destroy the freedom of the press.'[32] If this then results in defamatory statements being published, the court recognised that in such a case the publisher could be held liable for damages after the fact: 'if he publishes what is improper, mischievous or illegal, he must take the consequence of his own temerity.'[33] This case was decided in 1932, before defamatory speech was recognised as 'protected speech,' i.e. speech that is protected by the First Amendment.

The court subsequently extended the prohibition against injunctions to orders designed to protect national security. In the famous Pentagon Papers case,[34] an employee who worked at the US Department of Defense stole a classified document relating to Vietnam policymaking. When two newspapers to whom the employee had delivered the document, sought to publish it, the US government pursued declaratory and injunctive relief to prevent the publication. The court emphasised that any system of prior restraints will suffer from a heavy presumption against its constitutional validity, when it comes to be adjudicated, and that a claimant who petitions for such constraint will bear a very heavy burden of justification for the imposition of such a restraint. On the facts, the court concluded that the government had failed to meet its burden.[35] As a result, the newspapers were free to publish the document even though it had been stolen. Following the Pentagon Papers case, courts can only grant a prior restraint if the state concerned showed that it would otherwise suffer direct, immediate, and irreparable damage.

Compelling reason necessary for restriction of freedom of expression

Finally, and most importantly, a state cannot restrict freedom of speech (based on the content of the offending speech) unless it can prove a *compelling* reason

29 *Near v Minnesota*, 283 US 697 (1931).
30 Ibid, 704.
31 Ibid, 713–715.
32 Ibid, 713–714.
33 Ibid, 714.
34 *New York Times Co. v US*, 403 US 713 (1971).
35 Ibid, 714.

to do so – put another way, if there is any other less draconian way of protecting the interest concerned, that state will not be able to do so by restricting freedom of speech.[36] Again, the reason for this relates to the emphasis on participation of everyone in the public discourse in the US, and the US shows a remarkable 'hostility to the content-based regulation of public discourse.'[37] US law clearly distinguishes between content-based and content-neutral restrictions: Restrictions for the former are based on the content of the message, whilst restrictions for the latter are based on reasons unrelated to the message such as time, place, or manner speech.[38] Content-based restrictions are seen as being likelier to skew public debate, and for this reason the US regards contents-based restriction of speech with suspicion and the presumption is that it is unconstitutional.[39] Perhaps the starkest contrast that could be given as an example is the fact that Holocaust denial, prohibited in many Western democracies, would count as protected speech under the First Amendment in the US. To name one example, in Germany Holocaust denial is punishable under sections 130 and 185 of the German Criminal Code.[40]

Against this background we need to note that US law recognises reputation as a right worth protecting before the law of defamation itself is examined. Supreme Court Justice Potter Stewart stated in *Rosenblatt v Baer* (1966) that an individual's right to protection of their own good name

> [r]eflects no more than our basic concept of the essential dignity and worth of every human being – a concept at the root of any decent system of ordered liberty. The protection of private personality, like the protection of life itself, is left primarily to the individual States under the Ninth and Tenth Amendments. But this does not mean that the right is entitled to any less recognition by this Court as a basic of our constitutional system.[41]

36 Barendt, note 19, 51.

37 Weinstein, note 16, 81.

38 Ibid.

39 Howard, note 14, 114. See also Stone, G 'Free Speech in the Twenty-First Century: Ten Lessons from the Twentieth Century,' in Koltay, A (ed), *Comparative Perspectives in the Fundamental Freedom of Expression* (Wolter Kluwer, Budapest, 2015), 124–125.

40 For a comparative analysis of US and German law in this regard see Brugger, W 'Ban on or Protection of Hate Speech – Some Observations Based on German and American Law' (2002) 17 *Tulane European and Civil Law Forum* 1. For the ECtHR jurisprudence in this field see Lobba, P 'Holocaust Denial before the European Court of Human Rights: Evolution of an Exceptional Regime' (2015) 26 *European Journal of International Law* 237.

41 *Rosenblatt v Baer*, 383 US 75, 92 (1966) (Stewart, J., concurring). Justice Stewart's words were quoted with approval in the Court's landmark decision in *Gertz v Robert Welch, Inc.*, 418 US 323, 341 (1974), and more recently in the Court's reinterpretation of *Gertz*, in *Dun & Bradstreet, Inc. v Greenmoss Builders, Inc.*, 105 S. Ct. 2939 (1985).

We can now turn to the way in which US courts balance speech and reputation when these come into conflict.

Contemporary US defamation law

Turning to defamation specifically, the almost visceral distrust of governmental restriction of free speech is particularly evident here. However, this was not always the case. Until 1964, US defamation law did not differ fundamentally from the common law of defamation. Before that time, defamation liability rules were determined largely by the individual states who were free to strike the balance they deemed appropriate between speech and protection of reputation. Where this balance was struck differed from state to state. The reason for this disparity was because for much of US history, the First Amendment constitutional free speech guarantee did not apply to the states, and therefore, the states possessed broad authority to determine the content of defamation liability rules. This situation changed in 1940 when the Supreme Court incorporated the First Amendment into the Fourteenth Amendment (the due process clause) and made it applicable to the states.[42]

Until the 1960s, the general approach of US jurisprudence was to treat common law actions for defamation and privacy as posing no threat to free speech values. Judges reasoned that the right to speak freely was predicated on the corresponding responsibility not to abuse such right by speaking in ways deemed tortious under state law. Further, because the common law of defamation includes elements and defences designed to accommodate free speech concerns, the courts did not generally see any constitutional concerns in the existence and operation of these civil actions.[43] Thus, up until 1964, to a large extent US jurisprudence on defamation mirrored the common law. This changed fundamentally after the landmark decision in *New York Times v Sullivan* (1964).[44]

New York Times v Sullivan

This case should be understood in the context of the social upheaval in 1960s America, more specifically the civil liberties struggle in the American South. A publication in the *New York Times* discussed an incident involving police and students in Alabama, and allegedly defamed the local police commissioner, who subsequently sued.[45] The relevant Alabama law required, at the time, that the defendant should prove the truth of their assertions. This reflected the

42 *Cantwell v Connecticut*, 310 US 296, 303 (1940).

43 Goldberg, JCP and Zipursky, BC *Torts: The Oxford Introductions to US Law* (OUP, Oxford, 2010), 308.

44 *New York Times Co. v Sullivan*, note 3.

45 Ibid, 267.

common law reverse burden of proof still operant in England and Wales. Also reflecting the English common law characterisation of defamation as being actionable *per se*, the Alabama law allowed the jury to presume damages without any need to prove pecuniary injury.[46] The claimant Sullivan offered no proof of reputational harm but instead relied on the common law presumption of harm. He won his case in the Alabama court, where the jury awarded him $500,000 in compensatory and reputational damages. On appeal, this verdict was affirmed.[47] The matter then went on further appeal to the federal Supreme Court.

The US Supreme Court for the first time held that the First Amendment sets limits on the common law of libel and slander. The majority opinion, authored by Justice William Brennan, held that a government official cannot recover for defamatory falsehood published innocently or as a result of mere carelessness. Instead, such official has to prove with clear and convincing evidence that the statements were published with actual malice. This means, first of all, that the reverse burden of proof was done away with for these types of defamation claims: A public official who brings a defamation suit must bear the burden of proof on the question of truth.[48] Furthermore, not only did the plaintiff henceforward bear the burden to prove that the defamatory statement was false, but they also had to prove that it was made with actual malice.[49] This is defined as knowledge of, or reckless disregard for, the statement's falsity. In other words, the defamation claimant must prove that the defendant knew the statement was false or acted in reckless disregard for whether it was true or false.[50] In the court's view, the mere fact that an official's reputation had suffered injury 'affords no more warrant for repressing speech.'[51] The court, in reversing the state judgments, and in rejecting the common law presumption of damages and reverse burden of proof therefore struck the balance between speech and reputation firmly in favour of freedom of expression.

Sullivan declared a 'profound national commitment to the principle that debate on public issues should be uninhibited, robust, and wide-open, and that it may well include vehement, caustic, and sometimes unpleasantly sharp attacks on government and public officials.'[52] Recognising that 'erroneous statement is inevitable in free debate,' the court held that there must be 'breathing space' for free expression.[53] The court did this by fundamentally departing from the common law in three ways – restoring the burden of proof to where it belongs in civil cases (namely, with the claimant), casting aside the

46 Ibid.
47 Ibid, 260.
48 Ibid, 279–280.
49 Ibid.
50 Ibid.
51 Ibid, 272.
52 Ibid, 270.
53 Ibid, 271.

presumption of falsity, and changing the nature of the claim from one of strict liability to one based on fault.

From public officials to public figures

Sullivan on its facts concerned government officials, or public officials. However, the Supreme Court, after *Sullivan*, quickly extended the scope of the limitation on defamation actions. The most significant extension of the constitutional limits introduced by *Sullivan* occurred once it was decided in *Curtis Publishing Company v Butts* (1967)[54] to apply such limits not only to public officials but to any public figure.[55] The court explained that a public figure is either a 'general purpose public figure,' meaning a household name, or a 'limited purpose public figure,' meaning a person who involved themselves in a matter of public concern and who were then allegedly defamed in connection with such matter.[56] In *Curtis* this meant the commander of the Mississippi Highway Patrol was seen as a 'public official' within the meaning of the actual malice standard. Similar examples include a state court judge.[57] This means that an ordinary citizen who is defamed in connection with their voluntary participation in a debate or an event that has caught the public's eye has to, in effect, go through the same procedure as a public official: They have to prove actual malice, falsity, and actual damage to reputation. It is clear that the Supreme Court felt that freedom of speech is such an important constitutional principle that it is necessary to block not only government actors from using civil defamation actions to suppress political speech but also to create the widest possible space for public discourse without fear of being sued for libel.

Purely private figures: Gertz

The constitutional limitations introduced by *Sullivan*, therefore, apply to public officials as well as public figures. But what about private individuals who fall under neither category? For these claimants, defamation actions are subject to lower evidentiary standards. The Supreme Court in *Gertz v Robert Welch* (1974)[58] did not extend the actual malice standard to private individuals even though they may be involved in matters of public interest. This case involved a lawyer who had acted on behalf of the family of a victim of police brutality. He was subsequently described by far-right media as involved in a communist plot to discredit local police. The issue before the court was whether acting in

54 *Curtis Publishing Co. v Butts (Conjoined with Associated Press v Walker)*, 388 US 130 (1967).
55 Ibid, 132.
56 Ibid, 154–155.
57 *Rinaldi v Holt, Rinehart & Winston, Inc.*, 42 N.Y.2d 369, 366 N.E.2d 1299, 397 N.Y.S.2d 943 (1977).
58 *Gertz v Robert Welch*, 418 US 323 (1974).

this way rendered the lawyer a limited purpose public figure. The answer to this, the court held, was negative.

The next question was then what a purely private figure suing for defamatory speech on a matter of public concern must prove in defamation actions. The court's answer was that the claimant has to prove that the defendant acted at least *carelessly* with respect to the truth or falsity of their statement. In other words, where a private person claims in defamation, the defendant can successfully raise a defence that they actually and reasonably believed their statement to be true (even if it is not). However, it remains clear that there can nevertheless be no liability without proof of fault. What is more, even private individuals may not recover presumed or punitive damages without proving actual malice. More specifically, *Gertz* means the following: If the claimant can only prove carelessness, they can only claim special damages and will have to prove actual loss;[59] if the claimant can prove actual malice, then they can claim general damages, which include presumed damage (which is the common law rule) and punitive damages, without having to prove actual loss.[60]

If a case involves a private individual involved in a purely private matter, with no public interest, the court suggested in *Dun & Bradstreet, Inc. v Greenmoss Builders, Inc.* (1985)[61] that states are granted great latitude to define defamation standards. For example, the states might allow claimants to recover presumed or punitive damages without proof of actual malice.[62]

Comparison to UK defamation law

It is clear that the level of constitutional protection accorded to defamatory speech depends on the status of the defamation claimant, with the highest protection given to speech concerning public officials, or public figures where the public interest is concerned. In these instances, the 'actual malice' requirement makes it all but impossible for these figures to succeed in defamation claims. The fault element here therefore includes intention, which is a subjective element, with concomitant evidentiary difficulty. For 'purely private' claimants, more leeway is allowed, with states being able to set their own defamation rules. However, it must be noted that even in the last category the US defamation claimant still faces a much more difficult evidentiary task than their UK counterparts, as they still need to prove falsity or at least negligence. In both instances the claimant shoulders the burden of proof and also needs to prove damages.

The US law of defamation is therefore clearly fault-based. The whole burden falls on the claimant to prove not only fault but also falsity. As far as public

59 Albeit this can include, for example, emotional distress caused, job loss, etc.

60 *Gertz*, note 58, 348–349. See also Goldberg and Zipursky, note 43, 326.

61 *Dun & Bradstreet, Inc. v Greenmoss Builders, Inc.*, 164 US 749 (1985).

62 Ibid, 760.

officials and other public figures are concerned, actual malice must be proved by the claimant. The burden falls on the claimant to prove that a defamatory and false statement concerning them was published by the defendant, and that the defendant acted not only with intent but with actual malice. By contrast, liability in England and Wales remains strict, with no fault requirement. There, the burden of proof remains largely on the defamation defendant. Under the English common law, the claimant merely had to present the court with a *prima facie* defamatory statement. The burden then shifted to the defendant to convince the court that they had one of several possible defences, including that of truth. This reverse burden of proof survived the 2013 reforms largely intact, as is clear from the preceding discussion in chapters 1 to 3. Although the UK Defamation Act 2013 significantly improves the scope and ease of possible defences, the burden of proof still shifts onto the defendant as soon as the claimant has convinced the court that there was a defamatory statement published that harmed (or was likely to harm) their reputation.

It is also worth noting that the effect of the abolition of the presumption of falsity goes much further than a substantive change of the law, to significant concomitant procedural changes. Andrew Kenyon's comprehensive empirical research in this regard show how profoundly litigators experienced the effect of changing the burden of proving falsity:[63] First, the plaintiff was made to prove falsity with *clear and convincing evidence* and, second, after the case of *Anderson v Liberty Lobby*, the plaintiff had to prove it quite early in the pre-trial process or face defeat.[64] This meant that not only did defamation claimants now face an uphill battle as far as the substance of the law was concerned, they also faced difficulties on a practical level in the courtroom. Compared to common law jurisdictions, the effect of this was that in the US far fewer defamation cases tend to even make it to trial in the first place.[65] Furthermore, in the event that they do, they are then subject to strict review by appellate courts: Under *Sullivan*, in order to ensure that constitutional standards have been met, appellate courts have a duty to review the trial facts, with the facts relevant to actual malice being particularly significant.[66]

As far as compensatory damages in defamation actions in the US are concerned, it is for the court to determine whether a particular harm can be compensated in this way and for the jury or other trier of fact to determine the amount of damages recoverable as compensation.[67] As to punitive damages, if the matter concerned a private individual, it fell to the jury to decide whether the defamatory matter was published with knowledge of its falsity, or with

63 See Kenyon, AT *Defamation: Comparative Law and Practice* (Routledge, New York, NY, 2007), chapters 8 and 10.

64 *Anderson v Liberty Lobby*, 477 US 242 (1986).

65 Kenyon, note 63, 252–253.

66 *Sullivan*, 376 US 254, 285 (1964).

67 Restatement (Second) of Torts (1977) Division Five – Defamation, section 616.

reckless indifference as to truth or falsity, or solely for the purpose of causing harm to the plaintiff. Only in these instances would the plaintiff be entitled to punitive damages.[68]

Where the Constitution is engaged, i.e. where the matter concerns public officials or public figures, punitive damages cannot constitutionally be awarded if the defendant was merely negligent in failing to ascertain the falsity of the defamatory communication. In other words, negligence does not suffice for the fault requirement here, but actual malice needs to be proven before punitive damages may be awarded.[69]

The requirement to prove damages, be they compensatory or punitive, stands in contrast to the common law of defamation in England and Wales which was actionable *per se*. Although section 1 of the Defamation Act 2013 now requires the claimant to prove actual or likely harm to their reputation, this still pales in comparison to the evidentiary burden placed on the US litigant in this regard.

The 2013 reforms did not bring about any significant convergence with US law. Nevertheless, some similarities do exist. In both jurisdictions the requirement of publication means the communication of the statement to someone other than the claimant and in both jurisdictions the 'multiple publication' rule is retained. This means that each such communication is a separate tort – technically there are as many instances of publication as there are people who read/heard/saw the communication. A mass publication, such as a broadcast or online statement, gives rise to as many causes of action as there are viewers, listeners, or readers. It does not give rise to a single cause of action, as is the position in some other jurisdictions where the principle that there is only a single cause of action is known as the 'single publication' rule. The 'multiple publication' rule also includes the doctrine of republication, i.e. the notion that someone who published something that contained another's defamatory statement is treated as a publisher and can be sued in their own right. There are of course qualifications to this, and the Defamation Act 2013 restricts this in sections 8 and 10. But the possibility to sue multiple publishers for the same statement still exists in both jurisdictions.

However, there is one major caveat to this. Even after the liberalised regime ushered in by the 2013 Act, the situation *vis-à-vis* internet service providers (ISPs) in this regard still differs greatly across the two jurisdictions. In the US, providers and users of interactive computer services, including ISPs, content hosts, and online search engines, enjoy complete statutory immunity from suit as regards the publication of information provided by others. For example, section 230(c) of the US Communications Decency Act 1996[70] contains a broad immunity from liability for internet intermediaries and others who

68 Ibid.
69 Ibid, section 621 comment d.
70 Communications Decency Act 1996 47 USC.

facilitate or participate in the publication of online defamatory statements that they did not create. The section reads as follows, under the following heading:

> **Protection for 'Good Samaritan' Blocking and Screening of Offensive Material**
>
> (1) Treatment of publisher or speaker
> No provider or user of an interactive computer service shall be treated as the publisher or speaker of any information provided by another information content provider.
>
> (2) Civil liability
> No provider or user of an interactive computer service shall be held liable on account of–
>
> (A) any action voluntarily taken in good faith to restrict access to or availability of material that the provider or user considers to be obscene, lewd, lascivious, filthy, excessively violent, harassing, or otherwise objectionable, whether or not such material is constitutionally protected; or
>
> (B) any action taken to enable or make available to information content providers or others the technical means to restrict access to material described in paragraph (1).

As can be seen, the section was intended to protect internet intermediaries who removed offensive material from their computer systems or websites from free speech suits by the providers of the material, even where the removed material was constitutionally protected.[71]

Thus, the very existence of this statutory provision indicates the fundamental difference between the two jurisdictions: Whereas in England and Wales ISPs and the like need statutory intervention in order to protect them from *defamation* suits for statements posted by others, in the United States statutory intervention was deemed necessary to protect ISPs and the like from suit by publishers on *free speech* grounds. In other words, in the former it is about what gets published and in the latter about what does not. Either way, ISPs are placed in the position of judging whether statements ought to be published and the desirability of placing this editorial burden on these businesses is questionable.

The final similarity relates to defamation defences in the two jurisdictions. Even though the constitutional protection defendants in the US enjoy ever since *Sullivan*, by means of its powerful limiting action, effectively supersede the very need for common law defences, these defences nevertheless still exist. So just as in England and Wales, defendants may rely on, *inter alia*, absolute or qualified privilege, truth, reportage, and fair comment on public issues.

71 *Zeran v America Online, Inc.*, 958 F Supp 1124 (ED Va., 1997), 1134.

Analysis

Here it is pertinent to again revisit the landmark ruling in *New York Times v Sullivan* and to reflect on how and why it heralded such a marked break with the then long-established common law.[72] The Supreme Court justices found it troubling that the decisions of the state trial judge had stretched the common law definition of defamation to its breaking point by allowing the jury to conclude that the publication identified Mr Sullivan himself when it spoke only of law enforcement bodies in general. This is similar to the way false innuendo still operates in UK defamation law, and it also reflects the continued and growing importance of pre-trial hearings on meaning in the UK. The jury was able to give a grossly excessive damages award because they did not consider any evidence (nor was any evidence tendered) of actual damage to the plaintiff's reputation. This of course reflects the English common law characterisation of defamation as actionable *per se* and, until the UK Supreme Court decision in *Lachaux*,[73] continued to be the case in England and Wales.

It is interesting to note that contemporary US textbook writers unhesitatingly describe the lower courts' judgments in *Sullivan* as 'a thinly veiled effort by State and local governmental officials to suppress criticism of their policies.'[74] In this respect, they argue, the lawyers for the New York Times were right to argue that the tort of libel was in this particular instance operating as the equivalent of the sort of impermissible effort by government to censor political speech that founders like Jefferson and Madison had long ago decried as unconstitutional.[75] So strong were the feelings by the court that three of the justices (Black, Douglas, and Goldberg) wrote concurring opinions indicating that they would have gone further than the majority opinion by immunising from liability even those who, in bad faith or out of malice, publish defamatory statements in the course of addressing public affairs.[76]

The subsequent widening of the net from first public officials, to public figures, to even, in some instances, private figures also deserves some more reflection. The courts have indeed construed the public figure concept very widely. It has been broadened so much that 'everyone from the President of the United States to low-level government employees may be included in the category. Even football players and belly dancers have been judged to be public figures for purposes of applying *Sullivan*.'[77] It seems that if a person wields

72 Goldberg and Zipursky, note 43, 322.

73 *Lachaux v Independent Print Ltd and another* [2019] UKSC 27.

74 Goldberg and Zipursky, note 43, 322.

75 Ibid.

76 *New York Times Co. v Sullivan* 376 US 254, 270 (1964).

77 Anderson, DA 'Is Libel Law Worth Reforming?' (1991) 140 *University of Pennsylvania Law Review* 487, 502–503.

any influence at all, they may be at risk of being labelled a public figure. The result of being so labelled is, as pointed out earlier, the requirement of having to prove actual malice in defamation actions.

The realities of modern defamation litigation in the US further entail that even private figures who sue are forced to plead more than just actual damages. The reason for this is mainly because most lawyers, usually working under contingency fee agreements, are reluctant to take on risky defamation cases unless potential recovery is high.[78] This in turn leads to damage inflation by including presumed and punitive damages far in excess of actual damages. But when the claimant pleads presumed damages, the *Gertz* rule requiring actual malice, not just negligence, is activated and this adds to the claimant's burden of proof.[79] In the US, even though by the standards of England and Wales, defamation defendants are given almost unimaginable free speech protection, there are still those clamouring for even more protection. Hagans, for example, argues that all critical speech regardless whether it concerns public officials, public figures, or private persons, should find equal protection in the law,[80] and he quotes former Chief Justice Brennan: 'Truthful speech has value. False speech mistakenly believed to be true, while valueless, should be protected to avoid self-censorship of truthful speech. Known falsehood is neither valuable nor necessary to preserve free debate and thus has no constitutional protection.'[81]

This raises the question as to how the US law of defamation compares to England and Wales's post-2013, reformed defamation law. An interesting empirical study, conducted before, during, and after the *Reynolds* litigation in England and Wales, provides a starting point for analysis. Professor Russell Weaver, an eminent US scholar, together with American, British, and Australian counterparts, began a multi-year project designed to gain greater insight into how the media was functioning in the US, the UK, and Australia.[82] After conducting extensive interviews in these jurisdictions, Weaver and his research team found that the British media was nowhere near as aggressive or bold as their American counterparts and, indeed, that British media reporting was significantly affected by British defamation law.[83] In contrast, the interviews conducted over a period of years ultimately confirmed that the underpinnings of the *New York Times* decision were essentially correct. The conclusion was that the British media seemed to suffer from significant chilling of speech, whereas

78 Ibid.

79 Ibid. See also the discussion of procedural hurdles by Kenyon, note 63, chapters 8 and 10.

80 Hagans, WG 'Who Does the First Amendment Protect? Why the Plaintiff Should Bear the Burden of Proof in Any Defamation Action' (2007) 26(3) *The Review of Litigation* 613, 638.

81 *Dun & Bradstreet v Greenmoss Builders*, 472 US 749, 610 (1985).

82 This project culminated in a series of articles consolidated into the following monograph: Weaver, RL, Kenyon, AT, Partlett, DF and Walker, CP *The Right to Speak Ill: Defamation, Reputation and Free Speech* (Carolina Academic Press, Durham, NC, 2006).

83 Ibid, 183–200.

this did not apply to US media outlets at all.[84] Broadly similar conclusions were reached by other leading scholars including Professor Andrew Kenyon.[85]

Conclusion

Freedom of expression has been accorded a preferred position in the US constitutional hierarchy. Even though free speech absolutism has been rejected, free speech claims frequently prevail over other countervailing interests, such as many defamation claims.[86] To a much larger extent than in England and Wales, even after the inception of the 2013 Act, defamation in the US currently closely resembles the tort of negligence. The reasons for this convergence are twofold: Defamation in the US requires proof of *mens rea* in the form of intention/actual malice, and it requires harm actually suffered by the claimant, who bears the burden of proof. The result is that the pursuit of defamation litigation in the US has dropped to an extremely low level.[87] Thomas Jefferson's famous statement that freedom of expression 'cannot be limited without being lost'[88] clearly still reflects the core value of US jurisprudence in this area.

It is doubtful that lawmakers and the courts in England and Wales would ever want to go this far, but nevertheless, there are valid lessons that may be learnt from the US as far as the balancing of defamation law in favour of free speech is concerned. Perhaps the most valuable is the fact that defamation law in the US provides a paradigm for fault-based liability, where the burden of proof is firmly on the claimant and damages are calculated in a clearly defined manner. There are signs of convergence such as, for example, the section 1 requirement in the Defamation Act 2013 that claimants now have to prove harm to reputation. However, as is clear from the discussion in the preceding chapters, despite the 2013 reforms, English defamation law is still fundamentally different from that of the US. If the UK Defamation Act 2013 did not take the English law of defamation closer to its American counterpart, did it align more closely to other jurisdictions? In the next chapter the law of Germany, being another influential liberal democracy with constitutional protection of free speech, is examined.

84 Ibid, 131–200. See also Weaver, RL 'British Defamation Reform: An American Perspective' (2012) 63(1) *Northern Ireland Legal Quarterly* 97–117.

85 Kenyon, note 63; see also Partlett, D '*New York Times v Sullivan* at Fifty Years: Defamation in Separate Orbits,' Rolph, D 'Vindicating Reputation and Privacy' and Kenyon, AT and Richardson, M 'Reverberations of *Sullivan*? Considering Defamation and Privacy Law Reform,' in Kenyon, AT (ed), *Comparative Defamation and Privacy Law* (Cambridge University Press, Cambridge, 2016).

86 *Curtis Publishing Co. v Butts*, note 54; *Associated Press v Walker*, 388 US 130 (1967); *New York Times Co. v Sullivan*, note 3. This is also the case for many privacy claims – *Time, Inc. v Hill*, 385 US 374 (1967).

87 Weaver *et al.*, note 82, 6–7.

88 Note 9.

5 Defamation in Germany

Introduction

In this chapter, the focus moves to Germany and how its legal system treats defamation claims. Germany is a valuable comparator jurisdiction *vis-à-vis* the UK in general and England and Wales specifically for a variety of reasons. It is an influential and leading member of the European Union (EU), whose laws will continue to directly influence legal and political issues in the UK for an indefinite period of time. It is also a signatory of the European Convention of Human Rights (ECHR/Convention) and, as such, subject to the jurisdiction of the European Court of Human Rights (ECtHR), where its jurists continue to play a prominent role. For instance, both the current and former vice presidents of the court are German lawyers and academics.[1] Given the UK's ongoing participation in the Convention regime, the German influence in that forum will remain important. The German law as such also merits attention. Its roots are ancient and it represents one of the world's leading legal systems of thought. Since its coming into force on 24 May 1949, the German Basic Law (known as the *Grundgesetz*, the GG / Constitution)[2] has become one of the most influential constitutional systems in the world.[3] Commentators view the German model as on a par with US constitutionalism, with many states across Europe and Latin America, for example, emulating the German system.[4]

1 Anja Seibert-Fohr and Angelika Nussberger. www.echr.coe.int/w/anja-seibert-fohr. For the full list of current and past judges, see <www.echr.coe.int/Pages/home.aspx?p=court/judges>.

2 An official translation of the GG by Professors Tomuschat, C, Currie, DP, Kommers, DP and Kerr, R, in cooperation with the Language Service of the German Bundestag is available at <www.gesetze-im-internet.de/englisch_gg/index.html>. All references to the GG in this book are to this translation.

3 Hall, JB 'Taking "Rechts" Seriously: Ronald Dworkin and the Federal Constitutional Court of Germany' (2008) 9 *German Law Journal* 771.

4 Ibid, 771. See also: Kokott, J 'From Reception and Transplantation to Convergence of Constitutional Models in the Age of Globalization-With Particular Reference to the German Basic Law,' in Starck, C (ed), *Constitutionalism, Universalism, and Democracy – A Comparative*

DOI: 10.4324/9781003416005-6

As in the US, the rights engaged in a defamation suit also enjoy constitutional protection in Germany, but there are significant differences. One of these is the primacy that the Constitution accords to the right to human dignity, whereas by contrast in the US, free speech enjoys the strong First Amendment protection discussed in the preceding chapter. The content and operation of the German law balancing free speech with reputational interests form the subject of this chapter.

Some caveats for the common law scholar

Before examining the substantive law of a state in a comparative analysis, the system of law followed by the state itself, if different from that of the other comparator states, needs some attention. The US shares with England and Wales a common law tradition, facilitating the comparative analysis as many premises are the same. When looking at Germany, however, the analyst needs to bear in mind that the system of law is that of the civil law, and for the comparison to make any logical sense, systemic differences need to be borne in mind throughout. The relevant differences and characteristics unique to German law are first addressed before the substantive German law relating to defamation is analysed.

Specialisation and federalism

In Germany there is a plethora of different, specialised courts, each with their own practices. This is inevitably the result of the desire for increased specialisation which is an important characteristic of the contemporary German judicial structure. For instance, instead of one federal Supreme Court, there are five different supreme courts,[5] each with their own jurisdiction.[6] Keeping that caveat in mind, for our purposes the following two courts and their case law are important – the Federal Constitutional Court (*Bundesverfassungsgericht*, BVerfG) and the Federal Supreme Court (*Bundesgerichtshof*, BGH). The BGH is the Supreme Court for civil and criminal matters, whereas the Constitutional Court is entrusted with the task of ensuring the preservation of the Constitution and the control of the constitutionality of legislation and any other form of sovereign power in Germany. Concerning the control of the judiciary, the Constitutional Court is competent to decide whether a court (typically the court of last resort) has violated the constitution by not properly

Analysis (Nomos, Baden-Baden, 1999), 71–134; and Quint, P 'What is a Twentieth-Century Constitution?'(2007) 67 *Modern Law Review* 238.

5 'Oberste Gerichtshöfe des Bundes,' article 95 GG.

6 Together with the BGH four other supreme courts exist: the *Bundesverwaltungsgericht* dealing with administrative law; the *Bundesfinanzhof* dealing with financial matters; the *Bundesarbeitsgericht* tasked with labour matters, and the *Bundessozialgericht* which oversees social legislation.

considering its values and limitations. It does not, however, control the overall legality of the decision. Nevertheless, we need to keep in mind that the Constitutional Court outranks the other courts for most of our purposes – for one its competence is strictly confined to constitutional matters[7] so that it is not just another appellate jurisdiction. However, as it controls the constitutionality of every form of sovereign power in Germany, including the courts, and therefore can declare judgments unconstitutional and quash them, it should be considered superior to the five federal supreme courts.

As in the US, there is a very strong federal tradition in Germany. However, unlike in the US, the government maintains no federal courts at the first and second levels,[8] but instead each of the *Länder*/states has its own constitutional court ensuring that the relevant state constitution is observed. Federal devolution is observed and enjoys commitment at the highest levels. This means that the German administration of justice is considerably decentralised.[9] In such a system the chances are high for diverging case law from the different supreme courts on matters of substance. To resolve this conflict, and in order to ensure the unity of the federal law, a Common Senate (*Gemeinsame Senat*[10]) composed of judges from the five supreme courts rules whenever one of the supreme courts consciously departs from the case law of another supreme court. There are a number of other ways in which conflicts or potential conflicts are resolved, but luckily for our purposes the dangers of diverging case law in German defamation cases are rather low: First of all, the main competence lies with the BGH in civil and criminal matters, and the other supreme courts rarely deal with these questions. Second, there is a strong levelling effect of the constitutional case law of the Constitutional Court in this field. This is because the core legal issues are of a constitutional nature (articles 1 and 5 of the Constitution), and therefore, the standards of the Constitutional Court prevail and have to be applied by all the other courts. Another reason is that not every state constitution contains fundamental rights, and therefore, the relationship between the fundamental rights of the states and the fundamental rights at the federal level is heavily tilted towards the latter. This, combined with a rather complex provision in article 142 of the Constitution and the extensive jurisdiction of the Constitutional Court, means that in effect it is normally the Constitutional Court's own case law on article 5 of the Constitution, which sets the relevant standards in German defamation law.

For present purposes, therefore, focus remains on the BGH, which stands at the apex of the judicial hierarchy in civil and criminal matters and which

7 This is both in terms of the Constitution (article 93 GG) and the Act on the Federal Constitutional Court (Bundesverfassungsgerichtsgesetz – BVerfGG).

8 The one exception to this is the Federal Patent Court which acts only as an appeal court.

9 Markesinis, B, Bell, J and Janssen, A *Markesinis's German Law of Torts: A Comparative Treatise* (5th edn, Hart Publishing, Chicago, 2019), 2–3. All translations of German cases referred to in this chapter are from this book, unless otherwise stated.

10 Gemeinsamer Gerat der Obersten Gerichtshöfe des Bundes – (GmS-OGB).

hears cases from all civil and criminal German courts, and the Constitutional Court as the highest court for all constitutional matters in Germany.

Judicial precedent

In principle, the doctrine of binding precedent, as practiced in common law jurisdictions, is not known in German law. However, this does not mean that cases are not important, or indeed that there are no binding precedents at all. Applying the principles of *res judicata*, any given judgment of the Constitutional Court binds the parties as well as the institutions involved. Furthermore, all constitutional organs (i.e. the legislator, the government) and also the courts and the public administration, that means basically every institution that is exercising state power, is bound by the decisions of the Constitutional Court – in short, the Constitution as it is interpreted by the Constitutional Court.[11] In certain cases, such as if the Constitutional Court declares a statutory law unconstitutional, this decision has the same binding force as a statute itself.[12] In other words, a decision of the Constitutional Court is binding on the constitutional organs of the federal and state government; and, if after an appeal on a point of law, the Constitutional Court has reversed a decision of a lower court and sent the matter back for retrial, then the lower court is bound by the ruling of the Constitutional Court on the matter of law. In practice it also seldom happens that an inferior court would easily depart from the line taken by the Constitutional Court, especially if there is a series of decisions (*ständige Rechtsprechung*) with similar conclusions on the same issue.[13] Put another way, they are legally entitled to depart from the line, but in doing so, they take the likely risk that their decision will be reversed.

Because there is no general system of binding precedent in Germany, courts are not obliged to attempt the detailed consideration of material which is necessary in the common law in order to gauge whether the case under consideration is covered by earlier authority and if so, whether it is materially different and thus distinguishable on the facts. In practice, the higher courts and especially the supreme and constitutional courts tend to do this where they want to depart from an earlier line of case law.

Another feature in German case law which looks unusual to common law jurists is the detailed consideration of the views of German academic writers. The 'dominant opinion' (*herrschende Meinung*) as reflected in the majority of decisions as well as academic writing will enjoy strong persuasive authority. It even happens that academic discourse on a particular matter is so highly regarded by judges that their decisions sometimes contain a very

11 BVerfGG, para 31(1).
12 BVerfGG, para 31(2).
13 Markesinis *et al.*, note 9, 7.

lucid summary of the views of the academy.[14] To common law eyes, the fact that academic writing is accorded similar, and in some instances even higher authority than previous judgments doubtless appears somewhat unusual. Of course, the higher the court the more it relies on its own decisions, so that in the Constitutional Court, for instance, academic writing would normally only be considered in order to support a point in the existing case law or to develop a new line of reasoning. The supreme courts also tend to rely primarily on their own case law. Nevertheless, academic writing features in court decisions to an extent largely unknown in the UK. However, this could be seen as a result of the fact that the law is after all codified as Germany is a civil law jurisdiction, as well as a result of the education and training particular to German lawyers.

Codification

As with most civil law systems, technically only statute and to a (far) lesser extent custom are considered the true sources of law. Markesinis, a leading commentator on German law, remarked that all German judgments contain two reasons for their results – the published ones and the 'real' ones.[15] For a comparatist, especially one hailing from a common law jurisdiction, it is very important to note that the same importance could not be given to a German case *simpliciter* in the same way as it could be for an English case. To obtain a complete picture it is important to research beyond the text of a judgment and to furthermore, consider not only statutes but also other sources such as preparatory works and academic commentaries. Therefore, in order to begin to understand the true similarities and differences between the different legal systems, one needs to fully and properly study more than just German case law: The relevant statutory provision(s) as well as academic commentary also need serious scrutiny. Reading German cases, it is striking that although earlier case law does get quoted, this is usually by way of illustration or as examples of a particular established principle. But previous cases are not used as building blocks for the new decision – they simply are not given the same level of scrutiny as is usual in an English court. For a German judge the primary building block is the relevant statutory code, followed by the academic commentary on such code (which, however, very often relies on the existing case law – especially in defamation and free speech cases). The relevant code and provisions are referenced and interpreted deductively to the particular facts before the court. The level of detailed reasoning evident in English cases is generally absent in German counterparts, the idea being that all the necessary thinking on the topic had already been done by the drafting committee of the

14 Ibid, 6.
15 Ibid, 10.

code.[16] The German judge's task truly is to speak, not make, the law. In this the judge is further assisted by a well-developed fourfold method of statutory interpretation used to determine the true meaning of a law: First, the wording is considered, then the sense and purpose of the law, next its systemic role/position, and finally, its historic or purposive aims. Having said that, here again the Constitutional Court plays an exceptional role since it truly develops constitutional law and, as such, is less constrained by such judicial self-restraint.

The relevant codes play a prominent role in both the German legal system as well as in the German psyche. The Civil Code (the *Bürgerliches Gesetzbuch*, BGB), for instance, came into force on 1 January 1900 and symbolised the successful unification of the modern German state after decades if not centuries of tortuous negotiations. It put an end to a confusing diversity of local law, municipal law, and customary law.[17] The Civil Code consists of articles that are usually referred to as paragraphs. Some 30 paragraphs are devoted to the law of torts. Compared to the French Civil Code (the *Code Civil*), the BGB provides a much more systematic treatment of the subject, which reflects the exhaustive approach taken to the drafting of the law by German lawyers. The law of tort in the Civil Code is a mixture of general and particular provisions. This means that for some issues, a general directive only is given, transferring most of the burden from the shoulders of the legislators to the judge, whereas for others regulation is precise enough to largely do most of the heavy legal lifting for the judge, who is merely required to match the facts to the prescribed legal outcome.[18] If one examines the law comparatively, this means that the German system is positioned around halfway between the all-encompassing and open-ended system of general clause regulation found in the French *Code Civil*, on the one hand, and the traditional English writ system which resembled a distinct pigeonholing approach, on the other.

To recap, when examining German law one must bear these caveats in mind – namely, to focus on the relevant statutory codes, case law, and academic commentary when comparing the German law on defamation to that of the other jurisdictions examined in this book. The relevant statutory provisions include the Civil Code as well as the German Criminal Code, the *Strafgesetzbuch* (StGB), because the law which is compared with the common law tort of defamation can be found in both in Germany. As the German Constitution plays the most prominent role, the following discussion starts with an examination of the relevant provisions of the Constitution. After the relevant

16 Kötz, H 'Scholarship and the Courts: A Comparative Survey,' in Merryman, JH and Clark, DS (eds), *Essays in Honour of Henry Merryman on his Seventieth Birthday* (Duncker and Hamblot, Berlin, 1990), 190.

17 Wieacker, F *Privatrechtsgeschichte der Neuzeit unter Besonderer Berücksichtigung der Deutschen Entwicklung* (3rd edn, Vandenhoeck & Ruprecht, Göttingen, Niedersachsen, 2016), or the English translation of an earlier edition by Weir, T *A History of Private Law in Europe: With Particular Reference to Germany* (OUP, Oxford, 1996).

18 Markesinis *et al.*, note 9, 15.

codes, judgments of the Constitutional Court and the Federal Supreme Court are scrutinised. Finally, there follows an attempt to compare the relevant German law to the law of England and Wales and the US in order to once again address the central question – namely, how best to balance freedom of expression with the protection of an individual's right to their reputation.

Constitutional protection of the right to freedom of expression

As is the case in the US, freedom of expression enjoys constitutional protection in Germany. Article 5(1) of the Constitution states:

> Everyone shall have the right freely to express and disseminate his or her opinions in speech, writing and pictures and freely to obtain information from generally accessible sources. Freedom of the press and freedom of reporting via the radio, television and cinema shall be guaranteed. There shall be no censorship.

What is more, the state is under a positive duty to promote freedom of expression: Article 1(3) provides that the fundamental rights contained in the Constitution bind the legislature, the executive branch, and the judiciary as directly applicable law. Although there is no extensive case law on this positive obligation or obligation to protect, what is pertinent here is the doctrine of the Constitutional Court on the 'objective value' (*objektive Wertordnung*) that is inherent in all the fundamental rights and has to be considered even in private law contexts where the state (as the one directly bound by the fundamental rights) is not directly involved.[19] In this way speech protection seems to extend, in Germany, even beyond the strong constitutional protection guaranteed under the First Amendment in the US. Indeed, where the US Constitution paints a broad picture, the German Constitution goes into more detail: Not only is mention made of written and pictorial speech, but it is made clear that the free speech right comprises both the right to impart and the right to receive information, and both are separately recognised. The Constitutional Court explicitly stated that *Meinungsfreiheit*, or the right to express one's opinion freely, is separate from and does not form part of *Informationsfreiheit*, the right to receive information.[20] Furthermore, *Meinungsfreiheit* includes not only statements of opinion but also statements of fact, unless the person making the statement knows that the statement is false.[21] This becomes important when judging defamatory statements.

The previous chapter described how the First Amendment to the US Constitution prioritises the right to free speech over other fundamental rights. By

19 BVerfGE 82, 272/280; 86, 122/128 f; 107, 275/280.
20 *Leipziger Volkszeitung*, 27 BVerfGE 71 (1969).
21 Ibid.

contrast, in Germany the highest priority is given to the inviolable dignity of the human being. Article 1(1) of the Constitution states, 'Human dignity shall be inviolable. To respect and protect it shall be the duty of all state authority.' It therefore does not surprise that the right to freedom of expression is limited 'by the provisions of the general laws and statutory provisions for the protection of young people and the obligation to respect personal honour [*Recht der persönlichen Ehre*].'[22]

The high protection given to human dignity in German law is a direct result of the country's National Socialist past. In *Abortion Reform Law I* (1975), the Constitutional Court stated:

> The Basic Law contains principles . . . which can only be explained by the historical experience and by the moral-ethical recollection of the past system of National Socialism. The almighty totalitarian state demanded limitless authority over all aspects of social life and, in pursuing its goals, had no regard for individual life. In contrast to this, the Basic Law established a value-oriented order which puts the individual and his dignity into the very center of all its provisions.[23]

This theme runs through the most seminal cases in the broad area of personality rights: In *Lüth* (discussed further here), the Constitutional Court stated that 'the Basic Law is not value neutral,'[24] and in *Mephisto*[25] the Constitutional Court made it clear that the Constitution unifies a system of fundamental values, according to which the court would resolve cases.

Protection of reputation as a subcategory of personality rights

Whereas other jurisdictions may provide specific defamation legislation, the German defamation system is more differentiated.[26] Further to the duty on all state authorities to respect and protect the inviolable right to human dignity in article 1 of the Constitution, article 2[27] states that everyone has the right to the free development of their personality provided this does not infringe upon the rights of others or offend against the constitutional order or the moral code (*Sittengesetz*). These two provisions together with paragraphs 823 and 826 of the Civil Code create the constitutional basis for reputational (and privacy) protection, known as the general personality right (*Allgemeines*

22 Article 5(2).

23 *Abortion I*, BVerfGE 39, 1 (1975).

24 *Lüth*, BVerfGE 7, 198 (1958).

25 *Mephisto*, 30 BVerfGE 173 (1971).

26 For a detailed analysis about the origin of the strong personality rights in Germany, see Whitman, JQ 'The Two Western Cultures of Privacy: Dignity versus Liberty' (2004) *Yale Law Journal* 1180.

27 Para 1.

Persönlichkeitsrecht).[28] It is important at this stage to keep in mind the subtle difference between the overall guiding principle of article 1, human dignity, which is inviolable, and the general personality right, which is related to dignity but subject to the balancing exercise. In other words, the former cannot be infringed or restricted, whereas the latter can. The general personality right can more accurately be described as a bundle of rights that protect different aspects of an individual's personality from unauthorised public intrusions. The general personality right comprises a number of different rights such as the right to one's image, the right to one's name, and the right to oppose publication of private facts.[29] This means that the legal interests in privacy and reputation are not distinguished to the same extent as they are in the US and the UK. In Germany, they arise from the same constitutional basis. It also means that cases dealing with the general personality right may and do engage one right or a combination of or all of the rights just listed.

At first glance, it therefore looks as if the scales in Germany are tilted in favour of reputational protection *vis-à-vis* free speech, as the former forms part of the general personality right, which in turn resonates with inherent human dignity to a larger extent than the exercise of free speech. However, the Constitutional Court has recognised on several occasions that freedom of speech is a particularly important right that forms the basis of a democratic society and is indispensable for the free democratic fundamental order of the state and, furthermore, that free speech is also an emanation of the personality right.[30] In practice, reputational protection and free speech are balanced in a very nuanced and sometimes complex way in German disputes engaging these two rights, as will become clear from the following discussion.

Defamation law in Germany

In contrast to the UK and the US, where defamation suits are pursued through the civil courts, it is mostly a criminal offence in Germany. The law of libel and slander is governed mainly by part 14, paragraphs 185 to 200 of the German Criminal Code, which contains provisions punishing individual and collective defamation or insult (*Beleidigungsdelikte or Delikte gegen die persönliche Ehre*). 'Insult' and 'defamation' here are used in a wide sense (covering all criminal offences against honour) as well as in their narrower sense. In the narrow sense, 'insult' (*Beleidigung*) refers to the abuse of or an insult directed at the

28 The German Federal Constitutional Court acknowledged for the first time the general personality right in *Lebach*, BVerfGE 35, 202 (1973). For further details, see Schwartz, PM and Pfeifer, KN 'Prosser's Privacy and the German Right of Personality: Are Four Privacy Torts Better than One Unitary Concept?' (2010) 98 *California Law Review* 1925.

29 Coors, C 'Headwind from Europe: The New Position of the German Courts on Personality Rights after the Judgment of the European Court of Human Rights' (2010) 11 *German Law Journal* 527, 528.

30 See, for example, *Lüth*, BVerfGE 7, 198/208.

recipient in private and is covered by paragraph 185 only. As publication to a third party of the defamatory statement is a sine qua non for a defamation action in common law jurisdictions, the German offence of 'insult' therefore exceeds the scope of common law defamation law. If third parties were also made aware of the aggrieving statement, paragraphs 186 and 187 are engaged. The former covers defamation and the latter intentional defamation. Both provisions deal with factual assertions capable of reducing esteem for the victimised party, made in the presence of third parties. Put another way, defamation occurs when asserting or disseminating a fact related to another person which may defame them or negatively affect public opinion about them. Given the inclusion of 'insult' as an offence, it is therefore clear that the common law notion of defamation is narrower than the broad German notions of insult and defamation.

Insult is punished with imprisonment not exceeding one year or a fine. If the insult is committed by means of an assault, imprisonment of up to two years may be imposed.[31] Defamation is punished with a fine or imprisonment for up to one year. A sentence of imprisonment for up to two years can be imposed if the act is committed publicly or through the dissemination of written materials.[32]

Intentional defamation comprises intentionally and knowingly asserting or disseminating an untrue statement related to another person, which may defame them or negatively affect public opinion about them or endanger their creditworthiness. Punishment includes imprisonment not exceeding two years or a fine and, if the act was committed publicly, in a meeting, or through dissemination of written materials, imprisonment not exceeding five years.[33] It is clear that the fault element plays a major role in the German law on criminal defamation, in contrast to the UK where the tort remains one of strict liability. In terms of paragraph 192 of the Criminal Code, even disseminating factual statements may constitute criminal defamation – but this would only be the case if telling the truth is done in such a *manner* as to render the communication, objectively speaking, an insult. The objective insult itself is the reason for the criminal liability, not the factual statement. Still, this notion seems foreign to common law observers, where the truth of a statement, however egregious, remains the strongest defence against a defamation claim.

Specific provision is made for the defamation of 'persons in the political arena': In terms of paragraph 188, if a politician is defamed publicly, in a meeting or through dissemination of written materials based on the position of that person in public life, and if the offence could make their public activities substantially more difficult, the defamer may face imprisonment from

31 Para 185.
32 Para 186.
33 Para 187.

three months to five years, depending on whether the defamation was intentional.[34] In this regard, the German law agrees with the view of the European Court of Human Rights that politicians have to accept more insulting language than private individuals.[35] A leading case determined that the bar is high: Only statements that have the potential to undermine trust in the integrity of the official position would count.[36] Nonetheless, the protection accorded to politicians in Germany is in stark contrast to the fact that it would be almost impossible for politicians to sue in defamation in the United States.[37] In England and Wales, whilst political parties are unable to pursue a defamation suit, individual politicians may indeed institute a civil claim in defamation.[38]

It is also possible to bring a criminal prosecution in German law for violating the memory of the dead, meaning that unlike most common law jurisdictions including the UK, defamation suits may be brought in Germany to protect the reputation of a deceased person – although the longer ago the person died, the more difficult it would be to sue.[39] In Germany, publication generally occurs if the alleged false and/or defamatory material is read, heard, accessed, or seen. A single instance of publication may be sufficient to bring a case.

Paragraph 193 of the Criminal Code contains a defence similar to the common law defence of fair comment. Critical opinions about scientific, artistic, or commercial achievements are protected, except if the insult results from the form of the utterance or the circumstances under which it was made. The same reasoning applies to other similar instances, such as utterances made in order to exercise or protect rights or to safeguard legitimate interests, remonstrations, and reprimands by superiors to their subordinates, official reports or judgments by a civil servant.

An insult can only be prosecuted upon request by the alleged victim. An ex officio prosecution, i.e. on the initiative of the state, may be made if the insult comprised a persecution of the victim as a member of a group under the National Socialist or another authoritarian regime, if this group is a part of the population and the insult is connected to this persecution. If the victim objects to this, however, the offence may not be prosecuted ex officio.[40] Even

34 Paras 188(1) and (2).

35 *Insults against a Politician of the Green Party*, BVerfG, Beschl. v 19 December 2021–1 BvR 1073/20.

36 'Die Äußerung muss dazu das Vertrauen in die Integrität erschüttern können, derer der Betroffene zu seinem öffentlichen Wirken bedarf' (BGHSt 3, 73 (74); BGH NJW 1954, 649; MDR 1980, 455; LK-StGB/Hilgendorf Rn. 4; NK-StGB/Zaczyk Rn. 6).

37 See the discussion in chapter 4.

38 In *Goldsmith v Bhoyrul* [1998] QB 459 the English High Court held that the principle established in *Derbyshire CC v Times Newspapers Ltd* [1993] AC 534, preventing central and local government institutions bringing actions in defamation at common law on the ground that those holding office must remain open to criticism, extended also to political parties.

39 Para 189.

40 Para 194(1).

after the death of the victim, relatives retain the right to initiate a prosecution or to object to an *ex officio* prosecution.[41]

Not only are politicians allowed to institute defamation prosecutions, but so are public officials or their superiors on their behalf, as well as churches and religious associations.[42] And in perhaps the greatest contrast to the situation in English law, a legislative body of the German federation, a state in the federation, or any other political body within the Federal Republic of Germany may also institute a prosecution in defamation.[43] All indications however are that this remains mostly a theoretical possibility, with little to no evidence of the exercise of this power.

Finally, the preservation of legitimate interests as defined by paragraph 193 may preclude punishment of critical or negative judgments. It reads:

> Critical judgements concerning scientific, artistic, or commercial services, likewise statements made in the exercise of or in defense of rights or for the preservation of legitimate interests, as well as reproofs and reprimands of subordinates by superiors, official complaints or judgements on the part of a civil servant and similar cases are punishable only insofar as the existence of an insult arises from the *form* of the statement or from the *circumstances under which it occurred*. [Own emphasis]

The object of legal protection in these provisions is, as pointed out by Brugger,[44] the right to one's social worth (i.e. one's reputation or external honour) and also the right to be respected as a human being (i.e. one's internal worth or integrity). In this sense the German law of defamation has a far wider scope than that of the UK or the US. The question is whether this leads to an imbalance *vis-à-vis* free speech in Germany, and to answer that question, one needs to examine how the courts handle such conflicts. Here, one must remember that criminal defamation as well as a civil claim based on defamation are both subject to the overarching authority of the constitutional regime. Before examining an interesting recent example of how these areas interact, we need to complete the picture by also briefly examining the civil law on defamation in Germany.

The German Civil Code (*Bürgerliches Gesetzbuch*, or BGB) does not include any specific mention of the tort of defamation but nevertheless allow pursuing a tortious claim based on infringement of the personality right, which includes defamation. If criminal law provisions against insult and defamation apply, civil liability can often also be established in terms of the Civil Code.[45] Paragraph

41 Para 194(2).

42 Para 194(3).

43 Para 194(4).

44 Brugger, W 'The Treatment of Hate Speech in German Constitutional Law (Part I)' (2003) 4 *German Law Journal* 1, 15.

45 Para 823(2) BGB in combination with para 185(ff) StGB.

823(1) is significant for defamation claimants, as, read with article 1(2) of the Constitution, it is recognised as incorporating infringement of the very important 'personality right' (*Allgemeines Persönlichkeitsrecht*) as a basis for compensation in civil claims.[46] Because of the recognition of the personality right as a subjective right under paragraph 823(1) of the Civil Code, there are now additional cases that require the payment of damages which the drafters of the Code clearly did not originally have in mind, and for that reason, it is only applied in severe cases, where the relevance and the subjective element of the offence have to be taken into consideration. Remedies include monetary compensation but is restricted in case of non-pecuniary loss to only instances stipulated by law.[47] For example, payment of damages is required when the speaker is convicted of disseminating false assertions of fact about another person that subsequently damage that person's credit-worthiness.[48]

The following case study illustrates how the criminal and civil aspects of defamation interact and how the overriding authority of constitutional principles affect, or even dictate, what happens in the lower courts.

Case study: the Jan Böhmermann affair

In March 2016, satirist and comedian Jan Böhmermann included on his TV show a satirical poem about President Erdoğan of Turkey, accusing him of, among other things, repressing minorities, kicking Kurds, and slapping Christians while watching child porn. Böhmermann's expressed aim with his poem was to illustrate (and test) what would and what would not be permissible expression under German law. The poem was deliberately over-the-top at times, and Böhmermann pointed out throughout which sections of the poem would (in his opinion) be unlawful. He also stated that the wording was so clearly satirical that everyone would understand that it was not actually meant to be an insult but instead an attempt to educate the public. President Erdoğan thought otherwise and pursued the matter both in the civil and criminal court. First, he lodged a complaint against Böhmermann for insult under paragraph 103 of the Criminal Code. This rarely used provision prohibited insulting foreign heads of state but required that the government gave consent to the prosecution of such cases. The Turkish president received then-Chancellor Angela Merkel's permission for proceedings to go ahead. She stated that the German government would permit Erdoğan's action to proceed but also that the relevant paragraph of the law, which dated back to 1871, would then be repealed. Paragraph 103 was in fact repealed later on.[49]

46 BGHZ 199, 247.
47 Para 253 BGB.
48 Para 824 BGB.
49 The Act on the Reform of Criminal Offences against Foreign States of 17. July 2017, repealed para 103 StGB (Insult to Organs and Representatives of Foreign States) with effect from 1 January 2018 (Bundesgesetzblatt [Federal Law Gazette]) I 2017, 2439.

President Erdoğan was also vindicated in the civil court, where both the first instance and appeal courts held that freedom of expression in general and freedom to express satirical contributions in particular protect the expression of criticism in a pointed, polemical, and exaggerated way, but that this is subject to the proviso that the utterance really does constitute a criticism. Furthermore, the critique itself must contain elements that are related to the object of the criticism. The further the content of an utterance is removed from the object of criticism and focuses, without reference to it, on the mere defamation of the person in question, the lower the weight of freedom of opinion in dispute for the utterer in relation to the weight of the general right of personality of the person affected by the utterance.[50] The public utterance of several parts of the diatribe was thus considered illegal, and the satirist was silenced with a partial injunction with regards to certain paragraphs of the poem.[51]

Two further issues are important here: The outcomes in the criminal and the constitutional courts, respectively. In addition to seeking a civil law injunction in Hamburg, Erdoğan also filed a separate and more serious paragraph 185 criminal complaint alleging insult by Böhmermann.[52] However, the German prosecutors declined to continue with the criminal procedure, stating that in their opinion paragraph 185 of the Criminal Code had not been violated. Their reasons for this illustrate the primacy of the Constitution: They interpreted paragraph 185, read with the constitutional protection of freedom of expression, freedom of the arts and freedom of the press (three different constitutional rights) in this case not to have indicated an insult that met the threshold for a prosecution. This can be regarded as a victory for free speech, as the bar for criminal prosecution is clearly set very high – much higher than the civil standard in this case. But it is a pity that the matter didn't receive much detailed constitutional attention. The Appeal Court (BGH), without providing detailed explanation for its decision, declined to allow a further appeal. It did state rather tersely that the case did not have any fundamental importance, and neither did the development of the law or the safeguarding of uniform case-law require a decision.[53] The Federal Constitutional Court likewise made short shrift of Böhmermann's attempt to further pursue a constitutional complaint against the judgments of the lower instance courts. Like the BGH, the FCC did not allow the appeal to proceed on the basis that 'it had no prospect of success' but declined to give further reasons.[54] This refusal by the Constitutional Court to engage further with the matter has been severely criticised on

50 Kaufmann, S 'Freedom of Expression under German Law' (2022) 14 *Italian Journal of Public Law* 225, 231 citing the Higher Regional Court of Hamburg, Judgment of 15 May 2018, 7 U 34/17.

51 OLG Hamburg, Urteil vom 15 May 2018–7 U 34/17.

52 Editorial, 'The Guardian View on the Jan Böhmermann Affair: No Joke' *The Guardian* (22 April 2016).

53 BGH 30 July 2019, VI ZR 231/18.

54 BVerfG 26 January 2022. 1 BvR 2026/19, BeckRS 2022, 1484.

the grounds that it ignored obvious conflicts of fundamental rights and 'hid' behind the statutory possibility to leave decisions unreasoned.[55] Indeed, for the common law observer the choice not to provide reasons for a decision is indeed frustrating.

This matter illustrates several important aspects of how the German law operates, as it engaged the civil, criminal, and constitutional aspects of defamation. It showed that when a decision to prosecute is made, this is subject to the understanding that the Criminal Code can always be trumped by constitutional considerations such as protecting free speech. These considerations are important in the deliberations before a civil court too. In the latter the constitutional balancing exercise led to a partial injunction, which is clearly an attempt to balance the right to free speech with the personality right. But from a purely free speech perspective, the saga is troubling. Although the content of the 'poem' was inherently offensive, it did contain legitimate criticism and was directed against a public, not a private figure.

The German system favours a variety of remedies that place less emphasis upon money awards – for example, the publication of a counterstatement (*Gegendarstellungsanspruch*) or a claim for retraction (*Widerruf*).[56] Paragraph 200 of the Criminal Code also makes provision for the publication of the conviction upon application of the victim or a person otherwise entitled to file a request. The manner of publication is up to the court, with the aim of achieving parity; if the insult was committed through publication in a newspaper or magazine, the publication must also be included in a newspaper or magazine, if possible in the same one which contained the insult.

From these it is clear that defamation claims in Germany may be based on and pursued in the criminal and/or civil law arenas, but regardless of where the action arises and which code is applicable, constitutional considerations always rank uppermost. Against this background, we can now examine the relevant constitutional principles.

Guidelines from the German Federal Constitutional Court

From what has been discussed so far, it can be deduced that there are two facts particular to the German law which indicate very strong protection of reputation – retaining criminal defamation and conflating reputation with privacy as deserving of constitutional protection. However, reputation, or indeed any of the personality rights contained in the general personality right, does not always trump other concerns. Instead, the way in which the German law is set out results in a far more *ad hoc* and contextual analysis of competing interests. So, for instance, where political and other public discourse is concerned, there

55 Vasel, JJ 'Das Karlsruher Schweigen zur satirischen Schmahkritik' (2022) *Neue Juristische Wochenschrift* 740 ff.

56 Coors, note 29, 530.

is a presumption in favour of freedom of expression. Likewise, statements of opinion are accorded more protection than statements of fact. Relevant cases reveal the nuanced use of a constitutional balancing exercise (*Wechselwirkungslehre*) and that competing rights may be treated differently in differing cases, depending on the circumstances surrounding the facts.

Balancing exercise

German courts attempted to find a balance between competing rights from an early stage. A good case to start with when examining this balancing exercise is the seminal case of *Lüth*[57] as the Constitutional Court not only established the balancing formula but also confirmed an obligation on the German courts to apply the values underlying the Constitution to private law suits.

Decided relatively shortly after the Second World War, in *Lüth* (1958) the Constitutional Court established that the right to freedom of expression as enshrined in article 5(1) of the Constitution is limited not only by article 1 but also by provisions in general laws including provisions concerning defamation both in the criminal law[58] and in tort: The relevant Civil Code provisions prescribe that anyone who intentionally or negligently injures the life, body, health, freedom, property, or similar right of another is liable for any resultant loss,[59] and anyone who intentionally inflicts damage on another in a manner contrary to morality is obliged to compensate the other for the damage so inflicted.[60]

The case involved an action brought by a film director, Harlan, against Lüth, who had called for the director's film to be boycotted in protest against the director's past associations with the Nazi regime. The Hamburg Regional Court issued judgment in favour of the complainant, ordering the defendant, on pain of fine or imprisonment, to refrain from further calls for boycotting the film. Mr Lüth took the matter on appeal to the Constitutional Court, arguing that the Regional Court's judgment infringed his basic right to free expression of opinion as laid down in article 5(1).

The Constitutional Court noted that by prohibiting the complainant from making statements apt to lead others to join him in boycotting Harlan's films, the judgment clearly restricted the complainant's freedom to express his opinion. The Regional Court had granted the injunction as a matter of private law on the basis that the complainant's statements were tortious under paragraph 826 of the Civil Code. Thus, the public authority had restricted the complainant's freedom of expression on the basis of the plaintiff's private law claim.

57 *Lüth*, note 24.
58 *StGB* paras 185–194. See the previous discussion of the German law of criminal defamation.
59 Para 823.
60 Para 826.

The Constitutional Court in *Lüth* thus had to consider whether the fundamental rights in the Constitution constrained only the state or whether they prevailed against everyone in private legal relations. In other words, it was the classic constitutional question of whether there was horizontal application. The court emphasised that article 5(2) clearly shows that freedom of expression is not absolute but may be limited by the provisions of general law, as discussed earlier, as well as by specific laws, such as the law protecting the right to personal honour. The court held that the Constitution's fundamental rights were aimed primarily at protecting citizens against the state, but they also incorporated an objective scale of values which applied, as a matter of constitutional law, throughout the entire legal system. As such, the substance of the rights is expressed indirectly in the rules of private law, most evidently in its mandatory provisions. The court found that rules of private law may count as 'general laws,' which may restrict the basic right of freedom of expression under article 5(2). However, such 'general laws' must be interpreted in the light of the special significance in a free democratic state of the basic right to freedom of expression.

The court stressed that the Constitution protects not only the expression of opinion but also its inherent or intended effect on others, for the whole point of an expression of opinion is to have an effect on the environment of ideas. Thus, value judgements, which always have an intellectual aim, which is to persuade others, are protected by article 5(1). Put another way, it is the stance of the speaker as expressed in the value-judgment by which they hope to affect others which is principally protected by this basic right. In this sense the expression of opinion is free insofar as its effect on the mind is concerned, but that does not mean that one is entitled, just because one is expressing an opinion, to prejudice interests of another which are in their turn also deserving of protection. There has to be a balance of interests; the right to express an opinion must yield if its exercise infringes interests of another which have a superior claim to protection. Whether such an interest exists in a particular case depends on all the circumstances.[61]

The court reasoned that the rules of private law may well be ranked as 'general laws' in the sense of article 5(2) even though, up to then, the rights contained in the Constitution had been considered good only as against the state. The court came to the logical conclusion that if the fundamental right to free expression of opinion affects relations of private law as well and favours free expression of opinion against the fellow citizen also, then rules of private law which operate to protect superior legal interests must also be taken into account as possibly limiting the right. After all, if provisions of criminal law designed to protect honour or other essential aspects of human personality can set limits to the exercise of the fundamental right to freedom of expression, there is no good reason that similar provisions of private law should

61 *Lüth*, note 24, paras 36 to 39.

not equally do so.[62] However, the court held that in the context of public discussion, a presumption in favour of freedom of expression must be applied. Therefore, the court concluded that Mr Lüth's call for a boycott of Harlan's film was a valid expression of his right to free expression.

In summary, the balancing formula established by the Constitutional Court in this case enjoins the lower courts to weigh up the competing interests in freedom of speech and in personal reputation appropriately in the light of all relevant facts and law in each case. Defamation laws are not simply to be applied literally – in each instance the laws themselves must be interpreted and applied so they do not unduly restrict freedom of speech.[63] A noticeable characteristic of German case law is thus the detailed consideration given to all relevant factors, including all relevant laws, with the most weight accorded to overarching constitutional rules and fundamental rights. The example of the lower civil courts' handling of the Böhmermann case illustrate the point. This might also be a reason that there does not seem to be a significant chilling effect in Germany, despite its theoretically draconian criminal defamation law – a mandatory balancing exercise plus a body of case law stating explicitly the high value of free speech in a democratic order. The constitutional structure of the test favours free speech. In this regard the Constitutional Court issued a number of guidelines in subsequent cases.

In the *Soldiers are Murderers* (1995) case, the court emphasised that due weight should be given to the character of the speech or publication and the context in which it was made or issued.[64] If defamatory remarks are made incidentally in the course of a contribution to public discourse, then the speech should be protected from criminal or civil proceedings. The case concerned an appeal to the Constitutional Court about the criminal conviction for insult arising out of four conjoined cases,[65] and illustrate several important points about how competing interests are balanced by German courts. A detailed analysis of this case is therefore instructive.

The facts broadly concerned statements to the effect that soldiers are, *de facto* and of necessity, murderers. Individual soldiers, as well as the Federal Army itself, instituted and won criminal prosecutions against the appellants founded on insult[66] as well as the specific paragraph of the Criminal Code allowing state departments to sue for insult.[67] The Constitutional Court started off by reiterating that the statements for which the complainants had been punished for insult enjoy the protection of article 5(1) of the Constitution.[68] It also pointed out that, in contrast to assertions of fact, statements of

62 Ibid, paras 40–41.

63 Barendt, E *Freedom of Speech* (2nd edn, OUP, Oxford, 2005), 214.

64 *Soldiers are Murderers*, 93 BVerfGE 266 (1995).

65 1 BvR 1476/9; 1 BvR 1980/91; 1 BvR 102/92 and 1 BvR 221/92.

66 Para 185 StGB.

67 Para 194 StGB.

68 *Soldiers are Murderers*, note 64, para 101.

opinion are characterised by the subjective attitude of the person expressing themselves to the object of the statement. They contain the individual's judgement about facts, ideas, or persons. The protection of the basic right relates to this personal attitude. It therefore exists independently of whether the statement is rational or emotional, well founded or groundless, or regarded by others as useful or harmful or as valuable or valueless. The protection relates not only to the content of the statement but also to its form. The fact that a statement is formulated in a polemical or hurtful way does not remove it from the area of protection of the basic right.[69]

The statements for which the complainants had been punished for insult are opinions in this sense, which are always covered by the protection of the basic right. The complainants in their statements that soldiers are murderers or potential murderers did not claim that particular soldiers had committed a murder in the past. They were instead expressing a judgement about soldiers and about the profession of soldier which under certain circumstances compels the killing of other human beings. The criminal courts also proceeded on the basis that it was a value judgement, not an assertion about facts. It was clear to the court that punishment for these statements constituted an intrusion into the protected area of the basic right to freedom of expression.[70]

However, the court then went on to stress that the basic right to freedom of expression does not enjoy absolute protection. According to article 5(2), it is limited by the provisions of general statutes, the statutory provisions for the protection of young people, and the right to personal honour.[71] The court then examined whether the criminal provision is reconcilable with article 5(1), which primarily protects personal honour. Within the framework of the general right of personality derived from article 2(1) in combination with article 1(1), it explained that honour itself enjoys basic right protection. It can indeed be harmed by expressions of opinion. Therefore, article 5(2) of the Constitution expressly recognises protection of honour as a ground to justify limitations on the freedom of expression. But the court went on to say that it does not follow from this that the legislature could limit freedom of expression in the interest of personal honour as it pleases. Instead it should keep in mind the restricted right and avoid excessive limitations of free speech.

The court then turned its attention to the fact that this particular provision of the criminal code (paragraph 185) also extends protection to state institutions and not just to individuals. In this regard, the norm cannot be justified from the point of view of personal honour because state institutions have no personal honour, nor can they have the general right of personality. The court noted that instead paragraph 185 is justified as a protective norm in favour of

69 Ibid, paras 102–105.

70 Ibid, para 106.

71 Para 185 StGB, which forms the basis of the decisions that were being challenged, belongs to this category of general statutes protecting the right to personal honour.

state institutions as it ranks with the general laws in the sense of article 5(2) of the Constitution. State institutions cannot fulfil their function without a minimum degree of social acceptance. They ought, therefore, in principle to be protected from verbal onslaughts which threaten to undermine this. The criminal law protection ought not however to lead to state institutions being shielded from public criticism, even if it takes a harsh form. This should be guaranteed in a special way by the basic right to freely express an opinion.

Against this background the court then balanced the competing interests of the soldiers and the Federal army on the one hand and the conscientious objectors on the other. The court concluded that an article 5(1) balancing operation must be undertaken within the framework of the features of the definition of the statutes concerned. Paragraph 185 of the Criminal Code cannot be interpreted so that it extends the concept of insult so widely that it exceeds the requirements of the protection of honour or protection of institutions or leaves no more room for taking freedom of expression into consideration. Nor can it be interpreted in a manner which would deter people from exercising their right to free speech, which in turn would lead to even permissible criticism remaining unspoken through fear of sanctions. Therefore, having weighed up all the competing interests and rights, the Constitutional Court quashed the criminal convictions.

Soldiers are Murderers illustrated several relevant points – the manner in which reputation is protected through the criminal law of insult; the fact that criminal defamation may be pursued by individuals as well as institutions, such as the German army; the inclusion of reputation as forming part of the highest ranking right in German law; the right to human dignity; and finally, it illustrates that even so, it is subject to constitutional constraints that balances competing rights in a fact-specific context.

Public discourse, context, and the right to reply

Publication during public discussion is therefore protected by the presumption in favour of freedom of expression and therefore militates against the chilling of speech. In *Flugblatt*[72] a defamation conviction for publication of a leaflet concerning the involvement of two politicians in the 1939 invasion of Poland was quashed by the Constitutional Court as the lower court had failed to consider the political significance of the leaflet in furthering public discourse. It is only if the predominant character of a statement is not a contribution to political debate, but the disparagement of an individual that the statement should then be characterised as an insult.[73] A dispute between critics and an art professor was given the same treatment by the Constitutional Court, which held that the context of the debate had to be considered – namely, a contribution

72 *Flugblatt*, 43 BVerfGE 130 (176).
73 *Coerced Democrat*, 82 BVerfGE 272 (1990).

to a debate about the arts. In the same case the court upheld the 'retaliation' principle (*Gegenschlag*) in terms of which defamatory remarks that form part of a reply to a personal attack are protected speech.[74]

Status of the libel complainant

The Constitutional Court also takes the status of the defamation complainant into account. For example, the court stated that when the lower courts injuncted a Social Democratic Party candidate from repeating a charge that the Bavarian Christian Social Union was akin to a neo-Nazi party, this failed to respect his freedom of expression.[75] The reasoning in this is informed by the belief that anyone who engages voluntarily in public debate forfeits to some extent their right not to be criticised. Furthermore, a political party and individual politicians usually have sufficient opportunity and means to reply to insulting or defamatory attacks.[76] The Constitutional Court also distinguishes between citizens and the press. Although in general publishers may be required to substantiate their allegations, free speech protection requires that this burden should not be too high. Furthermore, the high standard of care expected of the press is not required for individuals because the latter do not have the same ability to conduct research and to check sources. In this sense the German courts echo the stance in English cases such as *Economou v de Freitas* [2018]:[77] In *Bayer-Aktionäre* (1991)[78] the Constitutional Court held that individuals are entitled to rely on uncontradicted press reports as a basis for making statements which turn out to be untrue and defamatory.

Opinions as opposed to abusive criticism

The Constitutional Court has held that more freedom should be allowed in the expression of opinion than for assertion of facts – this was clearly illustrated in the *Soldiers are Murderers* case discussed earlier. However, this is tempered by the key question whether the statement is primarily an insult or personal abuse, or whether it forms part of a contribution to public discussion. If the former, i.e. if the personal insult predominates, then the personality rights, including reputational protection, must prevail. Put another way, in principle, whether a statement should be punished as an insult or protected by freedom of expression must be decided by means of a balance. But when a statement is characterised as *Schmähkritik* (abusive criticism), freedom of expression is trumped from the outset – although it must be reiterated that the bar for what

74 *Römerberg*, 54 BVerfGE 129 (1980). See also *Schmidt-Spiegel*, 12 BverfGE 113 (1961).
75 *NPD Europas*, 61 BVerfGE 1 (1982).
76 Barendt, note 63, 215.
77 See the discussion in chapter 3.
78 *Bayer-Aktionäre*, 85 BVerfGE 1, 21 (1991).

is seen as abusive criticism was set very high in 'Solders are murderers.' In its more recent case law, the Constitutional Court expanded the net to include, for instance, hate speech: Insults that directly attack the human dignity of the plaintiff are to be treated similarly to *Schmähkritik*.[79] In other words, there is a distinction in the court's case law between the utmost protection of human dignity (understood narrowly) and the violation of personality rights (rooted in article 2(1) and subject to the balancing exercise.

Whether or not something is seen as abusive criticism and therefore severely sanctioned is decided by making an overall assessment of the content of the statement and also of whether the statement has a factual basis. Only if, on the merits of the case, a statement is aimed solely at the defamation of a person as such, such as in the context of a private feud, can an assessment be considered an insult; in that regard, the reason and context of the statement must be determined. If, on the other hand, the statement is, as is usually the case, in the context of a substantive dispute, a balance is needed which takes into consideration the importance of the statement in the specific circumstances of the individual case. Put another way, it is crucial to determine whether a statement should primarily be regarded as a direct insult or abuse of a person or whether the statement is an expression of an opinion. If the former, then the free speech right takes a back seat. If the latter, strong protection is given. The problem is that it is not always easy to make a distinction. If a statement is made up of a mix of invective and opinionated language, the statement should be characterised as an opinion: In this way free speech is protected.[80]

The case of Heinrich Böll (1980)[81] illustrates the importance of the distinction between an expression of opinion and factual allegations. Böll, a well-known author, brought a civil action against a broadcaster who quoted him inaccurately as stating that West Germany (as it then was) was rotten and that it mercilessly hunted down terrorists. The Constitutional Court held that the fundamental right to freely express an opinion protected in article 5(1) does not protect inaccurate quotation. On the facts of the case the broadcast misquoted the author, and the court held that misquotation amounts to the provision of false information. This accords with the common law in the US: Making untrue allegations of fact, knowing them to be false, falls outside any kind of free speech protection, and in both jurisdictions this will therefore not be covered by constitutional protection. However, it must be pointed out that the US Supreme Court allowed that not all misquotes were automatic grounds for a libel suit – a misquote first had to be false or substantially alter the speaker's meaning.[82]

79 See e.g. BVerfG, 19 May 2020, 1 BvR 2397/19.
80 Barendt, note 63, 216.
81 *Böll*, 54 BVerfGE 208 (1980).
82 *Masson v New Yorker Magazine*, 501 US 496 (1991).

The criminal or civil courts in Germany are tasked with finding meaning and to determine whether the statement complained of amounts to an insult or is defamatory of the complainant. These findings are then reviewable by the Constitutional Court, as arbitrary or incorrect decisions on meaning by the lower courts could prejudice the exercise of free speech rights. The *Coerced Democrat* (1990) case provides a good illustration.[83] An article was published concerning a number of politicians, including the complainant, and stated that they only became democrats out of necessity and furthermore satisfied the desire for strong government similar to the type provided by the Nazi führer. The courts at first instance found that this meant that the complainant was a barely concealed Nazi – and this was a serious insult. However, the Constitutional Court held that there was another possible meaning of the article – namely, that some Germans still longed for a strong leader and put the complainant in that role. According to the constitutional court's case law, it is necessary for a court to check all the potential (and plausible) meanings of a statement and look for the one that is not in violation of the personality right. If such a 'benevolent interpretation' is possible, there is, as a rule, no infringement of the personality right and the statement is covered by the protection of free speech even if other interpretations could be read as violations of the personality right. However, for *Schmähkritik*/abusive criticism, which is understood narrowly, there usually is no alternative plausible meaning so that the benevolent interpretation is not possible.[84]

Again, here we find parallels to US appellate court review of defamation cases, where the constitutional stakes mean that appellate review is much more extensive than in most areas of law. In Germany, though, constitutional oversight goes further and can be said to permeate all areas of law – all the balancing guidelines the constitutional case law has developed can be interpreted as elements of the principle of *proportionality* which is of paramount importance in German law in general.

In the most recent fully reasoned (i.e. full Senate) Constitutional Court decision (the 'Nazi Witch Trials' case)[85] the conflict between the right to freedom of expression and the protection of honour once again came under scrutiny. The complainant was the plaintiff in a civil court case, who criticised the conduct of the judge's trial as being 'more reminiscent of a medieval witch trial than of a trial conducted in accordance with the rule of law' and compared the proceedings to what he thought they must have been like in Nazi Germany. The complainant was found guilty of insult in terms of paragraph 185 of the Criminal Code. On appeal, the Constitutional Court held that this had been incorrectly classified by the lower courts as an insult. The main reasons

83 *Coerced Democrats*, 82 BVerfGE 272 (1990).

84 See, for instance, the '*Hang the Greens*' case: OVG Bautzen, Beschl. v 21 September 2021–6 B 360/21, NVwZ 2021, 1717.

85 *Nazi Witch Trials* 1 BvR 2433/17.

for this decision were as follows. The statements fell within the scope of the fundamental right to freedom of expression since the polemical or infringing wording of a statement does not, in principle, deprive it of the scope of the protection of the fundamental right. The fundamental right under article 5 does not apply without reservation but is limited in the provisions of the general laws, in this case in particular by paragraph 185 of the Criminal Code. Article 5 requires, in principle, a balancing of the impairment which threatens the freedom of expression of the person expressing himself, on the one hand, and the personal honour of the person affected by the statement, on the other. The right to sharply criticise measures by public authorities without fear of state sanctions is at the heart of freedom of expression, which is why it is accorded such relatively high weight when balanced against other rights. In particular, it does not allow the complainant to be limited to what is necessary to criticise the rule of law and thus deny him a right to polemical speech.

The court repeated that in the case of intentional insults, no balance is necessary between freedom of expression and the right to personality because then freedom of expression will be subordinate to the protection of honour. However, this is based on an objective assessment: As long as there is a link to a substantive dispute and the statements are not limited to a mere personal defamation or reduction of those affected by the statement, as in the case of the private feud, they will not be classified as an insult. Whether such a factual reference exists must be determined considering the reason and context of the statement. In this case, the court held that the statements complained of did not constitute an insult. The wording was directed against the conduct of the proceedings and not against the judge as a person. Historical comparisons with National Socialism or accusations of a 'medieval' attitude may have special weight in the context of the weighing up, but they do not justify the assumption of the existence of insult.

Since then, the court confirmed its strong protection of speech in this regard (i.e. concerning paragraph 185 of the Criminal Code) in a number of decisions and stressed the necessity for the competent criminal courts to balance very thoroughly the fundamental rights involved taking account of the particularities of the given case.[86] It constantly stresses the importance of opinions that contribute to a democratic exchange and criticise power rather than merely stir emotions.

In the *All Cops Are Bastards* (2016)[87] case, the Constitutional Court found that having ACAB (an acronym for 'all cops are bastards') printed on his trousers was a protected form of the complainant's right to freedom of expression under article 5 of the Constitution. The court of first instance in Munich

86 See e.g. BVerfG, Nichtannahmebeschluss vom 19. Mai 2020–1 BvR 2397/19, BVerfG, Stattgebender Kammerbeschluss vom 21. März 2022–1 BvR 2650/19, BVerfG, Stattgebender Kammerbeschluss vom 9. Februar 2022–1 BvR 2588/20.

87 *All Cops Are Bastards* 1BvR 257/14.

convicted the complainant of insult under paragraph 185 of the Criminal Code on the basis that the slogan on his trousers amounted to a personalised insult against individual policemen.

The Constitutional Court, however, found that the abbreviation on the complainant's trousers was an expression of opinion, showing his general disapproval of the police, and therefore fell under the constitutional protection of article 5. The court stated that the right to freedom of expression is subject to restrictions, including, as mentioned before, an insult under paragraph 185. However, the court pointed out that if the expressed criticism refers to a collective, it usually does not concern individual misbehaviour and the individual is less affected by the criticism. The court therefore disagreed with the lower courts' finding that the complainant's expression did not refer to the police as a collective but in particular to the specific policemen in the stadium. The Constitutional Court found that the expression referred to the police as a collective and the complainant's mere presence in the stadium with the knowledge that the police would be there and notice the printing on his trousers did not amount to an intention to insult specific individual policemen. Indeed, the court found that the acronym specifically referred to the police as a collective and was therefore protected under the right to freedom of expression under article 5 Constitution.

In the preceding chapter, it was shown that in the US there are strict guidelines from the Supreme Court on the way in which competing rights should be balanced in defamation actions. German jurisprudence in this area of law proceeds in a more contextual manner, but nevertheless there are relevant guidelines from the Constitutional Court, particularly emphasising that due weight should be given to the character of the statement. In the end, however, these guidelines allow for much contextual flexibility in the lower courts albeit subject to constant and sometimes strict scrutiny by the Constitutional Court that controls the lower courts' decisions on whether they have given sufficient weight to the relevant constitutional rights.

Analysis

A preliminary comparative analysis can now be attempted of the three jurisdictions discussed so far – England and Wales, the US, and Germany – to gauge how the competing interests in free speech and protection of reputation are handled. In all three jurisdictions, these rights are given strong legal protection, and the core question is to discover how they may best be properly balanced – one of if not *the* aim of the reform of the common law of defamation in England through the Defamation Act 2013. At first glance, taking the relevant codes into account, it looks as if the German defamation claimant is in a much stronger position than in common law jurisdictions: Not only is defamation defined more broadly to also include personal insult, it is also regarded and prosecuted as a crime without losing the right to pursue damages in a civil matter, plus the action survives the death of the defamed or insulted person, which is not the case in the US and England and Wales. But in reality the practice of defamation law in Germany tends to lead to a much more balanced result as free speech is also subject to constitutional protection and the strongly developed balancing exercise.

In fact, both the US and Germany differ from the UK in this key respect – namely, constitutional protection of free speech. In the UK, free speech is protected instead in the Human Rights Act 1998, which is an ordinary parliamentary statute. The question is therefore whether there is anything to be gained by protecting freedom of speech on a constitutional basis,[88] and therefore, we must start by first comparing the two jurisdictions that do so: Germany and the US.

The main difference between the German and US approach to defamation law can be explained by their respective understanding of the relative weight of certain constitutional norms. This is not surprising, as the two countries were created in different centuries and were furthermore shaped by entirely different sets of historical circumstances. Both countries are nevertheless leading models of liberal democratic constitutionalism, and at the end of the day, their common values outweigh their differences. Kommers explains the essential difference between the two jurisdictions by characterising the German Constitution as a constitution of dignity and the US counterpart as a constitution of liberty.[89] The German Constitution merges liberal constitutionalism with a strong commitment to social solidarity, and in so doing, it balances responsibilities with rights. The focus remains on proportionality. By contrast, American constitutional rhetoric focuses strongly on rights and the rule of law, and some would say that there is very little if any focus on the common good.[90] Put another way, in Germany human dignity informs all jurisprudence, and in the US this role is fulfilled by liberty.

In contrast to Germany, in the US the key case *New York Times v. Sullivan* (1964) has made it virtually impossible for a politician to collect damages for a defamatory statement of fact about his public conduct.[91] Whether this is entirely a good idea is debatable. It could indeed be argued that *Sullivan* and related decisions may have something to do with the increasing debasement and trivialisation of political debate in the United States. This is ironic when

88 Milo, D *Defamation and Freedom of Speech* (OUP, Oxford, 2008) argues that there are compelling reasons for the constitutional protection of free speech and examines the way in which this is achieved in several Commonwealth jurisdictions, including the UK, Canada, Australia, South Africa, and India, amongst others.

89 Kommers, DP, 'Can German Constitutionalism Serve as a Model for the United States' (2019) 20 *German Law Journal* 559, 561.

90 Ibid. See also Glendon, MA *Rights Talk: The Impoverishment of Political Discourse* (The Free Press, New York, NY, 1991).

91 *New York Times Co. v Sullivan*, 376 US 254 (1964).

one remembers the facts of *Sullivan*, which dealt with a powerful politician wishing to silence critique. An example of how the US absolutist interpretation of free speech may indeed work to shield powerful interest groups and wealthy individuals from state regulation of their political expenditures can be found in *Buckley v Valeo* (1976), where the court ruled that money is speech and thus struck down a federal law limiting the amounts of money any one candidate or organisation could spend in an election campaign.[92] The US speech law can therefore be criticised as lacking proportionality and balance – something which forms the very core of German constitutional jurisprudence.[93]

If *Sullivan* made it difficult for public figures to win defamation claims in the US, it may seem that the opposite is the case in Germany. Here, no distinction as to the status of the claimant is made, where the more prominent question is whether the speech contributed to public discourse rather than whom it concerned. Although politicians, public officials, state organisations, churches, and the like are all entitled to pursue defamation claims, the German courts do require of them to expect more scrutiny and critique than individuals. At first glance it may seem alarming, especially given the authoritarian history of Nazi Germany, that critique of government, state officials, military personnel, and politicians may be prosecuted as a crime under the guise of insult or defamation under the German criminal code. In this sense the German system seems to tilt in the same direction as the pre-reformed UK common law of defamation, i.e. favouring the defamation claimant. However, it is precisely in this area where the balance between the legislative, executive, and judicial branches of the German *Rechtsstaat* is beautifully illustrated: The courts, following the guiding principles of the German constitution, place very high value on the desirability of free and frank political speech and in their decisions reflect the notion that political parties and politicians, public organisations, and public figures ought to and must submit to higher levels of scrutiny and critique. This also illustrates the necessity of gauging German law by reference to statute, case law, and commentary.

Unlike in the UK and the US, in Germany personality rights including reputational rights are protected even after the death of the rights holder. The only proviso is that this is the case only as long as the non-material interests in the personality rights still exist. The powers associated with the personality right pass to the heir(s) of the holder of the personality right and can be exercised by them in accordance with the express or presumed will of the deceased.[94]

Other notable comparisons include the following: In Germany, as in the UK, the press is held to a higher standard than individuals, whereas in the US the press (as well as individuals who defame public figures, for that matter)

92 *Buckley v Valeo*, 424 US 1 (1976).

93 Kommers, note 89, 566.

94 *Marlene Dietrich*, 1 BGH ZR 49/97 (1999).

is almost unassailable, at least as far as 'public figures' are concerned. In German defamation cases, injunctions can be given very early on in proceedings, which sits uncomfortably with UK and especially US sensibilities about prior constraint.

In the end the German courts engage in a balancing exercise, utilising proscriptive statutory rules from a variety of statutes (criminal and civil codes, the Constitution) in a complex and fact-specific manner. The overall result is that the two competing interests, free speech and reputation, are balanced on an ad hoc basis which is very context-specific.

The German system of constitutional checks and balances regarding competing fundamental rights are flexible but may seem dauntingly complex in certain circumstances. The core challenge is this balancing exercise, and balancing tends to be inherently less predictable than written rules or (perhaps) a proper stare decisis doctrine. Nevertheless, the UK may consider the value of placing the norms on a constitutional basis, which means there is a guiding principle aiding decision-making. Although the laws of England and Wales do not extend constitutional protection to free speech as such, it does incorporate into its domestic law[95] the principles of the European Convention on Human Rights and these rights are strongly adhered to and implemented in UK courts.

The ECHR and the case law of the ECtHR are becoming increasingly important in German constitutional law as well since its Constitutional Court has obliged every court (including itself) to take the convention into account when interpreting and applying German law. It therefore comes as no surprise to note how well the jurisprudence of the ECtHR harmonises with that of Germany.

Against this background, the jurisprudence of the European Court of Human Rights, and especially its highly evolved balancing mechanism for weighing up competing fundamental rights, is examined in the next chapter.

95 By means of the Human Rights Act 1998.

6 Defamation in the European Court of Human Rights

Introduction

The preceding chapters noted that the vexing issue of balancing freedom of speech with the protection of an individual's reputation was one of the main drivers of the reformation attempt culminating in the Defamation Act 2013. Chapter 3 considered the effects so far of this reform, as evidenced from cases heard in England and Wales, and chapters 4 and 5 analysed the ways in which US and German law deal with this issue. It was further argued that the legislative attempt in England and Wales to redress the balance in favour of free speech does not go far enough. One of the areas that may have exercised an influence on the reform is the more or less co-synchronous jurisprudence in related areas coming from the European Court of Human Rights (ECtHR).[1]

In terms of the Human Rights Act 1998, English courts are under a duty to develop the law in accordance with the various rights and freedoms contained in the European Convention of Human Rights (ECHR).[2] This means that their decisions should, as far as not in conflict with primary legislation, be compatible with Convention rights: Section 2 of the Human Rights Act 1998 (the HRA) says this on the interpretation of Convention rights:

> (1) A court or tribunal determining a question which has arisen in connection with a Convention right must take into account any –
>
> (a) judgment, decision, declaration or advisory opinion of the European Court of Human Rights,
> (b) opinion of the Commission given in a report adopted under Article 31 of the Convention,
> (c) decision of the Commission in connection with Article 26 or 27(2) of the Convention, or

1 Also referred to in this chapter as 'the Court.'

2 Convention for the Protection of Human Rights and Fundamental Freedoms, as amended by Protocols Nos. 11 and 14.

DOI: 10.4324/9781003416005-7

(d) decision of the Committee of Ministers taken under Article 46 of the Convention, whenever made or given, so far as, in the opinion of the court or tribunal, it is relevant to the proceedings in which that question has arisen.'[3]

These obligations mean that courts are now able, in cases where Convention rights are potentially in conflict with common law principles, to depart from or develop the common law to resolve such conflict to favour rights such as the right to freedom of expression under article 10 of the ECHR. This right as well as others such as the right to a fair and public hearing under article 6, or the right to respect for private and family life under article 8 of the ECHR will doubtlessly continue to be used in support of competing interpretations of the Defamation Act 2013.[4]

It is therefore particularly important to examine the ECtHR's treatment of defamation, the Court's methodology and guiding principles, the possible influence of its case law on judicial reasoning in England and Wales, and lessons that may be learnt *vis-à-vis* the key question raised in this book namely how to achieve a proper balance between the protection of reputation and free speech in English defamation law. This chapter examines this fluid relationship, as well as the notion that the Court's conflation of privacy law with reputational rights has been and continues to be a significant issue for defamation jurisprudence in England and Wales.

The ECtHR: balancing competing rights

The ECtHR is an international court that was set up in 1959, with the stated aim of ruling on individual or State applications alleging violations of the civil and political rights set out in the European Convention on Human Rights (ECHR).[5] The Court monitors respect for the human rights of some 800 million Europeans in the 47 Council of Europe member states that have ratified the Convention. This entails cases involving rights set out in the Convention, such as the rights to life, fair hearings, respect for private and family life, freedom of expression, freedom of thought, conscience and religion, and the protection of property – to name but a few. Frequently disputes relate to discrete rights but often also relate to rights in competition with each other, in which case the Court is tasked with ensuring that a fair balance is struck between the relevant competing rights or interests.[6] The Court uses several devices or tools to assist in this exercise, such as allowing a margin of appreciation to member

3 See also sections 6(1), (2) and 3(1).

4 Collins, M *Collins on Defamation* (OUP, Oxford, 2014), 459.

5 Also referred to in this chapter as 'the Convention.'

6 *Von Hannover v Germany (No. 2)*, (Nos 40660/08 and 60641/08) [2012] EMLR 16, paras 98–99.

states, as well as utilising the doctrine of proportionality. These doctrines are discussed in the following sections.

Recognition of the chilling effect

The ECtHR often remarks that certain measures and sanctions interfering with the right to free speech may have a chilling effect on the exercise of the right to freedom of expression.[7] Although mention of the chilling effect is not limited to freedom of expression jurisprudence under article 10, it arises in that context most often. Furthermore, it has been applied in relation to a variety of state interferences, including, for example, abortion laws,[8] and interferences with the right of individual petition under article 34 of the Convention.[9] O'Fathaigh worked out that the phrase had been mentioned in over 100 judgments up to 2013 alone and remarked that it was therefore surprising that at the same time there had been a notable absence of scholarly attention to the judicial significance of the chilling effect principle.[10] How, then, does the Court address this issue? In essence, the ECtHR jurisprudence seem to indicate that only a narrow margin should be allowed to a state when the restriction of free speech concerns political speech or is likely to discourage people from making criticisms or contributing to public discussion of issues affecting the life of the community.[11] Therefore, it distinguishes kinds of speech and the level of protection that should be accorded to each.

The Court also states that it is of central concern to ensure that any measures taken by national authorities do not chill debates on matters of legitimate public interest.[12] The ECtHR recognises that free speech may be chilled in various ways for a variety of reasons, and it has specifically included and examined defamation in a number of cases, considered in this chapter. Furthermore, it recognises that chilling free speech could, in fact, be seen as a form of self-censorship.[13] More specifically, people may self-censor due to fear of disproportionate sanctions,[14] with the most obvious example here

7 Fathaigh, RO 'Article 10 and the Chilling Effect Principle' (2013) *European Human Rights Law Review* 304.
8 *Tysiaç v Poland* [2007] 45 EHRR 42, para 116; and *A v Ireland* [2011] 53 EHRR 13, para 178.
9 *McShane v United Kingdom* [2002] 35 EHRR 23, para 151; and *Colibaba v Moldova* [2009] 49 EHRR 44, para 68.
10 Fathaigh, note 7.
11 *Lingens v Austria* [1986] 8 EHRR 407 and Filipova, V 'Standards of Protection of Freedom of Expression and the Margin of Appreciation in the Jurisprudence of the European Court of Human Rights' (2012) *Coventry Law Journal* 64.
12 McGonagle, T, McGonagle, M and Fathaigh, RO *Freedom of Expression and Defamation – A Study of the Case Law of the European Court of Human Rights* (Council of Europe, Strasbourg, 2016), 24.
13 *Vajnai v Hungary*, No. 33629/06, ECHR 2008, para 54.
14 *Cumpănă and Mazăre v Romania*, [GC] No. 33348/96, ECHR 2004-XI, para 114.

being the fear of criminal sanctions for defamation. The ECtHR noted that in such a case, even in the event of an eventual acquittal, the mere existence of the fear of the sanction tends to discourage persons from making certain statements.[15]

Also relevant to the current discussion, the ECtHR explicitly stated that unpredictably large damages are capable of chilling free speech. In *Independent News and Media v Ireland* (2005)[16] it held that it is not necessary to rule on whether a specific damages award, such as the one under consideration, had in fact chilled speech; instead, 'as matter of principle, unpredictably large damages awards in libel cases are considered capable of having such an effect and therefore require the most careful scrutiny.'[17] The ECtHR went on to say that even if the assessment of damages in libel cases is an inherently complex and uncertain exercise, any such uncertainty must be kept to a minimum.[18]

The ECtHR further recognises that chilling free speech is detrimental to the whole of society.[19] In *Bladet Tromsø v Norway* (1999) it reiterated that when measures taken or sanctions imposed by the national authority are capable of discouraging the participation of the press in debates over matters of legitimate public concern, it is the duty of the Court to accord the issue the most careful scrutiny.[20] It must also be noted that it is the Court's expressed view that the press is the watchdog of society. In *Castells v Spain* it stated:

> It is nevertheless incumbent on it [the press] to impart information and ideas on political questions and on other matters of public interest. Freedom of the press affords the public one of the best means of discovering and forming an opinion of the ideas and attitudes of their political leaders. In particular, it gives politicians the opportunity to reflect and comment on the preoccupations of public opinion; it thus enables everyone to participate in the free political debate which is at the very core of the concept of a democratic society.[21]

Against this background, the ECtHR's jurisprudence on defamation as such can now be fruitfully examined.

15 *Altuğ Taner Akçam v Turkey*, No. 27520/07, 25 October 2011, (2016) 62 EHRR 12, para 68.
16 *Independent News and Media and Independent News Ireland Limited v Ireland*, No. 55120/00, ECHR 2005-V, (2006) 42 EHRR 46.
17 Ibid, para 114.
18 Ibid.
19 *Cumpănă and Mazăre v Romania*, note 14, para 114.
20 *Bladet Tromsø and Stensaas v Norway*, No. 21980/93 ECHR, 20 May 1999, para 64. See also *Jersild v Denmark*, (A/298), (1995) 19 EHRR 1, paras 31 and 35.
21 *Castells v Spain*, App No. 11798/85, 23 April 1992, para 42.

Developments in the ECtHR

Over the past two decades, two major channels of development in the field of defamation and freedom of expressions are interesting. On the one hand, there has been a move in the UK to right the balance between a tilt in favour of defamation claimants, arguably at the expense of the principle of freedom of speech in general. Almost during the same time frame, it can be observed that ECtHR jurisprudence has been moving away from the notion of giving precedence to freedom of speech when competing with reputation rights to regarding these as two equal rights to be balanced in the context of their own specific circumstances. As will become clear, these decisions followed from and built upon the fact that the ECtHR regards reputation as a subspecies of privacy and, as such, falling under the protection of the article 8 right to respect for private life of the Convention.

To fully understand the jurisprudence from the ECtHR on defamation, one therefore needs to also keep in mind relevant development in its treatment of the right to privacy. To do this, it is necessary to start by examining articles 10 and 8, as dealing specifically with reputation and free speech.

Freedom of expression

The relevant parts of article 10 of the Convention read (with my emphasis):

> 1 Everyone has the right to freedom of expression. This right shall include freedom to hold opinions and to receive and impart information and ideas without interference by public authority and regardless of frontiers . . .
> 2 The exercise of these freedoms, since it carries with it duties and responsibilities, may be subject to such formalities, conditions, restrictions or penalties as are prescribed by law and are necessary in a democratic society, in the interests of national security, territorial integrity or public safety, for the prevention of disorder or crime, for the protection of health or morals, *for the protection of the reputation* or rights of others, for preventing the disclosure of information received in confidence, or for maintaining the authority and impartiality of the judiciary.

Two things are notable here: Article 10 contains its own exceptions in paragraph 2, among which is specifically included the protection of reputation. The exception is narrowly construed in that it is triggered only when prescribed by law and deemed necessary in a democratic society. Secondly, the ECtHR recognises that the right to freedom of expression is (and should be) applicable not only to information or ideas that are favourably received or regarded as inoffensive or as a matter of indifference, but also to those that may be deemed offensive or shocking or that may disturb the state or any sector of the population: Such are the demands of pluralism, tolerance, and broadmindedness without which there can be no democratic society.[22]

This frames the debate, and within this broad and permissive framework the Court uses a standard test to determine whether a violation of article 10 is legally justified. In other words, the premise is that free speech is to be accorded the highest possible protection with the proviso that this is not absolute. Restrictions are possible: Paragraph 2 of article 10 sets out that free speech may be restricted provided that certain conditions are met. The justification for this is the notion that the right to free speech carries with it, certain corresponding duties and responsibilities. These duties and responsibilities are not clearly defined but would depend on the facts surrounding each individual case.[23]

First, the interference with free speech must be prescribed by law, which in turn speaks to its accessibility and foreseeability. Second, it must pursue a legitimate aim, these being the aims set out in article 10(2) and which include protection of reputation (i.e. defamation law broadly speaking). Third, the interference must be necessary in a democratic society, which is interpreted as meaning that it must satisfy a pressing social need and be proportionate to the aim pursued.

How the right to privacy being conflated with reputational rights led to a devaluation of the status of article 10

It is now necessary to examine article 8 of the Convention, which concerns the right to a person's private and family life and therefore can be seen as protecting the right to privacy. This right expanded through the jurisprudence of the ECtHR to include the protection of reputation. How this came about is examined in more detail further below. It is recognised that article 8 is only engaged if the attack on a person's reputation constitutes so serious an interference with their privacy[24] that it could be construed as undermining their personal integrity.[25] In *Axel Springer AG v Germany* (2012) the Court held that in order for article 8 to come into play, an attack on a person's reputation had to attain 'a certain level of seriousness and in a manner causing prejudice to personal enjoyment of the right to respect for private life.'[26]

Nonetheless, it must be noted that the expansion of privacy protection as such has arguably occurred to a certain extent at the expense of the right to

22 *Handyside v the United Kingdom*, 7 December 197, Series A, No. 24, para 49.

23 *Fressoz and Roire v France*, [GC] No. 29183/95, ECHR 1999-I, para 52.

24 In this chapter, the right to privacy refers to article 8(1) ECHR i.e. the right to respect for one's private and family life, one's home and correspondence, and may be used interchangeably.

25 *Karakó v Hungary*, No. 39311/05, 28 April 2009, para 23.

26 *Axel Springer AG v Germany*, [GC] No. 39954/08, 7 February 2012; [2012] EMLR 15, para 83.

freedom of expression. In *Flux v Moldova (No. 6)* (2008), for example, the dissenting judges severely criticised the majority judgment (in favour of privacy) as having 'thrown the protection of freedom of expression as far back as it possibly could.'[27] To understand this development, i.e. the article 10 versus article 8 question, we should reflect on the wording of the latter, the right to respect for private and family life:

1 Everyone has the right to respect for his private and family life, his home and his correspondence.
2 There shall be no interference by a public authority with the exercise of this right except such as is in accordance with the law and is necessary in a democratic society in the interests of national security, public safety or the economic well-being of the country, for the prevention of disorder or crime, for the protection of health or morals, or for the protection of the rights and freedoms of others.

The first case that dealt with a conflict between articles 8 and 10, that is, free speech and privacy, was *Lingens v Austria* (1986).[28] In this 1980s case the ECtHR found firmly in favour of free speech. The facts are illustrative of an often-repeated conflict between the two competing rights under discussion: The applicant (Mr Lingens) had been held liable for criminal defamation when he published two articles alleging that the Austrian chancellor had, amongst others, protected former members of the Nazi SS. It was agreed that Mr Lingens' conviction was indeed an interference by a public authority with his exercise of the article 10(1) right to freedom of expression: What was at issue was whether or not this interference was justified.

The Austrian government asserted that there was a conflict between two rights secured in the Convention – freedom of expression (article 10) and the right to respect for private life (article 8) and that these two rights should be balanced against each other.[29] The Court made short shrift of this argument by pointing out the public nature of the comments complained of as well as the fact that the claimant was a politician. It held that there was accordingly no need in this instance to read article 10 in the light of article 8.[30] The Court emphasised that the limits of acceptable criticism are wider when it concerns a politician as such than for a private individual. The reason for this is because politicians 'inevitably and knowingly' lay themselves open to close scrutiny by both journalists and the public at large. Because of this inevitable scrutiny, the politician must consequently display a greater degree of tolerance. It was held that without doubt, article 10(2) enables the reputation of all individuals

27 *Flux v Moldova (No. 6)*, No. 22824/04, 29 July 2008, para 17.
28 *Lingens v Austria*, 8 July 1986, Series A No. 103.
29 Ibid, para 37.
30 Ibid, para 38.

to be protected, and this protection of course extends to politicians too, even when they are not acting in their private capacity. But in cases like these, the requirements of such protection have to be weighed in relation to the interests of open discussion of political issues.[31]

The approach in *Lingens* can be summarised as holding that article 10 applications do not automatically engage article 8 but should be decided only on the exceptions raised in its own paragraph 2. This clearly placed the protection of free speech in a position of priority, at least as far as political speech is concerned.

However, it must also be noted that whilst concurring with the overall decision reached by the Court, Judge Thor Vilhjálmsson was of the dissenting opinion that article 10 of the Convention has to be interpreted and applied by taking the article 8 right to respect for private life, as one of the factors relevant to the question whether or not freedom of expression was subjected to restrictions and penalties that were necessary in a democratic society for the protection of the reputation of others. In later cases this notion gained traction.

A line of decisions followed which established that reputation is to be seen as falling under the protection accorded to privacy in article 8.[32] Subsequent ECtHR decisions therefore rejected the approach from *Lingens* that article 10 applications do not automatically engage article 8. This series of cases commenced in 2004 with *Radio France v France*.[33] In this case the court held that 'the right to reputation does indeed figure among the rights safeguarded by article 8 of the Convention, as an element of the right to respect for private life.'[34] In *Bédat v Switzerland* (2016)[35] the Court held that a person's right to protection of their reputation is encompassed by article 8 as part of the right to respect for private life,[36] and the same was confirmed again in *Einarsson v Iceland* (2018).[37]

In *Chauvy v France* (2005)[38] the Court held that the impugned interference was to be examined in the light of the case as a whole, including the content of the remarks held against the applicants and the context in which they made them. It was necessary to assess whether the interference in issue

31 Ibid, para 42.

32 *N. v Sweden*, No. 11366/85; Mullis, A and Scott, A 'The Swing of the Pendulum: Reputation, Expression and the Recentering of the English Libel Law' (2012) 63 *Northern Ireland Legal Quarterly* 27–58; *Chauvy & Others v France*, (64915/01) (2005) 41 EHRR 29; *Cumpana v Romania*, (33348/96) (2005) 41 EHRR 200; *Greene v Associated Newspapers Ltd* [2004] EWCA Civ 1462; [2005] QB 972; *Pfeifer v Austria*, (12556/03) (2007) 48 EHRR 175, paras 33 and 35; *In re Guardian News and Media Ltd* [2010] UKSC 1; [2010] 2 AC 697, paras 37–42.

33 *Radio France and Others v France*, No. 53984/00, ECHR 2004-II.

34 Ibid, para 31.

35 *Bédat v Switzerland*, [GC] No. 56925/08, 29 March 2016.

36 Ibid, para 72.

37 *Einarsson v Iceland*, App No. 24703/15 at para 33.

38 *Chauvy & Others v France*, (64915/01) (2005) 41 EHRR 29.

had been 'proportionate to the legitimate aims pursued' and whether the reasons adduced by the national authorities to justify it were 'relevant and sufficient.' In addition, it had to be established whether the national authorities had struck a fair balance when protecting two values at issue – namely, on the one hand, freedom of expression protected by article 10 and, on the other, the right of the claimants to protect their reputation, a right protected by article 8.[39] No explanation was given as to why the Court included the right to reputation as part of the right to privacy.

A more cogent explanation was provided in 2007 in *Pfeifer v Austria*.[40] The Court justified the inclusion of reputation under privacy protection by holding that a person's reputation forms part of their personal identity and psychological integrity and therefore also falls within the scope of their private life, and therefore the conclusion was that article 8 applies.[41] This mirrors the position in Germany where reputation rights are seen as part of the general personality right. It is interesting to note here that in his dissenting judgment Judge Schäffer agreed that freedom of expression does not automatically prevail over the rights of others if an applicant complains to the Court of an infringement of the right to freedom of information, and on the other hand, the protection of private life will not necessarily prevail over freedom of expression if the applicant complains to the Court of a violation of the right to respect for private life (for example, failure to protect their reputation).[42] But he then went even further and opined that the Court had a positive, i.e. affirmative, duty to balance at times multipolar rights – even if not raised *in casu*. In other words, where both values are at stake, the Court's balancing exercise ought not to depend on which particular article of the Convention had been relied on in the case before it. Howard highlighted this debate – namely, should the Court confine itself to the issues brought before it? Or should it be proactive and include what it regards to be relevant law even if not relied upon by the parties to the case?[43] Even where both conflicting rights are placed in front of the Court, there is a structural imbalance implicit in the way in which competing rights are adjudicated: It could be argued that invariably the right advanced by the applicant receives more attention from the Court than that advanced by the defendant, for the primary function of the Court would be to directly address the legal question posed by the applicant.[44] Tulkens agrees with this, concluding that 'the test of necessity would tend to lean in favour

39 Ibid, para H14 (j).

40 *Pfeifer v Austria*, No. 12556/03, 15 November 2007; (2009) 48 EHRR 8.

41 Ibid, para 35.

42 Ibid, O-II5 5.

43 Howard, E *Freedom of Expression and Religious Hate Speech in Europe* (Routledge, London, 2018), 47–49.

44 Brems, E 'Conflicting Human Rights: An Exploration in the Context of the Right to a Fair Trial in the European Convention for the Protection of Human Rights and Fundamental Freedoms' (2005) 27 *Human Rights Quarterly* 305.

of the applicant's right . . . this leads implicitly to establishing a presumption in favour of the applicant.'[45] The decision as to the relative weights of competing rights is also inescapably subjective – it would be virtually impossible for judges not to place value judgements on competing rights.

Furthermore, the parties may not be in a symmetrical position against each other: Tulkens gives the example of *Otto-Preminger-Institut v Austria* (1994)[46] where 'the possibility cannot be ruled out that the balance of rights was influenced more or less consciously' by the fact that what was on the scales was an individual filmmaker's right to freedom of expression, 'against the interests of all Catholics in the Austrian province of Tyrol.'[47] In this regard Howard rightly points out that the predisposition, be it conscious or subconscious, to give more weight to the majority view in a society should be handled circumspectly by the Court, as it is often the minority views and interests that most need to be protected.[48] The approach taken in *Pfeifer v Austria* was confirmed in *Karako v Hungary* (2011):[49] If only article 8 is raised by the parties, and a potential conflict exists with article 10, it is up to the Court to balance the competing articles notwithstanding whether the parties themselves had raised article 10. The effect of this on the concerns raised by Tulkens and Howard earlier are unclear.

In *Axel Springer v Germany*[50] the Court further attempted to clarify the relationship between freedom of expression and protection of reputation by reiterating that it regarded the right to protection of reputation as a right which is protected by article 8 of the Convention as part of the right to respect for private life. As such, when examining the necessity of an interference in a democratic society in the interests of the 'protection of the reputation or rights of others,' the Court stated that it may be required to verify whether the domestic authorities struck a fair balance when protecting two values guaranteed by the Convention, which may come into conflict with each other in certain cases. These could be, on the one hand, freedom of expression protected by article 10 and, on the other, the right to respect for private life enshrined in article 8. Likewise, in *Print Zeitungsverlag GmbH v Austria* (2013)[51] it was held that domestic courts were under a duty to verify whether the authorities struck a fair balance when protecting two values guaranteed by the Convention which may come into conflict with each other in certain cases, and

45 Tulkens, F 'Conflicts between Fundamental Rights: Contrasting Views on Articles 9 and 10 of the European Convention on Human Rights,' in *Venice Commission Blasphemy, Insult and Hatred: Finding Answers in a Democratic Society* (Council of Europe, Science and Technique of Democracy No. 47, Strasbourg, 2010), 125.

46 *Otto-Preminger-Institut v Austria*, No. 13470/87, 20 September 1994.

47 Tulkens, note 45.

48 Howard, note 43, 49.

49 *Karakó v Hungary*, note 25; (2011) 52 EHRR 36, paras 17 and 26.

50 *Axel Springer*, note 26; (2012) EMLR 15, paras 83 and 84.

51 *Print Zeitungsverlag GmbH v Austria*, No. 26547/07, 10 October 2013.

reiterated 'the right to protection of reputation is a right protected by article 8 of the Convention as part of the right to respect for private life.'[52]

Reputation rights were therefore (rightly or wrongly) elevated to the same status and protected in the same manner as privacy rights in the ECtHR, and from the case law it is clear that the Court has moved away from according primacy to free speech: It is regarded as equal in principle to other Convention rights. It then follows that the next question is how the Court determines which right should triumph in case of conflict. To answer this the discussion needs to return specifically to the right to reputation and defamation in ECtHR jurisprudence, and to examine how the Court balances these competing rights.

Balancing articles 10 and 8

To balance potential conflicts of article 8 and 10 interests, the Court has established the following general guidelines:[53] As a matter of principle, the rights guaranteed under either article deserve equal respect, and the outcome of an application should not, *a priori*, vary according to whether it has been lodged with the Court under article 10 of the Convention by the publisher of an offending article or under article 8 of the Convention by the person who has been the subject of that article. Accordingly, the margin of appreciation should, again, in principle be the same in both cases.[54] Where the balancing exercise between those two rights has been undertaken by the national authorities in conformity with the criteria laid down in the Court's case law, the Court would require strong reasons to substitute its view for that of the domestic courts.[55] In other words, there will usually be a wide margin afforded by the Court if the state is required to strike a balance between competing private interests or competing Convention rights.[56]

An examination of ECtHR jurisprudence furthermore shows that proportionality is the key to deciding cases where freedom of expression conflict with defamation, in substantially the same way as other instances where fundamental

52 Ibid, para 2.

53 As summarised in *Delfi v Estonia*, [GC] No. 64569/09, 16 June 2015, para 139. See also *Høiness v Norway*, No. 43624/14, 19 March 2019, para 66, and Aplin, T and Bosland, J 'The Uncertain Landscape of Article 8 of the ECHR: The Protection of Reputation as a Fundamental Human Right?' in Kenyon, AT (ed), *Comparative Defamation and Privacy Law* (Cambridge University Press, Cambridge, 2016), 265–290.

54 *Axel Springer*, note 26, para 87; *Von Hannover v Germany (No. 2)*, [GC] Nos 40660/08 and 60641/08, para 106, ECHR 2012 and *Mosley v the United Kingdom*, No. 48009/08, 10 May 2011, para 111.

55 *Axel Springer*, note 26, para 88, *Von Hannover (No. 2)*, note 54, para 107.

56 *Evans v the United Kingdom*, [GC] No. 6339/05, para 77, ECHR 2007-I; *Chassagnou and Others v France*, [GC] Nos 25088/94, 28331/95 and 28443/95, para 113, ECHR 1999-III; and *Ashby Donald and Others v France*, No. 36769/08, 10 January 2013, para 40.

rights conflict with each other.[57] Proportionality is further recognised as very important because of the chilling effect on public debate and on free speech that may be the result of defamation laws that may be overly protective of reputational interests and/or may provide for far-reaching remedies or sanctions.[58] These principles deserve some further attention.

Margin of appreciation

The Court recognises that the Convention may be interpreted differently across nations, and accords them a margin of appreciation within which the Court will not interfere. This doctrine was developed through the Court's case law[59] and is now enshrined in the preamble to the Convention.[60] A new recital has been added at the end of the preamble containing a reference to the principle of subsidiarity and the doctrine of the margin of appreciation. It is intended to enhance the transparency and accessibility of the Convention system and to be consistent with the doctrine of the margin of appreciation as developed by the Court in its case law.[61] Put another way, the member states enjoy a margin of appreciation in how they apply and implement the Convention, depending on the circumstances of the case and the rights and freedoms engaged. This reflects that the Convention system is subsidiary to the safeguarding of human rights at national level and that national authorities are in principle better placed than an international court to evaluate local needs and conditions.[62] Nevertheless, it needs to be remembered that the margin of appreciation goes hand in hand with supervision under the Convention system. In this respect, the role of the Court remains to review whether decisions taken by national authorities are compatible with the Convention, albeit having due regard to the state's margin of appreciation. The reason for the margin of appreciation doctrine lies in the absence of a European consensus on matters such as public morals, religion, decency, etc. and indeed whether such matters should be regulated in the first place, on the one hand, and the value placed on certain kinds of speech (such as political speech) in promoting democracy, on the other hand.

It could well be argued that there is evidence of a distinct 'procedural turn' inferred from the Court's jurisprudence, meaning that in most cases the Court

57 McGonagle *et al.*, note 12.

58 Ibid, 10.

59 *Handyside v the United Kingdom*, note 22, paras 47 to 50.

60 Protocol No. 15 amending the Convention for the Protection of Human Rights and Fundamental Freedoms (CETS No. 213). This Protocol was ratified by all Member States. <www.coe.int/en/web/conventions/full-list/-/conventions/treaty/213/signatures?p_auth=2XKbxmFx> last accessed 25 May 2019.

61 Council of Europe, Protocol No. 15 amending the Convention for the Protection of Human Rights and Fundamental Freedoms (CETS No. 213), Explanatory Report, para 7.

62 Ibid, para 9.

would draw a positive inference from due procedural diligence at the national level.[63] However, this does not go so far as complete deference – the Court still can and does use its own normative engagement on the issue in question, where it deems it necessary.[64] Carefully constructed and executed national decision-making processes would mostly indicate lenient review of the outcome by the ECtHR, whereas deficient processes would lead to a stricter review by the Court.[65] This stance is reflected, for example, in *Animal Defenders v United Kingdom* (2013) where the Court held that 'the quality of the parliamentary and judicial review of the necessity of the measure is of particular importance . . . to the operation of the relevant margin of appreciation.'[66]

TYPES OF SPEECH

One of the ways in which the margin of appreciation doctrine is applied to defamation cases in particular is by means of distinguishing between different types of speech. So, for instance, very little leeway for restricting free speech is tolerated when the speech is political expression, whereas it is up to each state how much free speech on matters such as religion, morals, etc. would be allowed. For instance, there will usually be a wide margin afforded by the Court if the state is required to strike a balance between competing private interests or competing Convention rights.[67] The Court therefore differentiates between kinds of speech, giving them higher and lower degrees of protection according to where they fit on a spectrum of speech. The important role of the press is also recognised. In *Dyundin v Russia* (2008) the Court held that in the context of the balancing exercise under article 10:

> [W]here the reporting by a journalist of statements made by third parties is concerned, the relevant test is not whether the journalist can prove the veracity of the statements, but whether a sufficiently accurate and reliable factual basis proportionate to the nature and degree of the allegation can be established.[68]

63 Propelier, P and Van de Heyning, C 'Procedural Rationality: Giving Teeth to the Proportionality Analysis' (2013) 9 *European Constitutional Law Review* 230, 248–249.

64 Arnardóttir, OM 'The "Procedural Turn" Under the European Convention on Human Rights and Presumptions of Convention Compliance' (2017) 15(1) *International Journal of Constitutional Law* 9, 10.

65 Ibid, 11.

66 *Animal Defenders v United Kingdom*, No. 48876/08, 22 April 2013, para 108. See also *Von Hannover v Germany (No. 2)*, note 6, paras 104–107.

67 See *Evans v the United Kingdom*, [GC] No. 6339/05, para 77, ECHR 2007-I; *Chassagnou and Others v France*, [GC] Nos. 25088/94, 28331/95 and 28443/95, para 113, ECHR 1999-III; and *Ashby Donald and Others v France*, No. 36769/08, 10 January 2013, para 40.

68 *Dyundin v Russia*, No. 37406/03, 14 October 2008 at para 35.

Similarly, in *Lingens v Austria* (1986) the Court placed great emphasis on the public nature of the comments complained of as well as the fact that the claimant was a politician.[69] On the basis of proportionality (discussed above), it held that there was accordingly no need in that instance to read article 10 in the light of article 8.[70] The Court stressed that the limits of acceptable criticism are wider as regards a politician, as such, than for a private individual. As stated earlier, the Court in effect reasoned that because politicians 'inevitably and knowingly' lay themselves open to close scrutiny by both journalists and the public at large, they had to display a greater degree of tolerance – grow a thicker skin, as it were. It was held that without doubt, article 10(2) enables the reputation of all individuals to be protected, and this protection of course extends to politicians, too, even when they are not acting in their private capacity. But in cases like these the requirements of such protection have to be weighed in relation to the interests of open discussion of political issues.[71]

From the preceding discussion it is clear that the Court, as a matter of principle, guarantees that the rights in articles 8 and 10 deserve equal respect, and the outcome of an application should not, in principle, vary according to whether it has been lodged with the Court under article 10 of the Convention by the publisher of an offending article or under article 8 of the Convention by the person who was the subject of that article.[72] The Court's view is that, therefore, the margin of appreciation should in principle be the same in both cases[73] but adjusted according to the types of speech under scrutiny.

Proportionality

Given the importance of the doctrine of proportionality both in the ECtHR jurisprudence as well as in the courts of England and Wales, it bears repeating what the doctrine actually means. The most well-known definition from English case law about proportionality, is a dictum of Lord Diplock, describing proportionality as meaning '[i]n plain English, "you must not use a steam hammer to crack a nut, if a nutcracker would do."'[74] In practical terms, the doctrine entails the following: Not only are the two rights themselves weighed up against each other in the context of each individual case, the Court will also assess the proportionality of interfering with either right. Under the proportionality doctrine, any limitation of a right must have a legitimate aim, and the limitation must be both rationally connected to and necessary to achieve the aim. What is more, there must be no less restrictive alternative than the

69 *Lingens v Austria*, note 11.
70 Ibid, para 38.
71 Ibid, para 42.
72 *Delfi v Estonia*, No. 64569/09, 16 June 2015, para 139.
73 Ibid. See also *Axel Springer*, note 26, para 87, and *Von Hannover v Germany (No. 2)*, note 66, para 106.
74 *R v Goldstein* [1983] 1 WLR 151, 155B.

limitation. In other words, if the aim can be fulfilled via a less restrictive alternative, then the limitation will be held to be disproportionate.[75]

In making the proportionality assessment in the case of an intermediate facing liability for defamatory postings by third parties, the Court has also identified the following specific aspects of freedom of expression as being relevant for the concrete assessment of the interference in question[76] – the context of the comments, the measures applied by the company in order to prevent or remove defamatory comments, the liability of the actual authors of the comments as an alternative to the intermediary's liability, and the consequences of the domestic proceedings for the company.[77]

In case of a successful claim in defamation, the nature and severity of the possible sanctions are also balanced against the interference with freedom of expression guaranteed by article 10. So even if a claim in defamation succeeds, the penalty imposed may be found to be disproportionate. For example, in *Cumpănă and Mazăre v Romania* (2004) the Court stated that the nature and severity of the penalties imposed are factors to be taken into account when assessing the proportionality of an interference with the freedom of expression guaranteed by article 10.[78] The Court must also exercise the utmost caution where the measures taken or sanctions imposed by the national authorities are such as to dissuade the press from taking part in the discussion of matters of legitimate public concern.[79] The fear of disproportionate sanctions is thus recognised by the Court as having a potentially chilling effect on free speech, and therefore proportionality must be very carefully maintained.

The English common law of defamation was also subjected to the proportionality test in several instances at the ECtHR.[80] Two cases suffice to illustrate the point. The first concerned the common law 'multiple publication' rule, and the second the issue of whether fees and costs associated with common law libel claims were disproportionate. In *Times Newspapers Ltd v United Kingdom* [2009][81] the issue was whether the 'multiple publication' rule as applied in the courts of England and Wales, following the rule in *Duke of Brunswick v Harmer* (1849),[82] was disproportionate. The 'multiple publication' rule entails that each publication of defamatory words gave rise to a fresh publication so that a new cause of action accrues whenever the words are read by users. Given the nature of internet publication and/or archiving,

75 *Sunday Times v the United Kingdom*, No. 6538/74, 26 April 1979, para 6.

76 *Høiness v Norway*, No. 43624/14, 19 March 2019, para 67.

77 *Delfi*, note 72, paras 142–143 and *Magyar Tartalomszolgáltatók Egyesülete and Index.hu Zrt v Hungary*, No. 22947/13, 2 February 2016, para 69.

78 *Cumpănă and Mazăre v Romania*, [GC] No. 33348/96, ECHR 2004-XI.

79 Ibid, para 111.

80 See for instance the discussion of the disproportionate costs regime in the 'McLibel' case (*Steel and Morris v UK* [2005] 18 BHRC 545) in chapter 2, para 4.1.1.

81 *Times Newspapers Ltd v United Kingdom (ECHR, 10 March 2009)* [2009] EMLR, 14.

82 *Duke of Brunswick v Harmer* [1849] 14 QB 185.

this could be very onerous. Although 'proportionality' is not mentioned in the case, the words 'proportionate' and 'disproportionate' did come up in the judgment repeatedly, thus indicating that the court regarded proportionality to be an important determinant. One of the key characteristics of the common law 'multiple publication' rule was that a historic defamation claim could be revived long after the original statement was made. The Court emphasised that while an aggrieved applicant must be afforded a real opportunity to vindicate their right to reputation, libel proceedings brought against a newspaper after a significant lapse of time may well, in the absence of exceptional circumstances, give rise to a disproportionate interference with press freedom under article 10.[83]

In *MGN Ltd v United Kingdom* [2011][84] the issue was whether legal costs which far outstripped the nominal damages awarded to the claimant under the UK's 'Conditional Fee Arrangements' regime[85] were disproportionate. The applicants, Mirror Group Newspapers, were required in the domestic litigation to pay legal costs, in addition to their own, in the sum of £1,086,295.47 after an award of damages of only £3,500 was awarded to the model Naomi Campbell in her privacy claim against them.[86] The applicants argued that the disproportionate costs amounted to an infringement of their article 10 right to freedom of expression. It is informative to contrast the UK House of Lords'[87] stance on proportionality in this regard with that expressed in the ECtHR: Lord Hoffmann in the House of Lords did express concern about the indirect effect of the threat of heavy liability in terms of costs on the newspaper's decisions as to whether to publish information which ought to be published but which carried a risk of legal proceedings against it. However, he considered that the newspaper's right could be restricted to protect the rights of Ms Campbell under article 8 and the right of litigants under article 6 to access to a court. He further considered that the applicant's argument confused two concepts of proportionality: Whereas the Civil Procedure Rules on costs were concerned with whether expenditure on ligation was proportionate to the amount at stake, the interests of the parties and other relevant factors, article 10 was concerned with whether the rule requiring unsuccessful defendants to pay the reasonable and proportionate costs of their adversary and contribute to the funding of other ligation was a proportionate interference given that the aim was to provide those other litigants with access to justice. He

83 *Times Newspapers*, note 81, para 48. *In casu*, the Court however held on the facts that the finding by the domestic courts that the applicant had libelled the claimant by the continued publication on the internet of the two articles was a justified and proportionate restriction on the applicant's right to freedom of expression: para 49.

84 *MGN Ltd v United Kingdom*, No. 39401/04 [2011] 1 Costs LO 84.

85 See also the discussion of conditional fee arrangements in chapter 3 and in particular the discussion of the Supreme Court decision in *Times Newspapers Ltd v Flood* [2017] UKSC 33.

86 See *Campbell v Mirror Group Newspapers Ltd* [2004] UKHL 22.

87 Now the Supreme Court.

considered that it had been open to the legislature to choose to fund access to justice in that way. He also considered that it was desirable to have a general rule in order to enable the scheme to work in a practical and effective way and that concentration on the individual case and the particularities of Ms Campbell's circumstances would undermine that scheme. This explains the House of Lords' decision that Ms Campbell's success fee should not be disallowed simply on the ground that the applicant's liability would be inconsistent with its rights under article 10.[88]

By contrast, the ECtHR held that there had indeed been a violation of article 10 of the Convention as regards the success fees payable by the applicant.[89] The Court considered 'that the requirement that the applicant pay success fees to the claimant was disproportionate having regard to the legitimate aims sought to be achieved and exceeded even the broad margin of appreciation accorded to the Government in such matters.'[90]

Other doctrines

Finally, brief mention should be made that the Court also utilises other interpretive principles, apart from those discussed earlier, to judge whether a particular limit on free speech is justified. These include the 'practical and effective' doctrine, the 'living instrument' doctrine, and the 'positive obligations' doctrine. The 'practical and effective' doctrine states that all rights guaranteed under the Convention must be 'practical and effective' and not merely theoretical or illusory.[91] In terms of the 'living instrument' doctrine the Convention is interpreted in Court as a living instrument that needs to be interpreted against present day conditions.[92] Finally, the positive obligations doctrine means that it is sometimes necessary for states to act, rather than just refraining from acting, i.e. affirmative action is sometimes indicated rather than refraining from interfering with individuals' human rights.[93]

It is now useful to look at a specific case study to illustrate the points made earlier by comparing two ECtHR cases with fairly similar facts. At this point a simple caveat must be made: For common law readers, compared to reported cases from the common law, jurisprudence from the ECtHR does not always very clearly state the reasons for decisions or the principles on which such decisions are based. Having said that, there is still much to be gained from delving into substantial judgments emanating from the ECtHR.

88 See *Campbell v MGN Limited (No. 2)* [2005] UKHL 61, paras 23–28.

89 *MGN Ltd v United Kingdom*, No. 39401/04 [2011] 1 Costs LO 84, paras 215–219.

90 Ibid, para 219. See also Hughes, K 'Balancing Rights and the Margin of Appreciation: Article 10, Breach of Confidence and Success Fees' (2011) 3(1) *Journal of Media Law* 29–48.

91 *Airy v Ireland*, 9 October 1979, Series A No. 32, para 24.

92 *Tyrer v the United Kingdom*, 25 April 1978, Series A No. 26, para 31; *Matthews v the United Kingdom*, [GC] No. 24833/94, ECHR 1999-I, para 39.

93 McGonagle *et al.*, note 12, 13.

Application in the ECtHR: a case study of Delfi v Estonia *and* Høiness v Norway

Unfortunately, the Court is not always as consistent as one would hope for in its application of the principles discussed earlier. This can be illustrated by the differing conclusions reached on very similar facts in *Delfi v Estonia*[94] and *Høiness v Norway*.[95] Both cases involved defamation claims by well-known figures against online publishers of 'below the line' comments made by anonymous members of the public. These are comments that are posted by readers of online articles 'below the bottom line' as it were, of the published article. 'Below the line' comments are usually anonymous and are not always moderated by the online publications. In both cases before the Court, the defendants exercised no editorial control over the comments, and in both they deleted the comments that were complained of very speedily. The ECtHR in both instances upheld the findings of the respective national courts – but in the case of *Delfi* this meant that the defamation claim succeeded whereas in *Høiness* the claim failed.

The different results from fairly similar facts could at first glance be read as an inconsistency on the part of the ECtHR. However, it could also be argued that the Court was merely exercising its commitment to allowing a wide margin of appreciation whilst reserving the option to engage normatively should the need arise, such as where the national courts clearly did not correctly balance relevant competing Convention rights. It is therefore worthwhile reflecting on these two judgments as a case study of how the Court, whilst applying the same principles to similar facts, could nevertheless reach different conclusions.

Delfi v Estonia

It makes sense to start with the earlier case as it was subjected to a much more thorough treatment by the Grand Chamber of the ECtHR. In *Delfi* the applicant company were the owners of the *Delfi* news portal, with large readership in Estonia and Lithuania. *Delfi* had published a critical but non-contentious article about a large public limited company, 'SLK,' which in turn elicited 185 comments in a 24-hour period, 20 of which were identified as containing personal threats and were offensive against the sole shareholder of SLK.[96] SLK successfully sued the defendant in libel based on these 'below the line' comments, despite the fact that most of the comments were made anonymously and that there was evidence that the defendant had in effect censored many of the most inflammatory statements and had removed the offensive comments

94 *Delfi*, note 72.
95 *Høiness v Norway*, No. 43624/14, 19 March 2019.
96 *Delfi*, note 72, paras 11–17.

when requested.[97] The ECtHR affirmed this decision and held the internet portal (that is the publisher of an online newspaper) liable for offensive comments made by its readers.

The parties did not dispute that the domestic courts' decisions in respect of the applicant (the publishing company Delfi) constituted an interference with its freedom of expression, but the applicant contended that this was not justified. Another contention – namely, the possibility of suing the makers of the statements rather than newspaper – was given short shrift by the Court: In principle, this was possible, but in reality, many of the posts were anonymous and the identity of the potential defendants was thus very difficult if not impossible to ascertain.[98]

In its reasoning the Court stated that when examining whether there is a need for an interference with freedom of expression in a democratic society in the interests of the 'protection of the reputation or rights of others' (as stipulated in article 10(2)), the Court may be required to ascertain whether the domestic authorities have struck a fair balance when protecting two values guaranteed by the Convention which may come into conflict with each other in certain cases – namely, on the one hand, freedom of expression protected by article 10, and on the other, the right to respect for private life enshrined in article 8.[99] However, the Court stopped short of suggesting that the article 8 right to privacy had come into play, stating that for the article 8 right to protection of reputation to be engaged, the attack must be made in a manner causing serious prejudice to the personal enjoyment of private life.[100]

So how did it go about judging whether or not the defamation claim in Estonia had struck the correct balance? The Court reiterated the principle that an interference with the applicant's right to freedom of expression had to be 'prescribed by law,' have one or more legitimate aims in the light of article 10(2) of the Convention, and be 'necessary in a democratic society.'[101] The Court proceeded to accord various weights to factors that were to be placed on this balance. These can be summarised as three main areas of concern: The fact that the speech under scrutiny were uttered in the context of a commercial venture, foreseeability as a fault element, and the culpability of an internet intermediary.

In assessing the context of the comments, the ECtHR attached great weight to the fact that the *Delfi* news portal was a commercially and professionally operated site which actively encouraged comments in order to maximise advertising revenue.[102] As such, the anonymity allowed on the comments

97 Ibid, para 18.
98 Ibid, paras 84–87, 91.
99 Ibid, para 110.
100 Ibid, para 137.
101 Ibid, para 7.
102 Ibid, para 144.

section, whilst indubitably encouraging free speech, had to be weighed against the rights and freedoms of others in the light of this consideration.[103] This stance is clearly displayed by Judge Zupančič in his concurring opinion, when he stated 'to enable technically the publication of extremely aggressive forms of defamation, all this due to crass commercial interest, and then to shrug one's shoulders, maintaining that an Internet provider is not responsible for these attacks on the personality rights of others, is totally unacceptable.'[104] Serious issue can be taken with this stance,[105] and it is submitted that the correct position is that espoused by Judges Sajó and Tsotoria in their dissenting opinion, where they argued that to find that responsibility of any speaker, including the press, is enhanced by the presence of an economic interest is going too far. Furthermore, they pointed out, this is not in line with previous case law.[106]

The comments in question had been insulting, threatening and defamatory. The Court clearly placed a high value on the fact that the nature of these comments was foreseeable by the applicant. The article's nature was provocative, and as such, the Court opined that the applicant should have expected offensive posts and therefore have exercised an extra degree of caution so as to avoid a defamation action. The applicant did use filters, and it did remove offensive comments when notified. However, the Court found that the former was easy to circumvent and the other measures were ineffective to prevent harm being caused to others. This essentially moves away from a traditional requirement of actual knowledge to the lesser requirement of constructive knowledge and arguably creates strict liability for the dissemination of such comments.[107]

It is widely recognised that there are clear differences between a traditional media publisher and a news intermediary. It could therefore be argued that the relative ease with which the Court accepted an intermediary as a publisher of the comments indicate that the Court failed to truly distinguish between the two.[108] The reality, it is submitted, falls somewhere in between, with the Court recognising that in this case the applicant, albeit an internet intermediary, did exercise some editorial control over the comments. The Court stressed the measure of editorial control exercised by the applicant. The publication of both the news articles and also subsequent readers' comments was part of the applicant company's professional activity. Its advertising revenue depended on the number of readers and/or their comments. Furthermore, publishing on

103 Ibid, para 147.

104 Ibid, Concurring Opinion of Judge Zupančič.

105 See Hall, J 'User-Generated Content on the Internet, and Intermediate Liability for the Dissemination of Unlawful Comments in the European Court of Human Rights' (2017) *Nottingham Law Journal* 103, 107–108.

106 *Delfi*, note 72. Joint Dissenting Opinion of Judges Sajó and Tsotoria, para 28.

107 Hall, note 105, 108.

108 Ibid, 107.

a large internet news portal, such as that of the applicant means that a wide audience is reached. The Court noted that

> the applicant company – and not a person whose reputation could be at stake – was in a position to know about an article to be published, to predict the nature of the possible comments prompted by it and, above all, to take technical or manual measures to prevent defamatory statements from being made public.

It was also significant, as an indication of editorial control, that the actual writers of comments could not modify or delete their comments once posted on the *Delfi* news portal and that only the applicant itself could do this.[109] Finally, the Court noted that considering that the applicant company was a professional operator of one of the largest internet news portals in Estonia, a damages award given by the domestic court to the equivalent of EUR 320 in non-pecuniary damages could not be seen as disproportionate.

The impact of this case mainly relates to the increasing possibility faced by publishers for being found liable for 'below the line' comments over which it may be difficult to exercise editorial control. However, the case is further significant because it set the precedent that an attack on personal honour and reputation must be sufficiently serious before article 8 of the Convention will be engaged.[110] In this respect it is congruent with the 'serious harm' threshold set in English defamation law, discussed in the previous chapters.[111] In this sense also it clarifies the line of cases discussed earlier, which stated that the Court was under a duty to include an article 8 analysis in cases engaging article 10, i.e. by stating *when* this duty was triggered.

The same issues came before the Court again in the following case.

Høiness v Norway[112]

In November 2010, a series of objectifying and vulgar comments about a prominent Norwegian lawyer and television personality, Mona Høiness, were posted on a discussion forum operated by the online news portal *Hegnar Online*. Ms Høiness sued the news portal and its editor for defamation, averring amongst others that her honour had been infringed. As to the fact that the discussion forum was distinct from the editorial content of the online edition, she argued that the defendants had the same editorial responsibility for the comments as if they had been letters from readers printed in a

109 Para 89.

110 Para 137.

111 See the discussion of section 1 of the Defamation Act 2013 and the related jurisprudence in chapter 3.

112 *Høiness v Norway*, No. 43624/14, 19 March 2019.

newspaper.[113] At first instance and at appeal, the Norwegian courts held that, in accordance with the penal code governing defamation in Norway, the claim could not succeed as the defendants had not acted negligently – they had taken down the offending statements within seconds of being notified.[114] Furthermore, the courts were of the view that the anonymous statements in the forum, albeit tasteless and vulgar, were not sufficiently 'serious' to found a libel claim. In fact, the court at first instance remarked that 'most readers would find that the comments said more about those posting them than about the people mentioned in the comments.'[115]

Permission to appeal to the Norwegian Supreme Court having been denied, the applicant-initiated proceedings at the ECtHR, averring that the domestic authorities, by not sufficiently protecting her right to respect for her private life (and requiring her to pay the defendants' costs in her failed claims against them), had acted contrary to her article 8 rights.[116] However, in a marked departure from their decision on similar facts in *Delfi*, the ECtHR did not uphold her claim. It held that the domestic courts had acted within their margin of appreciation when seeking the balance between Høiness's article 8 rights and the defendants' opposing right of expression under article 10. The Court followed its precedent from *Delfi* by reiterating the seriousness threshold before article 8 is engaged.[117] In this regard, the Court also considered the kind of speech that was complained of. The ECtHR considered it unnecessary to examine the nature of the impugned comments in depth because they did not amount to protected speech, such as hate speech or incitement to violence.[118]

The decision in *Delfi*, being delivered by the Grand Chamber of the ECtHR, was much more detailed than the Court's later decision in *Høiness*. In *Delfi*, for instance, the Grand Chamber of the Court examined in detail not only its own relevant jurisprudence but also other relevant international law principles,[119] and it paid special attention to relevant European Union instruments[120] and case law from the Court of Justice of the European Union (CJEU).[121] In particular, the Court examined the CJEU decision in *Google*

113 Ibid, para 22.
114 Para 39.
115 Para 26.
116 Para 48.
117 *Høiness*, note 112, para 64.
118 Ibid, para 69.
119 See *Delfi*, note 72, paras 44–47 for the Court's discussion of Council of Europe documents and paras 48–49 for the United Nations Human Rights Council's report by the special rapporteur on the promotion and protection of the right to freedom of opinion and expression (A/HRC/17/27 of 16 May 2011).
120 *Delfi*, note 72, paras 50–51. The Court scrutinised, in detail, Council Directives on electronic commerce (Directive 2000/31/EC); and Directive 94/38/EC on information provision and rules.
121 *Delfi*, note 72, paras 53–57.

Spain SL (2014),[122] which is known as the case that established the European 'right to be forgotten.' The CJEU considered that a fair balance should be sought between the legitimate interest of internet users in having access to the information and the data subject's fundamental rights. The data subject's fundamental rights, as a general rule, overrode the interest of internet users, but that balance might, however, depend on the nature of the information in question and its sensitivity for the data subject's private life and on the interest of the public in having that information. The CJEU held that in certain cases the operator of a search engine was obliged to remove from the list of results displayed following a search made on the basis of a person's name links to web pages, published by third parties and containing information relating to that person, even when its publication in itself on the web pages in question was lawful. This is now generally known as the 'right to be forgotten.'

The Court in *Delfi* then noted the CJEU *Papasavvas* (2014) case,[123] which concerned a defamation claim against an internet intermediary for statements made on its online platform. The CJEU found that, since a newspaper publishing company, which posted an online version of a newspaper on its website, had, in principle, knowledge of the information which it posted and exercised control over that information, it could not be considered to be an 'intermediary service provider' within the meaning of the E-Commerce Directive, whether or not access to that website was free of charge.[124] Thus, it held that the limitations of civil liability specified in the Directive[125] did not apply to the case of a newspaper publishing company which operated a website on which the online version of a newspaper was posted, that company being, moreover, remunerated by income generated by commercial advertisements posted on the website, since it had knowledge of the information posted and exercised control over that information, whether or not access to the website was free of charge. It is surprising that the CJEU in *Papasavvas* nowhere considered the arguably relevant free speech implications of the claim[126] and also that this omission was not noted by the ECtHR in its scrutiny of that case in *Delfi*.

Be that as it may, what is clear from these two apparently contrasting cases is that the threshold that must be surpassed before liability in defamation is imposed by the Strasbourg court is set very high. Up until recently, the bar for liability at the domestic level may have been set considerably lower, making it difficult for domestic decision-makers to impose the domestic legislation

122 *Google Spain SL and Google Inc.*, CJEU Case C-131/12, 13 May 2014.
123 *Sotiris Papasavvas*, C-291/13, 11 September 2014.
124 Articles 12 to 14 of Directive 2000/31/EC.
125 Ibid.
126 For information on the CJEU's stance in this area, see Jones, M 'EU Law Relating to Online Infringement of Personality Rights – Is EU Law Effective in Preventing Forum Shopping for the Pursuit of Actions Arising from Online Infringement of Personality Rights?' in Weaver, RL *et al.* (eds), *Privacy in a Digital Age Perspectives from Two Continents* (Carolina Academic Press, Durham, North Carolina, 2017), 47, 66–68.

whilst adhering to their obligations to apply the legal principles flowing from the ECHR and ECtHR. This has become even more of an issue given the slew of recent legislative efforts to curb undesirable online speech in a number of jurisdictions, including the European Union, the UK, and Germany. In the EU, the Digital Services Act,[127] fully operational from 2024, strengthens and retains the essence of the notice and takedown procedure.[128] Germany's Network Enforcement Act (NetzDG) mandates that social media companies delete what it calls 'manifestly unlawful' posts on their platforms within 24 hours of being notified or risk facing fines up to £44 million. The UK's recently enacted Online Safety Act 2023 (OSA) goes even further – whereas the EU Digital Services Act stops short of enabling member states mandating the monitoring of user content, and whereas the NetzDG at least requires 'manifestly unlawful' before such intervention, the OSA places a duty of care on social media platforms to protect users from not only illegal content but also much more fuzzily defined 'harmful' content. A new regulator will be responsible for drawing up codes of conduct and with powers to impose a range of sanctions, including fines, if the duty of care is not met. The statutory duty of care will be imposed on a whole range of digital players of all sizes and would force them to put in place a range of measures to protect their users from 'online harms.'[129] It is clear that these moves are not exactly favourable for free speech. What is less clear is how the decision in *Høiness* will interact with these examples of domestic legislation from Convention members.

Analysis

The United Kingdom is a signatory to the European Convention of Human Rights. As such, and in terms of the Human Rights Act 1998, English courts are under a duty to develop the law in accordance with the various rights and freedoms contained in the Convention. It also means that their decisions should, as far as not in conflict with primary legislation, be compatible with Convention rights,[130] and this in turn means that the courts are under an obligation to consider the decision emanating from the ECtHR on Convention interpretation and application.

But apart from this legal obligation, it is also very useful from a purely theoretical, and/or a comparative legal perspective, to take note of ECtHR case law. It seems as if the senior judiciary in their deliberations are increasingly,

127 Regulation (EU) 2022/2065 of the European Parliament and of the Council of 19 October 2022 on a Single Market for Digital Services and amending Directive 2000/31/EC (Digital Services Act).

128 See Church, P and Pehlivan, CN 'The Digital Services Act (DSA): A New Era for Online Harms and Intermediary Liability' (2023) 4(1) *Global Privacy Law Review* 53–59.

129 See Jones, M 'Regulation of Online Speech in the UK' (2024) 55(2) *University of the Pacific Law Review* 261 for a discussion of the Online Safety Act.

130 Section 2 of the Human Rights Act 1998.

in addition to common law jurisdictions, also referring to European decisions both from the ECtHR and the CJEU.[131] It may be very fruitful to keep a close eye on defamation judgments from the ECtHR in general as these provide a handy summary of the way in which the tension between free speech concerns and reputational and/or privacy rights are resolved in other European countries. In this way the ECtHR jurisprudence could be viewed as a mirror of the zeitgeist concerning these issues and of intrinsic value.

From the preceding discussion, a few issues relevant to the central themes of this book deserve to be highlighted.

Balancing speech with reputation

In moving away from treating the right to reputation as a narrowly construed internal exception to article 10 rights and according it the status of a fully fledged right to be balanced on equal terms with freedom of expression, it may be queried whether the ECtHR is taking sufficient account of the potential chilling effect on freedom of expression. It could very well be argued that there is currently an almost Europe wide trend towards restrictions on speech. This is evidenced by both pronouncements, such as the *Google Spain* 'right to be forgotten' cases,[132] as well as tightening of regulation of speech, such as the recently enacted General Data Protection Regulation (GDPR),[133] the Digital Services Act, the NetzDG, and in the UK, the Online Safety Act. Given that a balance skewed against free speech is a spectre that the UK only recently tackled with some will in the Defamation Act 2013, it may be of some concern that it seems as if the direction in which the ECtHR is heading is more commensurate with a conservative approach to judicial interpretation of the 2013 Act. For these reasons, what happens in Europe should be of concern to freedom of speech advocates in the UK.

The proportionality test

At first glance the ECtHR's adherence to the proportionality principle is laudable. But it needs to be kept in mind that proportionality as such is a relative concept, with this question always remaining: Relative to what? It has been

131 Gilliker, P *The Europeanisation of English Tort Law* (Hart Publishing, Oxford and Portland, Oregon, 2014).

132 Note 122.

133 Regulation (EU) 2016/679 ('GDPR') adopted on 27 April 2016. The GDPR came into force in 2018. For a critique of European data protection laws, see Pearce, H 'A Systems Approach to Data Protection Law and Policy in a World of Big Data?' (2016) 22(4) *Computer and Telecommunications Law Review* 90, 90–93; and on some of the implications of the GDPR see Jones, M 'Privilege, Power and the Perversion of Privacy Protection,' in Weaver, RL *et al.* (eds), *Comparative Perspectives on Privacy in an Internet Era, The Global Papers Series* (Carolina Academic Press, Durham, North Carolina, 2019), vol VII, 141–164.

pointed out that although proportionality matters very much in law, its moral dimension is elusive. A reference to this principle could be regarded as being elliptical since there is no moral principle to act proportionately *tout court*. For example, it is usually a specific type of action that one should take in proportion to a specific factor; one should use force in self-defence in proportion to the seriousness of the threat that the attacker poses, or one should punish in proportion to the gravity of the wrong.[134]

In this sense, what may be interpreted as a recent procedural shift in the balancing exercise performed by the ECtHR may prove to be of concern as it may well come at the cost of the Court's willingness to engage with issues at a normative or substantive level.[135] This brings us back to the fact that the ECtHR started out with giving free speech a lot of weight and now see it as only one of many rights.

Margin of appreciation: types of speech

The Court differentiates between kinds of speech, giving them higher and lower degrees of protection according to where they fit on the spectrum of speech. This makes sense and reflects the position in many other jurisdictions, including those subject to the jurisdiction of the ECtHR.

Finally, it must be noted that the vote to leave the European Union does not affect, without more, the UK's relationship with the ECtHR and its jurisprudence and therefore until such time as (and if) the UK ends this relationship, the ECHR and the decisions by the ECtHR will continue to play an important part in domestic jurisprudence.

Against this background, i.e. the of jurisprudence from a supranational jurisdiction and court which the courts in England and Wales are to a certain extent bound to follow, the comparative analyses undertaken in this book may now be assessed in full in the next and final chapter.

134 Letsas, G 'Proportionality as Fittingness: The Moral Dimension of Proportionality' (2018) 71(1) *Current Legal Problems* 53, 54–55, 86.

135 See the earlier discussion, as well as the comments by Propelier and Van de Heyning, note 63.

7 Analysis and conclusions

It has long been argued that the UK common law of defamation chilled free speech. Litigation was costly, protracted, and complex. The structure of the tort favoured claimants, with the aid of several legal presumptions whose inherent merit was (and remains) questionable. Academics, consumers, scientists, victims of crime, journalists, and others complained about being silenced in freely disseminating opinions and thoughts. High-profile instances of libel tourism resulted, prompting various actors including the United States federal government, the European Parliament, and the UK government itself, to call for reform. The Defamation Act 2013, which came into effect in 2014, was an ambitious and long-awaited attempt at redressing the balance. This book attempted to gauge the effectiveness of the UK Defamation Act 2013 in achieving the primary aims for which it was enacted. Of these, the key question informing this enquiry is to which extent the Act succeeded in redressing the balance between freedom of speech on the one hand, and the protection of reputation, on the other. Under this broad umbrella closely related issues were examined, such as whether the inequality of arms between defamation claimants and defendants were resolved by the Act and whether the issue of libel tourism (itself an indication of the imbalance between the parties in a defamation suit) was adequately addressed. In addressing these issues, three main premises were followed: The analysis was confined to those aspects of the Defamation Act 2013 that bear on the restriction of freedom of speech; the terms freedom of speech, freedom of expression, and free speech were used interchangeably; and the corresponding law in three key foreign jurisdictions were examined to try and gauge insights and bases of comparison. These jurisdictions are the United States (US), Germany, and the case law of the European Court of Human Rights (ECtHR).

The main argument throughout this book has been that although the Defamation Act 2013 goes a long way towards redressing the balance in favour of free speech, it does not go nearly far enough – especially when a more holistic view is taken and further threats to free speech are considered, such as emanate from rapidly evolving areas of law, including privacy, data protection, and online regulation.

DOI: 10.4324/9781003416005-8

The value of a comparative analysis

A comparative analysis of relevant jurisdictions is a valuable exercise, not only in the abstract, but also in practical terms. Globalised speech magnifies both the potential for almost limitless and free expression, but this is at the cost of potentially devastating harm to individuals' reputation. It also certainly poses difficult private international/choice of law problems and, where a particular jurisdiction becomes known as claimant-friendly, serves to encourage forum shopping. This was a particular problem for the UK, as it was (rightly or wrongly) seen as the 'libel capital of the world.' The European Parliament in 2012 termed the UK libel law the most claimant-friendly in the world. It was also seen as a national humiliation when in 2010 the US promulgated laws rendering defamation awards granted in English courts unenforceable in the US. Given the increasingly interconnected nature of the world, negative sentiment such as these expressed by traditional allies and trading partners of the UK are doubtless of concern to policymakers. Domestic defamation reform, therefore, had an international element, and as a result, it is fruitful to compare the legal landscape in prominent and relevant jurisdictions. A brief aide-memoire as to the choice of comparator jurisdictions: The US is the logical first choice for a comparator jurisdiction where freedom of expression is strongly protected. The continental perspective is reflected in the choice of examining the legal regime in Germany, a leading member of the European Union. Out of the European jurisdictions, Germany makes a natural choice because, just like the US, its laws operate under a strong and well-developed element of constitutional protection given to the competing rights under consideration. To supplement this, relevant case law from the ECtHR is also examined. As the members of the EU are signatories of the European Convention of Human Rights (ECHR) for which the ECtHR is the dispute resolution body, an array of continental thought on defamation and free speech is available. ECtHR judgments are also important because of the commitment of the UK through the Human Rights Act 1998 in honouring and implementing the provisions of the ECHR.

Before focusing on the core enquiry of this book and proffering some thoughts on successes, best practices, missed opportunities and tentative suggestions, a brief synopsis of the key concepts from each chapter:

Reputation, speech, and the events that led to the Defamation Act 2013

Chapter 2 reflected on the two central concepts which are engaged by defamation law – namely, reputation and free expression. Both of these values were examined through the lens of societal interests. The chapter first examined the reasons that free speech is, or should be, legally protected. Several of the most important theoretical bases underlying the value of free speech allocate the benefit of free speech in this manner. For instance, John Stuart Mill's stated goal in *On Liberty* was to identify the nature and limits of the power which can be legitimately exercised by society over the individual. His famous argument from truth emphasises the interests of society in discovering the truth. The argument goes that society should not merely tolerate but embrace speech that is considered objectionable. There are four main reasons for this: Nobody is infallible, and therefore, we must be open to the possibility that an opinion that deviates from the mainstream might be true. Next, even where an argument is substantially wrong, it may still contain a portion of truth that is missing from the accepted opinion. If the prevailing opinion is completely true, it still needs to be open to challenge for it is only through frequent challenge and vigorous defence that those who hold the opinion can fully understand the rational grounds for the opinion. Finally, related to the last point and of particular importance to our current analysis, Mill argues that in the absence of vigorous debate, the meaning of the doctrine itself will be in danger of being lost, or enfeebled, and deprived of its vital effect on character and conduct. In short, an argument may persuade the audience members to change their minds, or it may cause them to defend their stance on the matter. Either way, the focus is on the argument, the message, and the speech rather than the speaker. The speaker has the right to free speech only as a function of delivering the message.

Free speech is also defended through the lens of citizen participation in a democracy. Exponents of political speech emphasise the importance of the electorate being able to access a variety of opinions on political and social matters. A further theory explores free speech as an aspect of individual self-fulfilment or autonomy and holds that the justification for freedom of speech proceeds from the right of an individual to consider all the arguments and views that may determine their course of action. Of course, the liberal notion of individual autonomy also includes the speaker's right to determine the content of their speech. The categorisation of the right as being a societal good is clear.

Against this background, the *raison d'être* for defamation law, i.e. reputational interest, was examined next. It is commonly accepted that reputation could be regarded as personal property, or as part of a person's honour, or as a function of the inherent dignity of all human beings, and thus worthy of protection for one or all or a combination of these reasons. It was submitted that it is often overlooked that there is also a clear societal interest underlying these values.

The image of the market society underlies and informs the view of reputation as property. This view resonates strongly with the pervasive neoliberal worldview and also explains why non-human actors, such as companies, are able to sue in defamation. In short, this view of reputation sees it as a form of intangible property that may be damaged and, as such, result in monetary loss which can be compensated. When looking at the next view of reputation, that of 'honour,' it is interesting to remember that the civil law of defamation in England in large part developed because the Star Chamber outlawed duelling, the traditional means of restoring honour. The modern conception of 'honour' arguably confuses the external concept of honour with the internal concept of the inherent dignity of man and may be reflected in the grand and ongoing project of the current and previous century – namely, the idea and practice of human rights. However, all the elements of a cause of action in defamation in the common law confirm that what is protected is an external conception of image rather than an internal conception of self. This is later contrasted with the German and, to an extent, also the ECtHR's interpretation of reputation at least overlapping with the subjective element of inherent human dignity. Everything that the claimant needs to prove in a UK defamation trial focuses on the attitudes of the community – that the statement identified the claimant directly or indirectly, that it was defamatory, and that it was made public through publication to a third party. As such, it is the projection of the self to society that the law protects and it is argued that this is, in the UK at least, the core interest protected by defamation law. The common denominator in reputation as property and as honour is the involvement of society, of other people. The value of the company's reputation is determined by society's view, as is the *de facto* reputation of the individual.

It was therefore argued that reputation as the focus of defamation law is a societal construct that seeks to mediate the relationship between individuals and the society in which they exist. Whereas any single one of these reasons (property, honour, dignity) seem inadequate to fully explain the law's protection of reputation, when taken in combination a more coherent rationale emerges. The importance placed on one aspect of reputation over another also goes some way in explaining the differences in legal norms and approaches across the jurisdictions examined in this book. For instance, in Germany the constitutional emphasis is on human dignity, and this is clearly reflected and indeed imbedded in the German law of defamation. In the US, where the primary constitutional norm is freedom of expression, reputation can rightly be seen as relegated to property – valuable property but no more than property. In England and Wales, the notion of reputation as a person's abstract 'other,' i.e. their honour, survives the legislative reform.

Lord Nicholls in *Reynolds* explained how reputation is important both to the individual concerned and to society more generally:

> Reputation is an integral and important part of the dignity of the individual. It also forms the basis of many important decisions in a democratic society which are fundamental to its well-being: whom to employ or work for, whom to promote, whom to do business with or vote for. Once besmirched by an unfounded allegation in a national newspaper, a reputation can be damaged forever, especially if there is no opportunity to vindicate one's reputation. When this happens, society as well as the individual is the loser. For it should not be supposed that protection of reputation is a matter of importance only to the affected individual and

> his family. Protection of reputation is conducive to the public good. It is in the public interest that the reputation of public figures should not be debased falsely. In the political field, in order to make an informed, choice, the electorate needs to be able to identify the good as well as the bad.[1]

Societal interests in free speech and reputation can therefore be brought squarely into Mill's argument from truth, and the scene was therefore set to evaluate the Defamation Act 2013 from this perspective. It bears repeating that one of the main drivers of legal reform was the chilling effect of the common law of defamation on free speech. It was argued that the main reason for this was the unequal playing field between defamation claimants and defendants. The structure of defamation law and litigation itself handed an advantage to the claimant for which, it is submitted, there exists no real justification. Several characteristics of the common law combined to give an unfair advantage to libel claimants. The costs associated with bringing or defending a defamation claim were prohibitive. In the absence of a tribunal or other alternative dispute resolution forum for defamation, court remained the only option for such disputes, with the result that it seemed that only the rich and powerful had unfettered access to legal protection of their reputations. Impecunious defendants, faced with potentially being bankrupted by defending their words in a libel claim, could be bullied into silence by the mere threat of being sued. When McDonald's' defamation suit against critics turned into the longest and most expensive civil trial in UK history, the UK defamation law regime was confirmed as being inadequate in terms of access to justice when the matter was adjudicated by the ECtHR.

Furthermore, three principles peculiar to the common law fundamentally favoured defamation claimants – a legal presumption that the allegedly defamatory statement was false, combined with an irrebuttable presumption of damages, and finally the strict liability nature of libel and some slander claims. Milo referred to these as the 'potent trilogy of defamation law,' which combined to place a de facto reverse burden of proof on the defamation defendant. If one accepts that there is no inherent reason to accord such advantage to the defamation claimant, and that it tilts the balance in favour of reputation and away from speech, the logical conclusion is that in order to address free speech concerns, the advantage given to defamation claimants needed to be removed. A level playing field needed to be ensured in the defamation trial. This and addressing free speech concerns were stated reasons for the reform of the defamation law which culminated in the Defamation Act 2013.

1 *Reynolds v Times Newspapers Ltd* [1999] 3 WLR 1010, para 201D with Lord Cooke of Thorndon and Lord Hobhouse of Woodborough concurring.

The Defamation Act 2013

Chapter 3 scrutinised the Defamation Act 2013 and case law subsequent to its coming in force in 2014. The discussion was loosely delimited by examining whether and to what extent the 2013 reforms addressed a particularly potent trilogy of legal presumptions assisting the defamation claimant – namely, the presumptions of falsity, harm, and strict liability. At the debates for the Defamation Act 1996, it was suggested that the burden of proof be placed on the claimant to prove that the defamatory words of which they complained were false. However, this idea got no traction, and neither did the notion of abolishing no-fault liability for defamation. It was argued that this was an unfortunate choice, as a true commitment to free speech would have been reflected in aligning the law in this way. Placing the burden of proof on the claimant would have meant that the press, and others, would be free to raise questions about the conduct of people, such as, for instance, Jimmy Savile.

The most far-reaching and meaningful change to the law was effected by the inclusion of the requirement in section 1 of the 2013 Act which states that a statement is not defamatory unless it causes (or is likely to cause) serious harm to the reputation of the claimant. However, the question as to what constitutes serious harm proved to be difficult to resolve and gave rise to debate about whether or not this section abolished the common law presumption of harm. The issue went all the way to the Supreme Court in *Lachaux*,[2] where it was held that 'serious harm' within the meaning of section 1(1) cannot be demonstrated only by reference to the inherent tendency of the words themselves, as was the case under the common law. The Supreme Court therefore held that not only is the threshold of seriousness raised, but proof is also now required, on the facts, that the impact of the words was to harm the claimant's reputation. This was a strong indication by the Supreme Court that the lawmaker intended to make a major change rather than just to raise the bar. Since this significantly adds to the evidentiary burden faced by the defamation claimant, it goes a long way towards tilting the field more level with the defamation defendant and, in that way, may be seen as a gain for free speech advocates. Indeed, the statistics which reflect a significant drop in defamation claims being pursued might very well signal that many would-be claimants realise that they would fail at this first hurdle and decide not to pursue a claim at all: For example, the Ministry of Justice 2022 statistics report a 60% decrease in the number of defamation claims issued in London, compared to 2021,[3] while independent observers consider even that number to be too conservative.[4]

2 *Lachaux v Independent Print Ltd and another* [2019] UKSC 27.

3 Ministry of Justice, Civil justice statistics quarterly <www.gov.uk/government/statistics/civil-justice-statistics-quarterly-january-to-march-2022> accessed 31 October 2023.

4 Inforrm Blog, *Judicial Statistics, 2022: A 60% Decrease in Issued Defamation Claims but Doubts Remain over the Reliability of the Figures* (21 June 2023), <https://inforrm.org/2023/06/21/

In a nod to the impact of the McLibel litigation, for the serious harm threshold in section 1(2), in case of bodies trading for profits, harm is not 'serious' unless it has caused or is likely to cause serious financial loss to the body. Section 1(2) also gave rise to interpretational difficulties, but it is submitted that the Supreme Court's decision in *Lachaux*, even though it did not address the issue of corporate claimants directly, provides clarity here too. If the presumption of damage did not survive for section 1(1), it cannot survive for section 1(2), as the latter is meant to be a narrower construct than the former.

The presumption of falsity was addressed next. Under the common law, upon proof by the claimant that a defamatory statement of fact identifying the claimant had been published, a presumption arose that the statement was false. The legal burden of proof then shifted to the defendant to prove that the statement was substantially true. Lord Lester, veteran campaigner for libel reform, arguably voiced the frustration of many critics when he stated that '[v]illains can (and frequently do) recover substantial damages in libel without having to show that what has been published about them is false.'[5] However, policy-makers, jurists and other commentators proved to be remarkably resistant to the idea of abolishing this presumption, and it remains firmly entrenched.[6] The arguments in favour of retaining the presumption can be summarised as comprising a reluctance to break with longstanding precedent; the notion that reputation deserves to be protected robustly in this way by the courts; the conviction that the existence of robust defences, such as honest opinion and truth, mitigates the harshness of the presumption; and the argument that burdening claimants with proving falsity requires them to prove a negative.

It was submitted that these reasons are unsatisfactory, especially given that the English law of defamation remains committed to the proposition that a claimant is not entitled to recover damages for injury to a (positive) reputation which they do not in fact have. Here it is necessary to pause and reflect again on the concept of reputation, for this is what defamation exists to protect. As stated earlier, all the elements of a cause of action in defamation confirm that reputation is an external conception of image, rather than an internal conception of self and it is the projection of the self to society that the law protects. Therefore, an individual's reputation is determined as a matter of objective fact. Nor can the reasons for retaining the presumption of falsity be justified in the light of the societal interests underlying the right to free speech discussed earlier. Surely, the argument from truth would be best served if the person

---

judicial-statistics-2022-a-60-decrease-in-issued-defamation-claims-but-doubts-remain-over-the-reliability-of-the-figures/> accessed 31 October 2023.

5 *Hansard* HL Deb Col 240 (2 April 1996).

6 Attempts to change the burden of proof failed in Australia too: See New South Wales Law Reform Commission, *Defamation*, Report 75 (NSW Law Reform Commission, Sydney, 1995) and the earlier *Defamation*, Discussion Paper 32 (NSW Law Reform Commission, Sydney, 1993).

who is best placed to know the factual statements concerning themselves, that is the claimant, is put to the proof. It is therefore unjust that the truth (or not) of a statement allegedly affecting the claimant's reputation remains a burden that should be borne by the defendant. This is especially so, given that there are other areas of law in which the claimant is required to prove falsity, such as malicious falsehood and negligent misrepresentation. Nor is this a universally accepted notion outside of the UK – in the United States the burden is on the claimant to prove falsity.

So two out of the three main structural issues that were identified as being problematic in the common law of defamation remain fundamentally unaltered by the Defamation Act 2013. The main difference is that now the serious harm threshold falls to be decided on facts rather than on a presumption arising from the import of the words complained of. Whilst this is positive news from a free speech perspective, overall the Act still amended the law in a piecemeal rather than a revolutionary fashion. The procedure faced by parties to a claim of defamation is streamlined and slimmed down but still remains a daunting prospect. The burden of proof remains largely on the defendant. This brings us then to the Act's changes affecting the defamation defendant.

The 2013 Act shrinks the potential pool of defamation defendants, through sections aimed at preventing libel tourism and curbing the potential liability of intermediaries. Together with other legal changes such as the reform of conditional fee arrangements, it will indubitably reduce costs both in terms of potential damages awards and legal costs. The fact that, for all intents and purposes, jury trials are now abolished for defamation claims should also keep costs and damages awards down. The Johnny Depp trial outcome is perhaps a stark illustration of the result of 'depriving' a libel claimant of the right to a jury trial. Despite all this, costs nevertheless remain a very large problem, as legal aid is still not available except for defendants facing a defamation claim by a multinational corporation. Costs and complexity mean that the reformed defamation law of England and Wales can still be criticised from an access to justice perspective. Also, since the costs of defending a defamation claim are still potentially high and prohibitive, it is debatable whether the chilling effect on free speech has been adequately addressed in the reforms.

Prior to the 2013 reforms, calls were made that English defamation law should be developed so that expression on matters of public concern or public interest should receive greater protection than other speech. To a large extent this already happened in the courts in England and Wales. The common law Reynolds defence, for example, protected *prima facie* defamatory statements published on matters of public interest. Defamation judges making short shrift of vexatious claims reflect this principle. The inclusion in the Defamation Act 2013 of a defence specifically protecting speech on matters of public interest further sharpens the protection given to this type of speech. Here we need to pause and reflect on the saga of Mr Serafin, a litigant in person whose trials and tribulations experienced during his 'day in court' may serve as a cautionary tale to other would-be libel claimants. Albeit obiter, the Supreme Court in *Serafin v Malkiewicz* [2020] clarified that the section 4 'publication on a matter of public interest' defence did not comprise a development or extension of the common law defence but a powerful and more defendant-friendly defence in its own right.[7] The Act also provides stronger protection for opinions, as opposed to statements of fact. This tilts the balance firmly in favour of free speech, and so it was confirmed in *Banks v Cadwalladr* [2023].[8]

Finally, however, it is concluded that the Defamation Act 2013, by declining to fundamentally change the structure of the law of defamation, and choosing instead to mostly codify and change parts of the common law, may have missed a golden opportunity. This is all the more so, given that alternatives are available – the entire area could have been more closely aligned with the fault-based regime of negligence, for example. There is no reason that the tort of negligence could not *prima facie* be extended in scope to also protect reputation. It must be borne in mind that defamation was initially a tort based on fault in the form of malice, but it metamorphosed – in a transition that was 'neither smooth nor unanimous'[9] to a tort of strict liability.[10] What is more, a close reading of the Defamation Act 2013 and the case law that followed shows that fault, having been absented from the elements of defamation more or less because of the vagaries of the tort's peculiar history, is increasingly evident in defamation, in some form or other. For example, the way in which the judge determines the meaning of the words complained of, the 'hypothetical ordinary reasonable reader' test, is very reminiscent of the 'reasonable man test' used to determine fault in negligence. But fault is particularly evident in the defences. For instance, the structure of the publication on a matter of public interest (section 4) defence is fault-shaped in that the defendant is *prima facie* liable but will be absolved from liability if he proves that he acted responsibly. So while it could be observed that the standard of liability in defamation is strict, it is defeated by a *culpa*-shaped defence. To extend this reasoning, when examining most of the defences and their importance in defamation law, it is clear that fault does play a role in defamation law. The question remains why this is placed in the evidentiary burden of the defendant and not the claimant. The fact that the Defamation Act 2013 deals primarily with defences reflect the fact that it has not brought about a fundamental change from the common law in this regard. It could be argued that the recently enacted Online Safety Act (2023), by placing a duty of care on online intermediaries, has in

7 *Serafin v Malkiewicz & Ors* [2020] UKSC 23.

8 *Banks v Cadwalladr* [2023] EWCA Civ 219.

9 Mitchell, P *The Making of the Modern Law of Defamation* (Hart Publishing, Oxford, 2005), 101–113, 112–113.

10 *Jones v E Hulton & Co* [1910] AC 20 HL.

effect made online speech subject to a fault-based regime. If this is the case for speech, it becomes even less clear why it should not also be the case for defamation.

What is more, there is ECtHR jurisprudence precedent for treating defamation as fault based. This means that strict liability is indeed capable of being successfully challenged as being incompatible with article 10 of the ECHR, but it seems that it is possible only on an *ad hoc* basis, depending on each case's facts rather than on a systemic and principled basis. In *O'Shea*, for instance, the court held that the particular facts of the case placed an impossible burden on the defendant and served no pressing social need: Clearly, here a factual weighing up/balancing exercise was undertaken by the court. In this case, a pornographic website used in its advertisement a photograph of a woman bearing a striking resemblance to the claimant, who alleged that she was identified by the photograph. In the judgment of the court, article 10 of the ECHR here outweighed the claimant's dependence on the strict liability characteristic of English libel law.

Although the Act 'abolished' various common law defences, such as justification, fair comment and privilege, it seemed at first, going by judgments emanating from the Court of Appeal, as if this amounted to no more than repackaging each of them with a statutory variant that merely amended or expanded the defences to varying degrees. A good example of this was the initial treatment by the courts of the new defence contained in section 4 of the Defamation Act 2013, 'publication on a matter of public interest.' It purports to abolish and replace the very important 'responsible journalism' defence commonly referred to as the Reynolds defence, which originated from the case of *Reynolds v Times Newspapers Ltd* [1999][11] in which a list of indicators of responsible journalism standards prior to publication was formulated. Section 4 aims to replace these criteria for responsible journalism with a test of 'reasonableness of belief' in the public interest of the statement published. At first it seemed that far from being buried, *Reynolds* and the checklist approach it elicited seemed to have survived, and its principles were held to continue to apply by courts including the Court of Appeal in *Economou v de Freitas* (2018).[12] It took a rather terse judgment from the Supreme Court in *Serafin*[13] to finally lay *Reynolds* and its checklist to rest. The section is clearly aimed at recognising the fact that the lines between individuals and the traditional press have become blurred in modern times and that so-called citizen journalists cannot be kept to the same high standards as professional journalists. This was indeed confirmed by the Court of Appeal in its interpretation of the section in *Economou*. But this is nothing new, and holding the press to a higher standard than individuals is a

11 *Reynolds v Times Newspapers Ltd* [1999] 4 All ER 609.
12 *Economou v de Freitas* [2018] EWCA Civ 2591.
13 *Serafin*, note 7.

principle adhered to across all the jurisdictions examined in this book with perhaps the exception of the US press as far as public figures are concerned.

What would have been the ideal outcome for a free speech activist, given free rein to reform the English common law of defamation? Our imaginary activist would surely first wish for the presumptions of harm and falsity to be abolished, and the tort's strict liability nature to be reformed into one that is based on fault. How far did the Act bring this about? To an extent, the presumption of harm is indeed abolished by the section 1 serious harm requirement, but the rest did not change. So how viable is a fault-based law of defamation? And is it likely or possible that the law can develop in that direction in England and Wales? Given the recent reforms and Parliament declining to follow this route, it seems unlikely in the short term. But the transformation to a fault regime happened in the United States, and it was driven by the jurisprudence of its Supreme Court. How this happened is informative.

United States

The US arguably places more emphasis on the participatory aspect of public discourse than virtually all other liberal democracies, which goes a long way to explaining why such a high premium is placed on free speech. Dworkin pointed out, 'we might have the power to silence those we despise, but it would be at the cost of political legitimacy, which is more important than they are.'[14] The US example clearly illustrates what a true commitment to the protection of free speech entails *vis-à-vis* defamation law.

In chapter 4 the way in which the US balances individuals' rights to free speech and reputation in its defamation law was examined. The first difference with the law of England and Wales is the fact that in the US, free speech is given constitutional protection. The First Amendment to the US Constitution states,

> Congress shall make no law respecting an establishment of religion, or prohibiting the free exercise thereof; or abridging the freedom of speech, or of the press; or the right of the people peaceably to assemble, and to petition the government for a redress of grievances.

Where the claimants are public officials, a libel claim cannot succeed unless the claimant can prove clearly that the aggrieving statement was not only false but that the author demonstrably *knew* that the statement was false. The rule was stated in *New York Times v Sullivan* (1964) by Brennan J and imposed

14 Dworkin, R 'Foreword,' in Hare, I and Weinstein, J (eds), *Extreme Speech and Democracy* (OUP, Oxford, 2009), ix.

as a constitutional safeguard against the possible chilling effect of libel law, as follows:

> [A] federal rule that prohibits a public official from recovering damages for a defamatory falsehood relating to his official conduct, unless he proves that the statement was made with 'actual malice' – that is, with knowledge that it was false or with reckless disregard of whether it was false or not.[15]

The 'actual malice' requirement was later extended from public officials to public figures as well,[16] and although claimants who are neither public officials nor public 'figures' do not have to prove actual malice, they still need to prove fault.[17] If the claimant can only prove carelessness, they can only claim special damages, and will have to prove actual loss;[18] if the claimant can prove actual malice, then they can claim general damages which include presumed damage (which is the common law rule) and punitive damages, without having to prove actual loss.[19] Compared to the law in England and Wales, the US law seems to be almost the exact opposite: Where the defamation claimant in England need not prove fault, the US claimant does, and in most significant cases this would mean actual malice; the claimant in England does not need to prove damages apart from harm to their reputation, whereas this forms a large part of the US claimant's burden of proof; and whereas it is up to the defendant in English courts to prove that the defamatory statement was true, US defamation law requires the claimant to prove that the defamatory statement was false. In brief, defamation law in the US provides a paradigm for fault-based liability, where the burden of proof is firmly on the claimant and damages are calculated in a clearly defined manner. If, to the English free speech advocate the United States represents the unattainable ideal, with priority for free speech baked into the constitutional cake, so to say, then a look closer to home may be a bit more realistic.

Germany

Chapter 5 therefore returned to Europe and examined an influential jurisdiction where not only free speech but also reputation as an aspect of individual personality rights are also given constitutional protection. The German law of

15 *New York Times v Sullivan*, 376 US 254 (1964), 279–280.

16 *Curtis Publishing Company v Butts* (conjoined with *Associated Press v Walker*) 388 US 130 (1967).

17 *Gertz v Robert Welch*, 418 US 323 (1974).

18 Albeit this can include, for example, emotional distress caused, job loss, etc.

19 *Gertz*, note 17, 348–349.

defamation consists of a mosaic of disparate rules drawn from civil, criminal and constitutional law. Perhaps the most surprising characteristic of this system, to common law sensibilities, is the retention of criminal defamation. This however is balanced by equally strong, and moreover, *constitutional* protection given to the right to free speech. To this must also be added the overarching due diligence owed in all application of the law to the inviolability of human dignity. The result is a complex and nuanced substantive law, but saved from unpredictability by a finely honed balancing exercise for instances where fundamental rights come in conflict. German cases are characterised by a detailed consideration of all relevant factors which are balanced against each other in sensitive ways relating to context, content and, in some cases, the parties concerned.

Although the German Federal Constitutional Court (*Bundesverfassungsgericht* or BVerfG) has formulated guidelines for balancing competing rights, these are not as straightforward as the rules formulated by the US Federal Supreme Court. In essence, the guidelines boil down to the balancing exercise which also features strongly in ECtHR jurisprudence. The complexity arises from the various and varying weights given to relevant factors or rights in a specific situation. For instance, if speech occurs in the context of public discussion, the German courts apply a presumption in favour of freedom of expression. This holds true, even if the defamatory speech was made only incidentally in the course of contributing to public discourse: The statements in the *Soldiers are Murderers* case, for instance, were protected from civil or criminal defamation proceedings in this way.[20] Another example of the differential weighting concerns politicians, political parties and other public figures. German jurisprudence extends the protection given to speech in the context of public discourse, to speech involving its key participants. The reasoning seems to be that by participating in public debate, and given their usually ample opportunities to reply to critique, politicians and political parties forfeit to some extent their right to be protected from insulting and defamatory statements. The contextualised nature of the Federal Constitutional Court guidelines is highly adaptable. It is also no jump of the imagination to see that German jurists have an influential role at the European Court of Justice as well as the European Court of Human Rights. Whereas English courts are not averse to obiter contemplation of comparable laws in other jurisdictions, these are of course in most instances, academic exercises at best. But the jurisprudence from the European Court of Human Rights (ECtHR) can be of direct consequence in UK courts.

European Court of Human Rights

Chapter 6 examined relevant ECtHR jurisprudence. In terms of the Human Rights Act 1998, English courts are under a duty to develop the law in

20 *Soldiers are Murderers*, 93 BVerfGE 266 (1995), discussed in chapter 5.

accordance with the various rights and freedoms contained in the European Convention of Human Rights (ECHR). For this reason alone, ECtHR case law on defamation, free speech, and privacy is important. UK courts are now enabled, in cases where Convention rights are potentially in conflict with common law principles, to depart from or develop the common law to resolve such conflict to favour rights such as the right to freedom of expression under article 10. So how does the ECtHR address the key question raised in this book – namely, how to achieve a proper balance between reputation and free speech?

In moving away from treating the right to reputation as a narrowly construed internal exception to article 10 rights and according it the status of a fully fledged right to be balanced on equal terms with freedom of expression, it may be queried whether the ECtHR is taking sufficient account of the potential chilling effect on freedom of expression. It could very well be argued that there is currently a Europe-wide trend towards restrictions on speech. This is evidenced by both pronouncements such as the *Google Spain* 'right to be forgotten' cases, as well as tightening of regulation of speech, such as via the General Data Protection Regulation (GDPR) the Digital Services Act, the NetzDG, and in the UK, the Online Safety Act. It will be interesting to see how the ECtHR interprets the relevant margins of appreciation should cases arising out of these measures come before it.

Out of the comparator jurisdictions examined, the methodology employed by the ECtHR seems to strike the best balance: Compared to the US, the competing rights are balanced more fairly as freedom of speech is not given a virtually unassailable status; compared to Germany, there is less complexity, and therefore, the results are more predictable, thus adhering to the virtue of legal certainty. This methodology is the balancing exercise contained in article 10(2) of the ECHR and which can be summarised as comprising a test of legality, necessity, and proportionality. For speech to be lawfully curtailed, there needs to be a valid legal reason, such as, for instance, safeguarding other personality rights, including the right to privacy and reputation; the curtailment needs to be necessary in the sense that no less restrictive alternative is available; and the restriction needs to be proportionate to the legitimate aim pursued.

This seems the fairest way of balancing competing rights, provided that one keeps in mind that proportionality as such is a relative concept, with the question always remaining: Relative to what? The margin of appreciation doctrine is important in this respect, as it allows member states to decide what is necessary in their particular, unique, democratic society. The ECtHR nevertheless does not interpret the margin of appreciation as granting unrestricted carte blanche to a member – the court remains empowered to give the final ruling in cases before it where it is of the opinion that the member state had exceeded what could reasonably be termed its margin of appreciation.

As in the other jurisdictions, the ECtHR differentiates between kinds of speech, assigning them higher and lower degrees of protection according to where they fit on the spectrum of speech. The highest protection is accorded to political speech and speech that contributes to the public debate. This makes sense and reflects the position in many other jurisdictions, including those that are subject to the jurisdiction of the ECtHR.

Out of the three comparator jurisdictions, the example set by ECtHR jurisprudence is the most valuable, workable, and practicable in UK courts. Out of the three jurisdictions it is also the only one whose pronouncements carry legal weight in the UK, and for that reason alone, they remain significant.

Conclusion

This book attempted to analyse whether the UK Defamation Act 2013 delivers on the promises of redressing the balance between free speech and reputation, primarily by levelling the playing field between defamation claimants and defendants in England and Wales. We started by examining the relative importance of freedom of speech and reputation and highlighted the societal interests in both as being instrumental in finding the right balance in case of conflict. The English common law of defamation was unique in several ways: It alone formed a specific interest-shaped tort in order to protect reputation, and furthermore, it protected this interest heavily by reversing the burden of proof and by its nature as a strict liability tort for the most part actionable *per se*. This book argues that there was nothing self-evident or compelling about this uniqueness. There is no principled reason for the law to be structured in this way. A comparison of the reasons for protecting speech on the one hand and reputation on the other would on the contrary suggest that the societal interest in free speech should rank at least equally with the individual interest in reputation. This means that at the very least the clear advantage accorded to reputation by the common law of defamation needed to be rebalanced in favour of free speech. This was indeed one of the stated aims for enacting the Defamation Act 2013.

However, although the balance is doubtless tilted much more in favour of free speech, the Act simply does not go far enough. No major structural changes were made to the common law. The focus is still very much on the defences, and to a very large extent, the defendant still shoulders the bulk of the burden of proof in court. The most fundamental change is to be found in section 1, dealing with the serious harm requirement, which was only recently clarified by the Supreme Court in *Lachaux*. While the court did not go so far as to categorically abolish the presumption of harm, it did state in no uncertain terms that reputational harm can now no longer be gauged just from the words complained of but must be determined by reference to the actual fact of their impact. This goes further than interpreting the 'serious harm' requirement as a mere threshold and places the burden of proving damage to their reputation on the claimant.

There are other welcome innovations and changes in the reforms. The demise of the jury trial is not to be regretted, nor is the impact of costs and procedural reforms. Still, the issue of costs and complexity could have been addressed in much more detail. Expanding the defence of publication in the public interest and of protecting opinion is to be welcomed by free speech advocates, as is the inclusion of protection for academic and scientific publications and internet intermediaries. But it remains unclear to what extent the vexing issue of balancing freedom of speech with the protection of an individual's reputation is really addressed.

To that aim, a bird's eye view of three other jurisdictions were given. For a complete contrast, the law of the United States showed that a fault-based regime for defamation cases would indeed result in more freedom of expression. However, this is indubitably at the cost of other legitimate interests. The German system may seem byzantine in its complexity at first glance, but it does result in balanced outcomes, and the overarching constitutional guidance is valuable. The German law places great emphasis on proportionality and the balancing exercise that guarantees it. The latter is strongly reflected in the balancing approach taken by the European Court of Human Rights. The principles upon which the ECtHR resolve disputes in this area are clear and relatively easy to understand and follow. This is fortunate, given that UK courts are bound to interpret domestic laws in line with Convention rules and thus obligated to keep ECtHR jurisprudence in mind.

In the final analysis, the Defamation Act 2013 does make significant changes to the common law of defamation in England and Wales, but not as far reaching as free speech advocates may have wanted. Does it succeed in less chilling of free speech? This question becomes even more serious when considered in the light of a seemingly rising tide of threats to free speech, such as increased privacy claims against the media, draconian data protection laws, and the regulation of online speech in the UK and Europe. The German proportionality principle and the ECtHR's balancing approach are likely to become even more pertinent.

Many books and articles on defamation conclude with these words of Shakespeare's Iago: 'Good name in man and woman, dear my lord, / Is the immediate jewel of their souls: / Who steals my purse steals trash; tis something, nothing, / 'Twas mine, 'tis his, and has been slave to thousands; / But he that filches from me my good name / Robs me of that which not enriches him, / And makes me poor indeed.' But few remember to add that he went on to also say: 'Reputation is an idle and most false imposition; oft got without merit and lost without deserving. You have lost no reputation at all, unless you repute yourself such a loser.'[21]

21 *Othello*, Act III, scene iii.

Index

Made in the USA
Las Vegas, NV
19 September 2026

5971e895-ed99-49d9-8200-1c3ec7aa9a88R01